SACRED
MUSHROOM
OF VISIONS:
TEONANÁCATL

ALSO BY RALPH METZNER

Green Psychology: Transforming Our Relationship to the Earth

Sacred Vine of Spirits: Ayahuasca (Editor)

The Unfolding Self: Varieties of Transformative Experience

The Well of Remembrance: Rediscovering the Earth Wisdom Myths of Northern Europe

Opening to Inner Light: The Transformation of Human Nature and Consciousness

Through the Gateway of the Heart: Accounts of Experiences with MDMA and other Empathogenic Substances (Editor)

Maps of Consciousness: I Ching, Tantra, Tarot, Alchemy, Astrology, Actualism

The Ecstatic Adventure: Reports of Chemical Explorations of the Inner World

The Psychedelic Experience: A Manual Based on the Tibetan Book of the Dead (with Timothy Leary and Richard Alpert)

SACRED
MUSHROOM
OF VISIONS:
TEONANÁCATL

A Sourcebook on the Psilocybin Mushroom

Edited by Ralph Metzner, Ph.D.
with Diane Conn Darling

Park Street Press
Rochester, Vermont

Park Street Press
One Park Street
Rochester, Vermont 05767
www.InnerTraditions.com

Park Street Press is a division of Inner Traditions International

Library of Congress Cataloging-in-Publication Data
Teonanácatl
  Sacred mushroom of visions : teonanácatl : a sourcebook on the psilocybin
mushroom / edited by Ralph Metzner with Diane Conn Darling.
    p. cm.
  Originally published: Teonanácatl. El Verano, CA : Four Trees Press, c2004.
  ISBN 978-1-59477-044-9
  1. Mushrooms, Hallucinogenic. 2. Mycology. 3. Shamanism. 4.
Mushroom culture. I. Metzner, Ralph. II. Darling, Diane. III. Title.
  BF209.H36T46 2006
  154.4—dc22

                                                                    2005013502

Printed and bound in the United States

10 9 8 7 6 5 4 3

Text design and layout by Jonathan Desautels
This book was typeset in Sabon with Mason Alternate as the display font

THIS BOOK IS DEDICATED TO

MARÍA SABINA (1894–1985), Mazatec Wise Woman and Healer who spoke the Holy Language of the *niños santos* and preserved their spiritual wisdom.

ROBERT GORDON WASSON (1898–1986), scholar, world traveler and ethnomycologist who rediscovered the *teonanácatl* cult of the indigenous people of Mexico and brought the gifts of this ancient religion to the modern world.

ALBERT HOFMANN (who celebrated his ninety-ninth birthday in 2005), scientist, alchemist and nature mystic who found the Stone of the Wise, identified the crystal essence—psilocybin—of the holy mushroom, and fathomed the secret of the Eleusinian Mysteries.

TIMOTHY LEARY (1920–1996), psychologist, visionary philosopher, and trickster, who ate the sacred mushroom and inspired a generation to "go out of your mind and come to your senses."

TERENCE MCKENNA (1946–2000), scholar, bardic seer, emissary from the mushroom world, who mapped the hidden landscape of hyperspace, communed with alien intelligence, and showed the way to join the cosmic community.

Acknowledgments

The editors acknowledge with gratitude

Visionary artist Robert Venosa, for permission to use his magnificent painting Shroomglow (oil, collection of Glenn Bailey) on the cover of the first edition of this book, published by Green Earth Foundation, 2004. See: www.venosa.com.

Elizabeth Gordon and the late Bob Wallace for financial support on the first edition.

Kathleen Harrison, for permission to use her drawings of the psilocybe life-cycle, and the Bee-Mushroom Goddess from the Tassili Plateau.

———

The information provided in this book is for educational, historical, and cultural interest only and should not be construed as a guide to or advocacy of the use or ingestion of the teonanácatl mushrooms. The psilocybe mushrooms, wild or cultivated, as well as substances derived from them, are controlled substances under U.S. laws. In no way should the material in this book be taken to advocate, explicitly or by implication, the use of these mushrooms or any other illegal substance. Neither authors nor publisher assume any responsibility for physical, psychological, or social consequences resulting from the ingestion of these mushrooms or their derivatives.

Contents

VISIONARY MUSHROOMS OF THE AMERICAS

RALPH METZNER, PH.D.

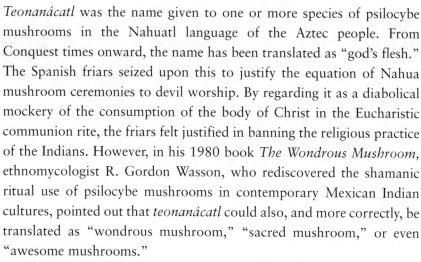

Teonanácatl was the name given to one or more species of psilocybe mushrooms in the Nahuatl language of the Aztec people. From Conquest times onward, the name has been translated as "god's flesh." The Spanish friars seized upon this to justify the equation of Nahua mushroom ceremonies to devil worship. By regarding it as a diabolical mockery of the consumption of the body of Christ in the Eucharistic communion rite, the friars felt justified in banning the religious practice of the Indians. However, in his 1980 book *The Wondrous Mushroom,* ethnomycologist R. Gordon Wasson, who rediscovered the shamanic ritual use of psilocybe mushrooms in contemporary Mexican Indian cultures, pointed out that *teonanácatl* could also, and more correctly, be translated as "wondrous mushroom," "sacred mushroom," or even "awesome mushrooms."

What is clear, both from the accounts of the Spanish chroniclers and from the accounts of modern anthropologists, is that these vision-inducing mushrooms were (and are) revered by the Indians for providing deep spiritual insight and inspiration. The names given to the mushrooms by some of the Mexican Indian tribes—Mazatec, Mixtec, Zapotec, and others—confirm the reverence and affection the mushrooms inspire: "holy lords," "little saints," "children" *(los niños),* "dear little ones that spring forth" *(nti-xi-tho,* Mazatec), "little princes." The Aztecs also called them "little flowers," although fungi do not bloom. For them "flower" was a metaphor, as it was for the Maya, for whom "flowering dreams" refers to ecstatic visions.

In 1957, Wasson published in *LIFE* magazine his account of a mushroom session with a Mazatec *curandera* in a remote mountain village in the state of Oaxaca. The psilocybe mushroom exploded into Western consciousness and during the transformative 1960s, thousands of hippies trekked to the mountains of Oaxaca, seeking consciousness-expanding mushroom experiences. This development was much to the dismay of Wasson and other conservative researchers, who felt that this kind of activity cheapened and desacralized the religious dimensions of the mushroom experience.

Wasson had become friends with Albert Hofmann, the brilliant research chemist of the Sandoz pharmaceutical company in Switzerland. About ten years earlier, in 1943, Hofmann had discovered the astounding mind-expanding effects of lysergic acid diethylamide (LSD), a compound derived from the ergot fungus that grows on rye and other grains. Upon obtaining samples of the Mexican mushroom from Wasson, Hofmann was able to identify and then synthesize the psychoactive ingredient, which he named *psilocybin,* after the psilocybe mushroom. Thus Western scientific and psychiatric research with psychedelic hallucinogens was linked with ancient Meso-American shamanic practices that used visionary mushrooms as well as plants.

After the initial wave of North American and European magic mushroom hunters had descended on the mountain villages of Mexico, reports started appearing that psilocybin-containing mushrooms were not limited to Mexico. In fact, they could be found in many parts of the world, including Hawaii, South America, Europe, and Southeast Asia—and were particularly widespread in the American Pacific Northwest coastal areas, due to the abundant rainfall. To date, several new species and varieties of psilocybin-containing mushrooms have been identified. The chapters by John Allen and Paul Stamets in this volume describe the worldwide distribution and ecology of these psychoactive mushrooms. More extensive and detailed information can be found in two books by Jonathan Ott (1976, 1978); in German mycologist Jochen

Gartz's *Magic Mushrooms Around the World* (1996); and in Paul Stamets's *Psilocybin Mushrooms of the World* (1996). Both of the latter two books are illustrated with full-color photographs, an essential feature for safe identification of mushrooms in the wild. None of the psilocybin-containing species of mushrooms outside of Mexico are known to have been associated with shamanic healing practices.

In addition to the increasing discovery and identification of wild-growing psychoactive mushrooms, a major boost to free-lance personal explorations of visionary mushroom experiences occurred when relatively simple techniques of home cultivation of major species, especially *Psilocybe* (originally *Stropharia) cubensis,* were developed and published. One of the first was the cultivation guide written by the McKenna brothers, under the pseudonyms O. T. Oss and O. N. Oeiric (1976), which has sold over one hundred thousand copies. The spread of mushroom cultivation provided thousands, perhaps millions, of individuals in North America and elsewhere easy access to powerful tools for exploring the visionary dimensions and potentials of human consciousness. These tools and the experience they afforded have inspired the growth of a "mushroom culture," including visual, literary, and musical arts as well as ritualistic dance forms, such as the Grateful Dead "shroom" events. Because of the controlled legal status of psilocybin mushrooms, cultivation methods will not, of course, be described in this book.

Psilocybin, and the mushrooms from which it was first isolated, falls into a group of substances that defy classification. Besides psilocybin, they include: mescaline, derived from the Mexican and North American peyote cactus; DMT (dimethyltryptamine) and several of its chemical relatives, which are the psychoactive component of the Amazonian visionary concoction *ayahuasca,* as well as of plant-derived snuff powders known as *cohoba* or *epena*; the infamous LSD, originally derived from the ergot fungus that grows on grains; ibogaine, derived from the roots of the central African *Tabernanthe iboga* tree; and many others. As plant extracts or synthesized drugs, these substances (and others with similar properties that were discovered in laboratories but are not known to have been used in shamanic rituals) have been the subject of a large number and variety of scientific research studies over the past fifty to seventy years (in the case of mescaline and peyote, going back over one hundred years). The research studies have primarily had as their aim the elucidation of the basic chemistry and pharmacology of these substances; secondarily, exploration of their potential applications as adjuncts to psychotherapy; and, in a few cases, their application in the expansion of consciousness, enhancement of creativity, and amplification of spiritual exploration and religious experience.

In a kind of testament to the bewildering variety of effects that these substances can elicit in human observers, they have been called by a variety of names that reflect the different backgrounds and mind-sets with which they have been regarded. The first psychiatric researchers called them *psychotomimetic* ("madness mimicking"), seeing them as training tools for psychiatrists. Those who wanted to use them as adjuncts to psychoanalysis called them *psycholytic* ("mental pattern loosening"). Humphrey Osmond, the English psychiatrist who pioneered the use of LSD in the treatment of alcoholism and who gave Aldous Huxley his first mescaline experience, coined the term *psychedelic* ("mind manifesting"). This term was adopted by the Harvard psilocybin research projects.

The older term *hallucinogenic* ("hallucination inducing") was universally rejected by those investigators who had actually experienced these substances, since it was clear that they do not cause one to see hallucinations in the sense of illusions: rather one sees all the ordinary objects of the sense world *plus* another whole range of energies and phenomena normally not seen. However, etymology reveals that the original meaning of the Latin verb *alucinare*, from which "hallucination" is derived, means to "roam or wander in one's mind." This is actually a fairly appropriate metaphor for the experience—a journey in the mind, in consciousness; a "trip," as it became known colloquially.

The term *entheogenic* ("connecting to the sacred within") was coined in the 1980s by Wasson, Ott, and others to refer to plant or fungal substances that have a role in traditional shamanic rituals. These scholars wanted to avoid the associations of "psychedelic" with the counterculture of the 1960s, since many such substances were known and used in places and in times far removed from that particular historical context.

In my book on the Amazonian shamanic hallucinogen ayahuasca (Metzner 1999), I pointed out that the discovery of psychedelic mind-expanding substances such as LSD and DMT, as well as the rediscovery of indigenous shamanic practices involving entheogens, and the diffusion of these practices into the creative counterculture, all seem to have catalyzed a series of profound socio-cultural transformations.

A powerful resurgence of respectful and reverential attitudes toward the living Earth and all its creatures seems to be a natural consequence of explorations with visionary plant or fungal teachers. This revival of entheogenic shamanism can be seen as part of a worldwide response to the degradation of ecosystems and the biosphere—a response that includes philosophical movements such as deep ecology, ecofeminism, bioregionalism, ecopsychology, herbal and natural medicine, organic farming and nutrition, and others. In each of these movements individuals are expressing a new awareness, or rather a revival of ancient awareness, of the organic and spiritual interconnectedness of all life on this planet (Metzner 1999).

My interest in consciousness-expanding substances began when I was a graduate student research assistant to Timothy Leary on his Harvard University Psilocybin Research projects. Later, through contact with the work of anthropologist Michael Harner and others, I become aware of shamanic teachings and practices around the globe involving nonordinary states of consciousness in which the shaman seeks otherwise hidden knowledge (a process called "divination") and healing. The two main types of methods for inducing the shamanic "journey" or altered state of consciousness are psychoactive plants or fungi, and rhythmic drumming; the latter more in the Northern Hemisphere parts of Asia, Europe, and America; the former more in the tropical and subtropical areas of central and South America, Africa, and Asia (presumably because of the greater profusion of plant life of all kinds).

I have come to see the revival of interest in shamanic practices as expressions of a worldwide seeking for the renewal of a spiritual relationship with the natural world. Over the past two millennia Western civilization has increasingly developed patterns of domination and exploitation based on an arrogant assumption of human superiority. This dominator pattern, which, from the point of view of Earth's ecosystems, functions like a pathogenic parasite, has involved the gradual desacralization, objectification, and exploitation of all nonhuman nature and its inorganic substrate. Indigenous peoples with shamanic practices, though greatly reduced in numbers, have maintained beliefs and values that honor and respect the integrity, indeed the *sacredness of all of nature* in its infinite variety of manifestations. Their life-style includes rituals of remembrance of the living intelligences inherent in the natural world.

In the modern Western worldview dominated by materialistic-mechanistic science, such recognition of "spirits" in nature, or spirits of dead ancestors, is considered quite beyond the pale of reason or proof. The spiritual dimension of life is more or less associated with institutionalized religion, completely dissociated from nature. "Spiritual" and "natural" are virtually considered opposites. However, those seekers who are partaking again of the sacramental plants and mushrooms of earlier times and cultures are rediscovering a sense of the sacredness of nature that is not at all incompatible with the curiosity and respectful knowledge-seeking of a scientific explorer or researcher.

Even the scientific study of consciousness, long considered out of the question in mainstream psychology or cognitive science, is coming into its own again. The *radical empiricism* philosophy formulated by William James over one hundred years ago provides an appropriate epistemological framework for the systematic study of subjective experience. Radical empiricism is "empirical" in that all knowledge is based on observation, i.e., experience; and it is "radical" in that no experiences are excluded from the field of study (James 1912/1996). Thus, this book, like the ayahuasca book, contributes to the developing database, so to speak, of experiences with visionary mushrooms by giving the descriptive accounts of experiencers in their own words. A second stage of scientific study would be to identify patterns in these experiences to see how they can be related the objective, material world. In this book we therefore also provide an overview of what the objective natural and social sciences (ecology, biology, chemistry, pharmacology, anthropology, and psychology) can tell us about these remarkable organic and spiritual beings and their profound impact on human consciousness.

THE KINGDOM OF FUNGI—EVOLUTION AND PSYCHOACTIVITY

Older biology texts, with their two- or three-fold division of the realms of life (single cells, plants, animals) arranged in the form of a tree with humans at the crown, often lumped mushrooms together with plants. This model is obviously anthropocentric: it erroneously equates evolution with "progress" and implicitly promotes a vision of *Homo sapiens* as superior to all other life forms—the "crown of creation"—by virtue of greater complexity of organization, and by virtue of coming later in time. But as Darwin had already noted, it is misleading to speak of "higher" and "lower" evolutionary forms, if this implies some kind of superior adaptation. Instead of the image of a ladder or tree with many branches, the evolution of species is now more accurately portrayed in the metaphor of a bush or multi-trunk tree. Stephen Jay Gould, in his book *Wonderful Life,* writes that "life is a copiously branching bush, continually pruned by the grim reaper of extinction, not a ladder of predictable progress . . . not the conventional tale of steadily increasing excellence, complexity and diversity" (Gould 1989). Or, in the most succinct definition, evolution is *changing adaptations to changing conditions.*

The new view of evolution, as now generally given in textbooks and accepted by leading biologists, involves a five-kingdom taxonomy first proposed by Robert Whitaker and described in detail by the microbiologist Lynn Margulis in the book *Five Kingdoms* (Margulis & Schwartz 1982). Instead of the image of the tree of life, Margulis uses the image of a hand with five fingers: the *monera* (bacteria) form the base of the hand and the thumb; the *protoctista* (water-dwelling microbes primarily), the palm of the hand and one finger; and plants, animals, and fungi (multi-cellular organisms), the three remaining fingers.

This model shows that each of the five kingdoms still continues to this day, with many successfully adapted life forms. The most significant division in this new taxonomy is between the *prokaryotic* (lacking a true nucleus) monera, the oldest organisms on Earth, and the *eukaryotic* (with a true nucleus) single-celled protoctista (and all subsequent multicellular forms). Margulis is one of the prime proponents of the theory that the simple bacteria evolved into eukaryotic organisms (which are generally much larger) by *endosymbiosis*—by incorporating themselves into larger, more complex cells and continuing their evolution as parts of the larger whole (as well as independently). From these eukaryotic cells evolved all other multicellular forms of life, including plants, animals, and fungi (Margulis 1998). This kind of evolution by incorporation, or *symbiogenesis,* may well provide a long-term model for human survival.

The three kingdoms of larger organisms have evolved characteristically different life cycles and ecological strategies for obtaining energy. *Plants produce* and *grow:* with chlorophyll-containing cells they capture sunlight (photosynthesis), convert it to the carbon compounds that nourish all animal life, and release oxygen that is then used by the aerobic animals. *Animals* (including the human kind) *consume* and *move:* they obtain nutrient energy from feeding on others, exchange the carbon dioxide they excrete for the oxygen produced by plants, and develop complex capacities for movement that symbiotically aid in the propagation of plants and fungi.

Fungi (which includes yeasts, molds, and mushrooms) *absorb* and *decompose:* they do not ingest food, they absorb minerals and other nutrients from the environment after breaking them down (decomposing), then secrete and transport complex chemicals out to plants with which they are in symbiotic association. An example is the mycorrhizal association between many species of fungi and the roots of trees, which association is fundamental to the ecological viability of forests. The sub-soil mycelial net is really the primary body of these fungi, with the mushrooms being the sexual organs that release billions of spores into the environment. Some mycelial nets, forming a single organism, have been found to be hundreds or even thousands of square miles in extent—making them by far the largest organisms on Earth.

Some fungi, like plants, are food sources for humans, either directly, as edible gourmet mushrooms; or indirectly, like the yeasts and molds used in the production of beer and cheese. Like plants, fungi may be poisonous and cause disease in plants or animals, or they may be medicinal. An example of the latter is the antibiotic penicillin, derived from a mold. Lynn Margulis writes: "various fungal strategies for survival include the production of complex organic compounds, such as the ergot and amanita alkaloids, which can induce hallucinations or even death in mammals" (Margulis & Schwartz 1982, p. 146).

We are touching here on the fascinating question of the ecological role and evolutionary origin of the psychoactive or visionary alkaloids found in plants, fungi, and even (rarely) in animals. The *Amanita* genus of mushrooms contain several extremely poisonous species, as well as the inconsistently hallucinogenic *Amanita muscaria*, or fly agaric, which played some role as a visionary adjunct in Siberian shamanism. This is the spectacular red mushroom with white spots, familiar to us from fairy tales, folklore, and myth—and which Wasson and some others believe played a central role as *soma* in the Vedic religion of ancient India (Wasson 1968; Heinrich 1982).

Ergot, a parasitical fungus of the genus *Claviceps* that grows on rye, barley, and other grains in Europe and the Middle East, was the cause of ergotism: hallucinations, burning sensations, gangrene, convulsions, insanity, and occasionally death. In Europe during the Middle Ages, outbreaks of ergotism, also known as "St. Vitus' Dance" or "St. Anthony's Fire," periodically infected whole communities that had eaten the infected grain. Ergot derivatives have *oxytocic* (stimulating uterine contraction) properties and were (and are) used for that purpose in obstetrics. Ergot is also the source of lysergic acid diethylamide, the most potent hallucinogen known, and as such may have played a role in the Eleusinian mysteries of Ancient Greece (Wasson, Ruck & Hofmann 1978).

In this book we do not deal with the amanita or the ergot alkaloids, both highly complex subjects in their own right. However, the question of the evolutionary origin of psychoactive, visionary fungi also arises in regard to psilocybe mushrooms. We have surviving traditions going back hundreds, perhaps thousands of years, of shamanic spiritual healing, diagnosis and clairvoyant divination with these inconspicuous-looking mushrooms. These mushrooms don't have sufficient toxicity, or even confusing hallucinatory effects, to deter any potential predator, so why did they evolve the capacity to produce hallucinogenic alkaloids? From a strict Darwinian perspective, of course, we don't ask the question *why*; we just look for adaptive strategies. The mycologist Paul Stamets (1996) has suggested that since humans and other animals readily and unconsciously carry microscopic spores around, perhaps the visionary psilocybe mushrooms have evolved symbiotically with humans—taking advantage of humans' interest in them to propagate themselves. This is the same ecological strategy used by fruiting plants that package their seeds in delicious fruits desired by humans and other animals.

So we have substances that, under certain conditions, cause poisoning and disease; in other forms they are used medicinally; and in certain other forms, by inducing divine visions they may have played a central role in the origin of certain religious traditions. While the production of toxins by a plant or fungus can be understood as a survival strategy, preventing it from being consumed by animals, it is more difficult to see an evolutionary strategy in the induction of religious visions in humans. Bright abstract pattern hallucinations could be confusing to an animal, thus, like a toxin, deter further attack on the plant or fungus. But insight and religious ecstasy? Perhaps our understanding of evolution and the symbiotic interactions between human culture and nonhuman nature needs to be reexamined.

Scholar-scientists not committed to a strict, reductionist Darwinian interpretation of evolution, including Pierre Teilhard de Chardin, have suggested that the evolution of plant and animal species involves ever greater complexity as well as consciousness (what Teilhard called the *within* of things). In an earlier essay (Metzner 1968), I suggested that if we assume that evolutionary processes are accompanied by development of a greater range of consciousness, perhaps consciousness-expanding substances play a role as a kind of evolutionary instrument or gnostic catalyst. This would account for the worldwide and historically documented role of plant- or fungus-based visionary substances in traditional systems of transformation, including shamanism, alchemy, and yoga (Metzner 1999). The independent scholar-philosopher Terence McKenna has taken this line of speculation a step further, proposing in his book *Food of the Gods* (McKenna 1992) that psilocybe mushrooms, with their perception-enhancing and consciousness-expanding properties, may have symbiotically contributed to the growth of language and therefore culture in early bands of hunter-gatherer hominids. We will discuss his ideas further below.

MUSHROOM SHAMANISM IN ANCIENT AND INDIGENOUS MESOAMERICAN CULTURES

Although "shamanism" is a term derived from the Siberian Yakut culture, it has come to refer to any of a group of practices that involve going into an altered state of consciousness for the purpose of healing or divination (Harner 1973). The psilocybe mushrooms have apparently been used in shamanistic ceremonies in Mesoamerica for hundreds, perhaps thousands, of years. Contemporary patterns of usage of the mushroom among indigenous communities in Mexico, although long unknown to Western science, are consistent with the use patterns for ayahuasca in South America, peyote in North America, and iboga in equatorial Africa: they are used ceremonially for obtaining spiritual visions of the land of the dead and for communing with the spirits of the natural world for healing and knowledge (Schultes and Hofmann 1979).

Miniature mushroom stones, some dating back to 1000 B.C.E, have been found in the lands of the ancient Maya in Guatemala, Ecuador, and Southern Mexico. Long misidentified, these are now understood as effigies of a mushroom deity: they may have a human or animal (jaguar, bird, monkey, hare) figure or face under the huge overshadowing mushroom cap. The pleated skirt on the one shown in the picture on the following page probably indicates a female deity, and the nine-point starburst around the head suggests a flower with radiating leaves, or the radiance of flowering visions induced by the mushroom. Finds of mushroom effigies in the tomb of Mayan nobles suggest an association with the Lords of Xibalba, deity rulers of the land of the dead, as described in the *Popul Vuh*.

Among the Spanish friars in sixteenth-century Mexico, the Franciscan Bernardino de Sahagún devoted himself to recording extensive descriptions and testimonies on the culture, history, and religion of the native peoples. The testimonies, recorded in Nahuatl and Spanish paraphrase, were preserved in numerous handwritten volumes known as the *Florentine Codex*. Wasson suggested that because Sahagún came from a family of Jewish converts in Spain, he perhaps had more instinctive sympathy for the conquered natives. In any event, his attitude, though pejorative, also had a certain kind of detachment and objectivity.

Among the otherwise meager material on mushroom use, there is one

Stone effigy of Mayan mushroom deity, dating from 300 B.C.E.
Height: 33.5 cm; from El Salvador. Probaby female (skirted), the figure has a nine-point
star halo and radiates beneficence. (Rietberg Museum, Zürich)

description of a mushroom ceremony that stands out: it describes prophetic visions that individuals had of themselves and others, including visions of their own death. The text begins by describing how the group of people came together to eat mushrooms: the blowing of a conch, fasting, except for taking chocolate and honey with the mushrooms, some dancing, some weeping, or sitting quietly (Wasson 1980, p. 206):

> One saw in vision that he would die, and continued weeping. One saw in vision that he would die in battle; one saw in vision that he would be eaten by wild beasts; one saw in vision that he would take captives in war; one saw in vision that he would be rich, wealthy; one saw in vision that he would buy slaves . . . one saw in vision that he would commit adultery—he would be stoned; one saw in vision that he would perish in water; one saw in vision that he would live in peace, in tranquility, until he died . . . However many things were

to befall one, he then saw all in vision. And when the effects of the mushroom had left them, they consulted among themselves and told one another what they had seen in vision. And they saw in vision what would befall those who had eaten no mushrooms, and what they went about doing. Some were perhaps thieves, some perhaps committed adultery. Howsoever many things there were, all were told—that one would take captives, one would become a seasoned warrior, a leader of the youths, one would die in battle, become rich, buy slaves . . . provide banquets, be strangled, perish in water. Whatsoever was to befall one, they then saw all in vision.

So here we have an account of classical visionary experiences in the form of divinations about one's own future and that of others. Those familiar with entheogenic experiences and practices will understand that these visions should not be considered undesirable effects of a drug or fungus. The visions one has are a function of the "set and setting," the intention or purpose of the ceremony; in other worlds, we must assume that the Aztec mushroom-eaters sought out those kinds of precognitive visions intentionally. Clearly, the experiences described in this informant's account are visions anticipating one's death, as might be found in the traditions of ancient mystery cults, or in contemporary research on "near-death experiences" (NDEs). Similar deathbed visions can be found in some of the experiences described in this book. They bring the individual to an enlarged and compassionate perspective that is informed by acceptance of one's own mortality.

Some of the visions described in the account are precognitions of one's future life-path—to be a merchant, a warrior, a "leader of youth." Others are healing visions that may be called "course corrections": here a person foresees the consequences of present bad actions, such as thieving, adultery, and so forth. These accounts are consistent with those described in the research with *hoasca* in Brazil, where subjects report seeing in vision the eventual consequences of their behavior and are thus enabled to move on to a road of recovery (Grob 1999). Interestingly, the Nahua account also includes mention of a kind of integrative discussion after the mushroom ceremony—very much in accord with the kinds of healing and divination sessions that contemporary seekers arrange.

R. G. Wasson, in his marvelous book *The Wondrous Mushroom—Mycolatry in Mesoamerica,* has pointed out that "flowers," botanically unspecified, are a huge recurring theme in Nahuatl poetry. He explains that for the Nahua poets and singers, "flowers" and "flowering" or "dream flowers" referred to the visionary experience induced by teonanacátl mushrooms. "The flowers took them to another world . . . a world that they called their *Tlalocan,* a world of strange and wondrous beauty, where they reveled in sensations beyond imagining." (Wasson 1980). Hence the poets would speak of "inebriating flowers" and "songs that inebriate," pointing to a quality of the mushroom experience often remarked on by inner space explorers: their ability to stimulate creative expression in voice, song, and poetry.

Xochipilli—Aztec "Prince of Flowers" in ecstatic visionary trance. Fifteenth century C.E.
(Museo Nacional de Antropologia, Mexico City; photo by Christian Rätsch)

The lovely songs come solely from His house,
from within the sky;
Solely from His house come the lovely flowers.

(WASSON 1980, P. 83)

It was Wasson too, who first identified the famous Aztec deity known as *Xochipilli,* the "Prince of Flowers," as the deity of ecstatic mushroom trance. The remarkable seated figure, dating from the sixteenth century and now in the Museum of Archaeology in Mexico City, wears a mask with hollowed-out eyes, his face lifted upward with a fixed gaze. This is a depiction of a man in ecstatic trance. His feet are crossed, toes curled, hands held lightly above the knees at the level of the heart. All around the base of the figurine as well as on his body are images of various flowers, including the hallucinogenic morning glory *(ololiuhqui),* and mushrooms in profile. This deity is a kind of Mesoamerican Dionysus, a god of rapture and inebriation. Wasson writes: "Here is the work of a master, a supreme carving of a man in the midst of an unearthly experience, the formal hieratic effigy of the God of Rapture, the God of Flowers (as the Aztecs put it): the god of youth, of light, of the dance and music and games, of poetry

Ceramic figurines, depicting singers and drummers, with mushroom-shaped head
protrusions. Southern Mexico, dated from the second century C.E.

and art; the Child God, the god of the rising sun, of summer and warmth, of flowers and butterflies, of the 'Tree-in-Flower' that the Nahuatl poets frequently invoke, of the inebriation mushrooms" (Wasson 1980, p. 59).

The suppression of the visionary mushroom cult by the Spanish clergy was effective and complete. For four centuries it disappeared from the memory of the general and scholarly public, so much so that at the beginning of the twentieth century some identified teonanácatl with the peyote cactus, and some questioned whether such a practice had ever existed. After Wasson rediscovered in the 1950s the practice of mushroom divination in the person of the famous Mazatec *curandera* Maria Sabina, it emerged that there were still practicing shamans among the Mazatec, Chinantec, Chatino, Mixe, Zapotec, and Mixtec of Oaxaca; the Nahua and possibly Otomi of Puebla; and the Tarascan of Michoacan. The Mazatec in the mountains of Oaxaca probably have the largest number of mushroom-using healers, though they are disappearing. There are three accounts in this book of Euro-Americans partaking of the mushrooms in small circles of people in the Mazatec country, under the guidance of Maria Sabina or another *curandero*.

According to anthropologist and Mayanist Christian Rätsch, who has made extensive studies of psilocybe and other shamanic entheogens, the Mixe people of Oaxaca (who, according to the linguistic evidence, may be descended from the Olmec, the oldest Mesoamerican culture) used several different species of psilocybe mushrooms in their religious life. From these cultures we have strange clay figurines (seen on the previous page), with a drum between the legs, and mushroom-like protrusions sticking out from the head on both sides; they look almost like antennae for cosmic visions and inspirations, which is a suggestive metaphor for the teonanácatl mushroom experience.

MARIA SABINA, R. GORDON WASSON, AND ALBERT HOFMANN

The encounter in 1956 between R. Gordon Wasson and Maria Sabina created an amazing bridge across times and cultures. Wasson participated in one of her all night mushroom *veladas* (vigils) and then published an account of his experiences in *LIFE* magazine in 1957. This opened Western minds and eyes to the incredible riches of knowledge and beauty in the ancient traditions of the sacred visionary mushroom. The world became aware of this wise woman—*sabia*—as a living representative of a lineage of shamanic healers, reaching back to pre-Conquest times, a lineage and tradition that had been presumed extinct. At the time he met her, Maria Sabina was a sixty-year-old traditional healer living and practicing her art secretly, known only to very few, in the tiny Mazatec village of Huatla de Jimenez in the state of Oaxaca.

R. Gordon Wasson was an immensely erudite scholar, banker, and amateur mycologist, who, with his Russian-born wife, Valentina, traveled the world seeking evidence in language, myth, and folklore of the connection between psychoactive mushrooms and the origins of religion. The Wassons observed a deep-seated attitudinal distinction between *mycophobic* and *mycophilic* cultures. Most Anglo-Saxons and Nordics were mycophobic (mushroom-fearing), whereas Slavic and Mediterranean peoples were examples of mycophiles (mushroom-lovers). The Wassons learned that the fly-agaric mushroom *(Amanita muscaria)* played a role in Siberian shamanism. They speculated that it might be the legendary soma of Vedic religion (Wasson 1968). Following the trail of Spanish accounts of the Aztec mushroom cult and the reports of a few anthropologists, he found the first strong support for his thesis when he became the first non-Indian to partake of the ancient mushroom ritual. In a paper on "The Hallucinogenic Fungi of Mexico—An Inquiry into the Origins of the Religious Idea Among Primitive Peoples," Wasson wrote: "As man emerged from his brutish past, thousands of years ago, there was a stage in the evolution of his awareness when the discovery of a mushroom (or was it a higher plant?) with miraculous properties was a revelation to him, a veritable detonator to his soul, arousing in him sentiments of awe and reverence, and gentleness and love, to the highest pitch of which mankind is capable . . . It made him see what this perishing mortal eye cannot see" (Wasson 1963).

Thomas Riedlinger, in his essay in this book, provides a more detailed account of the story of the founder of ethnomycology. The

Maria Sabina, mushroom curandera, in 1981, in Huatla. (Photo by Bonnie Colodzin; courtesy of Richard Yensen)

Wassons recorded one of the *veladas* and published the text of Maria's chants in Mazatec, with Spanish and English translations, as *Maria Sabina and her Mazatec Mushroom Velada*. Some years later an auto-biographical account of the life of Maria Sabina appeared in Spanish by Alvaro Estrada, a Mazatec-speaking friend from her home village. This was published in an English translation in 1981 as *Maria Sabina—Her Life and Chants* and surely represents a document unique in world literature, in that it is the first-person account of a shamanic practitioner speaking of her life, worldview, and practices that go back to the paleolithic depths of time.

Maria Sabina related that she discovered the magical effects of the mushrooms when as a seven or eight-year-old child playing in the woods with her sister, she ate some and found herself in a realm with lots of "children" *(los niños)*, who talked to her and played with her with great good humor and laughter. She knew that her father and grandfather used these mushrooms in healing. Ever after, she referred to the mushroom spirits as "los niños" and as she grew up she learned to consult with them when she needed help in healing. They might tell her about certain herbs at a particular place that she should find and apply to the patient. She became known as a gifted *curandera*, and devoted herself fully to her vocation—except during her two marriages, when she was raising her children.

"When I became a widow for the second time, I gave myself up for always to wisdom, in order to cure the sicknesses of people and to be myself always close to God. One should respect the little mushrooms. At bottom I feel they are my family. As if they were my parents, my book. In truth I was born with my destiny. To be a Wise Woman. To be daughter of *los santos niños* (the saint children)" (Estrada 1981).

During her veladas, Maria Sabina would sing and chant for hours, with percussive clapping and slapping her hands against her body, praying for the sick person, calling to the holy little ones, *los santos niños*. She would invoke the names of Christian saints and also the spirits of her native land, like the Lord of the Mountain and spirits of nature. Her words were mostly Mazatec, but sometimes included unknown words or repeated syllables, a kind of spirit language similar to that found among shamans around the world.

Her chanted statements would have the form of a first person declaration: "I am . . . woman, says" at the end. The syllable *t'so*, "says," is a kind of impersonal affirmation commonly found in trance mediums that indicate that it is not she, the personality that is saying these things, it is the mushrooms. Here are a few samples of her lines that give a sense of the awe and mystery that emanated from this tiny, humble woman, transformed into a powerful healer-shaman during her mushroom trance (Estrada 1981, pp. 105–190):

> *I am a woman who waits, says*
> *I am a daylight woman, says*
> *I am a Moon woman, says*
> *I am a Morning Star woman, says*
> *I am a God Star woman says . . .*
> *I am the doctor woman, says*
> *I am the herb woman, says . . .*
> *Our woman of light, says*
> *Our saint woman, says*
> *Our spirit woman, says . . .*
> *I am a lord eagle woman, says*
> *Our woman who flies, says . . .*
> *Our woman who looks inside of things, says*
> *You are the saint, says*
> *You are the saintess, says . . .*
> *I am a woman wise in medicine, says*
> *I am a woman wise in words, says*
> *I am a hummingbird woman, says*
> *Whirling woman of colors, says*
> *Woman of the sea, says . . .*

In one particularly powerful vision that Maria had when she was trying to heal her sister, who was very ill, she met beings she called "the Principal Ones, who inspired me with respect . . . of whom my ancestors spoke . . . I knew it was a revelation the saint children were giving me . . . I understood that the mushrooms were speaking to me. I felt an infinite happiness . . . On the Principal Ones a book appeared, an open book that kept on growing until it was the size of a person . . . It was a white book, so white it was resplendent. One of the Principal Ones spoke to me and said, 'Maria Sabina, this is the Book of Wisdom. It is the Book of Language. Everything that is written in it is for you. The Book is yours, take it so that you can work.' . . . At that moment, I began to speak. Then I realized that I was reading the Sacred Book of Language. The Book of the Principal Ones . . . And it's because the mushrooms are saints; they give wisdom. Wisdom is Language. Language is in the Book. The Book is granted by the Principal Ones. The Principal Ones appear through the great power of the *children*"(Estrada 1981).

She realized too that this was a divine or spiritual wisdom book that she was seeing and reading. In her personality she was a peasant woman who never learned to read. In her essence she was a spiritual giant, a *sabia*, a wise woman: "I am lord eagle woman, says . . . " After that vision and transmission of spiritual healing, she no longer saw the book "because I already had its contents in my memory." Her reputation as a healer grew and people came to her from far away with difficult problems, including possession by bad spirits.

"The mushrooms told me what the remedy was. They advised me what to do to cure them . . . And since I received the Book I have become one of the Principal Ones. If they appear, I sit down with them and we drink beer or *aguardiente*. I have been among them since the time when they gave me wisdom, the perfect word: the language of God . . .

"Language makes the dying return to life. The sick recover their health when they hear the words taught by the *saint children*. There is no mortal who can teach this Language" (Estrada 1981).

Wasson brought back specimens of the mushrooms that Maria Sabina and other

R. Gordon Wasson, ethnomycologist, in Mexico, 1955. (Photo by Allan Richardson; courtesy of Thomas Riedlinger)

Albert Hofmann with mushroom stone. (Photo by Christian Rätsch)

healers used and worked with the great French mycologist Roger Heim to identify them, name them, and publish the results of their findings in the mycology literature. Wasson also contacted Albert Hofmann, who identified the psychoactive principles in the visionary Mexican mushrooms as *psilocin* and *psilocybin*.

In 1962 Albert Hofmann and his wife accompanied Gordon Wasson and some other friends on a journey to Mexico to investigate the hallucinogenic plant now known as *salvia divinorum*. As part of this journey they also went to Huatla de Jimenez, where they met with Maria Sabina. Hofmann provided her with pills that contained the synthetic psilocybin, asking for her evaluation. She agreed to conduct a session with the synthetic tablets. At the end of the ceremony, Hofmann reported: "As we took leave of Maria Sabina and her clan at the crack of dawn, the *curandera* said that the pills had the same power as the mushrooms, that there was no difference. This was a confirmation from the most competent authority that the synthetic psilocybin is identical with the natural product" (Hofmann 1990). Maria Sabina also remarked that with the help of the tablets she would now be able to conduct mushroom healings even during the seasons when they normally don't grow.

This exchange between the traditional shamaness and the modern chemist constituted a respectful completion of the cycle of discovery and an honoring of the ancestral roots of knowledge. It is in marked contrast to the usual exploitative approach of contemporary pharmaceutical science, which seeks to isolate the chemical principles in traditional plant medicines and then proceeds to market those with no regard to the treasury of wisdom maintained by traditional shamans and healers.

Both Hofmann and Wasson made further profound contributions to our understanding of the role of psychoactive plant substances in the history of culture, especially religion. Working with plant specimens supplied by Wasson, Hofmann was able to identify LSD-like ergot alkaloids (ergine, ergonovine) as the psychoactive principle in several species of morning glories *(Ipomea violacea, Turbina corymbosa)*, which are known to the Aztecs as *ololiuhqui* and are still used shamanically by contemporary healers among the Mixtecs and Zapotecs (Schultes and Hofmann 1976; Ott 1993). Wasson also went on to write his major work *Soma— Divine Mushroom of Immortality* (Wasson 1968), which proposed that the legendary soma of Vedic religion was an extract of the fly agaric mushroom *(Amanita muscaria)*, which is known to have been used in Siberian shamanism. This thesis of Wasson, based on extensive ethnographic and linguistic evidence, has not found widespread agreement among researchers in entheogens, primarily because the experience induced by ingestion of fly agaric mushroom, even by Wasson's own account, is very mild and hardly comparable to the vivid and dramatic changes caused by tryptamines like those in psilocybe mushrooms. Finally, Wasson and Hofmann again collaborated, this time with Greek scholar Carl Ruck, to put forward the bold theory that the secret of the Eleusinian Mysteries, the elusive *kykeon* that was drunk by the initiates, may have been a detoxified extract of ergot, analogous to LSD, on the abundantly growing barley of that area (Wasson, Ruck, and Hofmann 1978).

CHEMISTRY, PHARMACOLOGY, AND PSYCHOLOGY OF PSILOCYBIN

Almost all the presently known psychedelic, hallucinogenic, or entheogenic compounds, whether occurring in plants or synthesized, belong to one of two chemical "families": the *phenethylamines* (which include mescaline, peyote cactus, San Pedro cactus, MDA, MDMA or Ecstasy, DOB, and others) and the *tryptamines* (which include DMT, psilocybin, ayahuasca, LSD, bufotenine, and others). Readers interested in more details of the chemistry of traditional entheogens and their plant sources, as well as newly synthesized psychoactive substances, are advised to consult the books by Alexander and Anne Shulgin (1991, 1997) and Ott (1993). Dozens of potentially psychoactive tryptamines have in recent years been identified in various plant sources, ranging from phalaris grasses, to acacias and mimosas. K. Trout (2002) gives detailed chemistry information on these discoveries up to the present time. Very few, if any, of these have any shamanic pedigree, i.e., documented use for shamanic healing and divination anywhere in the world. Whether they will prove to have applications in medicine or psychotherapy remains to be seen.

The chapter in this book by David Presti and Dave Nichols on the neurochemistry and pharmacology of psilocybin gives an overview of current scientific understanding of the intricate structural and functional interrelationships between the psychedelic tryptamine psilocybin and the endogenous tryptamines found in the brain. Of the four main neurotransmitters (norepinephrine, acetylcholine, serotonin, and dopamine), all of the known psychedelics interact primarily with serotonin. This has been known since the 1950s and is probably the reason for their "cross-tolerance" with each other. Cross-tolerance means that for a period of several hours after ingesting any one of the psychedelics, the individual will be "tolerant," i.e., experience reduced or no effects, from a normal dose of any of the others. The phenethylamines (e.g., MDMA) in addition affect norepinephrine, which is the neurotransmitter mostly involved with the effects of stimulants such as amphetamine (which is also a phenethylamine). This probably accounts for the more energized, stimulating properties of the phenethylamines as compared to the tryptamines. On the level of subjective experience, this can be observed if one compares the extremely rapid, almost percussive beat of the typical peyote chants, with the more sedate, mellow, and melodic spirit healing songs sung by *ayahuasqueros* and mushroom curanderas like Maria Sabina.

Research in the last couple of decades has extended scientific understanding of the complexity and pervasiveness of serotonin in the human brain and nervous systems. Current research has localized the main effect of psilocybin and other tryptamine psychedelics at one receptor site specific from the dozen or more that are receptive for serotonin. Neural circuits that use serotonin as their main neurotransmitter have been found in the limbic-mammalian brain systems that underlie much of our feeling life, especially the basic mammalian emotions (fear, rage, affiliation). Such neural circuits are also found in parts of the brain stem, called reptilian brain in Paul McLean's model. These findings are suggestively related to the sense of self-awareness, awareness of our evolutionary animal heritage, and the shamanic sense of connectedness or identification with animal consciousness. Perhaps most provocatively, serotonin has been found to be the main neurotransmitter for the "enteric nervous system," a system of one hundred million neurons distributed in and around the intestinal tract. This brain system is neuronally almost completely independent of the cerebral cortex. It is thought to be evolutionarily the oldest part of our nervous system (Gershon 1998). My speculation is that the role of serotonin in this brain system, and the possible effects of psychedelic drugs in it, may be the basis for experiences of evolutionary remembering, heightened instinctual or "gut-level" knowledge, and the healing of psychosomatic disturbances possible with psychedelics.

Serotonin is called a "mood regulator," bringing both anger and depression back to a central balancing point. Perhaps then, I may be allowed to speculate that it is serotonin that is involved in the "expansion of consciousness," the heightening of awareness and understanding that can bring about a more balanced emotional attitude. Serotonin may be the neurotransmitter for emotional intelligence or balance.

In addition to the action of tryptamines on serotonin receptors, there may be indirect effects of psilocybin on dopamine receptors as well. Some people speculate that dopamine is the neurotransmitter most involved in the experience of pleasure—for example, the "rush" of a cocaine high. The interaction with dopamine may account for some of the intense erotic-ecstatic sensations and feelings that can be part of the psilocybe mushroom effect.

Examination of the structural formulae of the entheogenic and endogenous tryptamines reveals striking similarities and parallels, which are suggestive of systemic interactive effects, though they do not prove them. The basic core molecule, tryptamine, consists of an indole ring and an amine side chain. It is biosynthesized in the body from nutritional tryptophan, one of the essential amino acids. Serotonin is *5-hydroxy-tryptamine (5HT)*, the tryptamine molecule with a hydroxy molecule in the 5-position. Serotonin itself cannot be absorbed via ingestion as it does not pass the "blood-brain barrier." It is synthesized in the brain (probably the pituitary and pineal glands) from tryptophan via the intermediate step of *5-hydroxy-tryptophan (5HTP)*. Both tryptophan and 5HTP can be absorbed orally and act to increase serotonin levels in the brain; both have been and are used in the treatment of depression. Numerous studies link depression, as well as anger, insomnia, and addictive cravings, to serotonin deficiency (Murray 1998), which is treatable with 5HTP. The well-known pharmaceutical creations known as the SSRIs (such as Prozac, Zoloft, and others) also act to increase the amount of serotonin at the synapses, but they do this by selectively inhibiting the "re-uptake" of serotonin, thus preventing its storage making it more available at the synapse.

When a double methyl group is added to the tryptamine molecule we have dimethyltryptamine (DMT), an extremely powerful hallucinogen that is found in several shamanic entheogenic plant preparations and endogenously in the human brain. DMT is synthesized in the brain's pineal gland. Some have speculated that DMT or one of its derivatives might be responsible for the vivid imagery of dreams and spontaneous visions. Dr. Rick Strassman, who completed an extensive psychiatric research project with DMT, calls it the "Spirit Molecule" and suggests that pineal-produced DMT is released in near-death experiences and other mystical revelations (Strassman 2001).

Psilocybin, the psychoactive principle in psilocybe mushrooms, is fairly rapidly changed into psilocin after oral ingestion, making the latter the active hallucinogen. Psilocin is *4-hydroxy DMT*, i.e., DMT with an additional hydroxy molecule at the 4-position. Physiologically, psilocin (and psilocybin and the mushrooms) produces moderately intense sympathetic nervous system activation within 30 minutes of ingestion, lasting for about 3–6 hours, depending on dosage. The most easily observable autonomic effects include pupil dilation and transient variations in heart rate and blood pressure. Researchers agree that these physiological changes are insignificant in comparison to the vivid perceptual, cognitive, and affective changes (Passie et al. 2002). Perceptual changes are of the kind typically found with other tryptamine hallucinogens, including DMT and ayahuasca: enhancement of all sensory modalities, synaesthesias, brightly colored kaleidoscopic visuals behind closed eyelids, perception of interconnected webs and lattices of energy patterns that seem to be full of spiritual and psychological meaning as well as visually gorgeous.

Although the focus of this book is on psilocybin and psilocin (and the mushrooms that contain these molecules), for the sake of comparison I will mention two other tryptamine derivatives that are of great interest for the understanding of the relationship between molecular structure and psychoactivity. If the hydroxy molecule is at the 5-position, we have *5-hydroxy-DMT,* or bufotenine, which is the main toxic ingredient in the exudates of many species of toads (Latin: *bufo*). Largely because of this structural similarity to DMT and psilocybin, bufotenine was placed on Schedule I during the prohibitionist frenzy of the midsixties, when LSD was also illegalized. Scientific researchers in the field however had never found any evidence to support its psychoactivity, and toad venoms are generally regarded as toxic rather than hallucinogenic (although they have found occasional use as homeopathic medicines). Very recent research by Manuel Torres, Jonathan Ott, and Christian Rätsch, has however established that among the Wichi of Southern Argentina, the ground seeds of *Anadenanthera colubrina,* known as *cebil,* are smoked or snuffed for shamanic divination; and the main psychoactive ingredient in cebil is bufotenine! (Ott 2001).

If a methoxy molecule (instead of hydroxy) is substituted at the 5-position with DMT, we have *5-methoxy-DMT,* or 5-meo-DMT, a substance as equally powerful as DMT, but more potent, i.e., the same effect is produced by a much smaller dose. This tryptamine derivative is the main psychoactive ingredient in shamanic snuffs, variously known as *cohoba, yopo, epena,* and other names, derived from two South American plant sources. These snuff materials have a long documented history of indigenous shamanic use: snuff trays and still viable seeds have been found in burial sites dated to 1500 B.C.E in the Atacama Desert of northern Chile. Also 5-meo-DMT is the psychoactive ingredient in the exudate of one species of toad, the Colorado River toad, that *does* have hallucinogenic effects—though no shamanic use of this animal hallucinogen is known to date (Ott 2001).

In the introduction to the ayahuasca book I pointed out that two analogies or metaphors for the drug experience have been repeatedly used by writers in both the psycholytic and psychedelic paradigms. One is the *amplifier analogy*, according to which the drug functions as a non-specific amplifier of perception of both inner and outer stimuli. This is the "cleansing of the doors of perception" of which William Blake wrote in his poetry, and which Aldous Huxley used to describe his first visionary experiences with mescaline. The other analogy is the *microscope metaphor*. It has been repeatedly said that psychedelics could play the same role in psychology as the microscope does in biology: opening up realms and processes in the human mind to direct, repeatable, verifiable observation that have hitherto been largely hidden or inaccessible. Both amplifier and microscope are technological metaphors for expanded perception and divination—the ability to see and hear more vividly, to see into other, normally invisible worlds or dimensions, and to obtain otherwise hidden knowledge (Metzner 1999).

Both the amplifier and microscope analogies help us to understand how the "set and setting," the internal expectations of the inner space voyager and the physical and social context of the voyage, act to determine the psychological content of the experience. This well-known relationship is amply documented in the experiential accounts in this book. When the set or intention is for healing of illness, as it was for most of the people who consulted Maria Sabina, then healings can take place; if people come looking for religious or spiritual insight or revelation, as was true for Wasson and many other seekers, then those kinds of mystical experiences can take place. In the naturalistic settings of the Harvard Psilocybin Project, described below, people had experiences of heightened self-awareness, interpersonal connection, and creative inspiration.

Psilocybin has been used as an adjunct to the therapeutic treatment of many psychological disorders, including anxiety, depression, sexual neuroses, obsessions, compulsions, and addictions. These studies are reviewed in the chapter by Torsten Passie. The two best-known application studies of psilocybin that came out of the Harvard Project—the Concord Prison study of rehabilitation, and the Good Friday study of religious experience—are also reviewed, with follow-up studies, in a separate chapter.

Let me return for a moment to the psychopharmacological hypothesis I ventured above—that the expansion of awareness induced by psychedelic tryptamines like psilocybin is a function of their raising levels of serotonin in key areas of the brain and nervous system. I had proposed (Metzner 1994) that one can regard transcendent experiences, as found in mysticism, as consciousness-expanding, and compulsive/addictive experiences as consciousness-contracting, fixating, and narrowing. It is then a natural step to explore the use of psychedelic substances in the treatment of compulsions and addictions (Halpern 1996). Before it was banned, LSD was used in several different centers as a treatment for alcoholism. Participants in the Native American Church peyote rituals, and participants in the Brazilian churches that use ayahuasca as their sacrament, report a marked decrease in alcoholism. Iboga, an African hallucinogen, has been tested in the treatment of cocaine addiction. Psilocybin is currently being tested in the treatment of obsessive-compulsive disorders, as discussed in the chapter of this book by Rick Doblin, on current research projects.

TIMOTHY LEARY AND THE HARVARD PSILOCYBIN PROJECT

In 1959, two years after R. Gordon Wasson had published his groundbreaking account of a sacred mushroom ceremony in *LIFE* magazine, Timothy Leary, a Harvard University psychology professor, while on vacation in Mexico, was given an experience with the mushroom that changed his life dramatically, causing him to devote the rest of his career and his life to explore the potentials of these substances for the understanding of the human mind and their implications for society. Albert Hofmann had succeeded in identifying psilocybin as the active ingredient of the mushroom and the Swiss pharmaceutical company

Sandoz, which had ten years earlier initiated experimental studies of LSD, also began to offer synthetic psilocybin to medical and psychological researchers. Thus it came about that psilocybin, the active ingredient of the Mexican hallucinogenic mushroom, was manufactured in tablet form by the Sandoz Company, which had a branch in New Jersey. They offered to supply the Harvard University professor with as much of the drug as he wanted, free of charge, for research purposes.

Thus begun the Harvard Psilocybin Project, which conducted studies of the psychedelic ("mind-manifesting") drug with convicts, creative artists, religious professionals, and graduate students—of whom I was one. I signed on to assist with the study that was going to give psilocybin to convicts in Concord Prison. Since Leary believed that we all needed to be familiar with the experience ourselves before providing it to someone else, I had my first psychedelic experience (with psilocybin) in 1961 at the age of twenty-five, as part of Timothy Leary's research project. Tim Leary's account of his dramatic first experience with the Mexican mushroom, as well as my account of my first encounter with psilocybin while a graduate student at Harvard, are reprinted in this book.

The Harvard Psilocybin Project was formed to investigate, from a psychological point of view, the astonishing properties of this mushroom chemical. From the start, Tim Leary adopted what he called an "existential-transactional" approach to this research. He rejected the impersonal clinical atmosphere of the traditional psychiatric experiment. Having taken the substance himself in a sacramental atmosphere, he knew how important it was to have a warm supportive setting if one is to experience the ego-shattering revelations of the mushrooms safely.

We used the term "consciousness-expanding" for the drug and the experience; which is reminiscent of the "consciousness-raising" language of women's liberation groups in the 1970s. This model was that if a safe, supportive set and setting is provided, with a small group of peers, the experience will probably be enlightening and productive. Another group of researchers in Menlo Park, California, including Willis Harman, Myron Stolaroff, Robert Mogar, James Fadiman, and others, were developing a *creativity* context for the drug experience: allowing for architects, artists, designers, scientists, and others to work on new problem-solving strategies during their session.

A similar attitude was adopted for the Concord Prison Project: rather than treating prisoners like guinea pigs in a lab experiment (as they too often are), we proposed providing them with insight-producing, "mind-manifesting," experiences, in which we also participated. The intention and hope was that the men would gain sufficient insight to allow them to make the kinds of changes in their lives that would reduce the rate of return to prison after release. The results of this two-year study were mixed: on the one hand there were many profound experiences of insight and changes on personality tests; on the other hand, it quickly became clear that actually reducing the recidivism rate was a much more difficult and long-term challenge.

Aldous Huxley was at MIT in 1960 and became an advisor to the Harvard Psilocybin Project. In 1953 and 1955, Huxley had published two widely read books on his mystical experiences with mescaline, *The Doors of Perception* and *Heaven and Hell*. Huxley described the experience at its best as a "gratuitous grace," providing access to what he called "Mind-at-Large," beyond the "reducing valve" of the ordinary egoic mind. He and Leary developed a strong rapport and had psilocybin sessions together during that period, working out a nonclinical, supportive, yet objective and safe framework for this kind of experimentation. It was Huxley who gave Leary the idea of adapting the *Tibetan Book of the Dead* as a kind of manual for spiritually-oriented psychedelic experiences—death-and-rebirth were to be seen as a kind of metaphor for the ego-transcendence and subsequent return of the typical psychedelic experience. The religious dimensions of psychedelic experience were also reinforced for Leary through his association with Alan Watts and Huston Smith, both of whom became participants in some of the studies.

The religious mystical approach to psychedelic drug-experiences was developed further during the time of the Harvard project by Walter Pahnke's epoch-making Good Friday Experiment, a carefully controlled scientific study of drug-induced religious experience. The set and setting of the experience were arranged to maximize the probability of religious experience: volunteer participants were students at a divinity seminary and the actual session took place in the basement chapel of a church where a Good Friday service with music and sermon was transmitted by speaker to the session room. The participants were divided into small groups, each with an experienced facilitator, and took either psilocybin or a placebo—with neither subject nor experimenter knowing who had which. Pahnke had culled a list of nine characteristics of mystical experience from the literature. He interviewed all subjects right after and a week after the experience. On all the criteria, the psilocybin group scored significantly higher than the placebo control group. In a twenty-five-year follow-up of this study, Rick Doblin found lasting impacts in many of the individuals who had participated in this study.

Gerald Heard, the distinguished English philosopher, friend of Aldous Huxley, and author of many books on the history of religion and mythology, visited the Harvard project early on and was very positive about the potential of psychedelics. He gave fascinating discourses on the role of psychedelic drugs in mystery cults in ancient times. He advised us not to publicize our findings, to stay underground, following the example of historical esoteric groups and secret societies. Needless to say, his advice was ignored; nothing could have been further from Tim Leary's whole nature. Both the Concord prison study and the Good Friday mysticism study attracted a huge amount of attention, both from the academic communities and from the general public. Psychedelic drugs were fast becoming sensationalized in the media.

During the years to come I often wondered what would have happened had we followed Gerald Heard's advice, thus letting psychedelic drugs become the exclusive province of a small group of visionary researchers and explorers. It did not seem to be the script we were called upon to follow. The experiences were too positive to not want to share them with everybody. It would appear that the time had come when this kind of experience should be made available to large numbers of searchers, so that "the doors of perception" could be opened, so that expanded consciousness was no longer something attainable only by rare individuals, but that it was here and now. The experience was a genuine view of what was possible. Those who felt the call to search could do so with a vivid knowledge of the goal.

The psilocybin project experienced increasing resistance from the Harvard University community. We were criticized that our research was loose and our approach uncontrolled and irresponsible. Let it be said here that these criticisms were prejudicial and not factual. To the contrary, as far as research is concerned, the project carried out and published several extensive statistical and questionnaire studies on the drug experience. No one was ever given a drug without their knowledge, or against their wishes, or without full and complete preparation before and support during the experience. Tranquilizer antidotes were always available but no one ever requested their use. The existence and reports of the psilocybin research project naturally stimulated a lot of interest among Harvard students and thus led indirectly to a good deal of drug self-experimentation. Supplies of mescaline, peyote, and other substances were at that time easily obtained by anyone with a little ingenuity. At that time, there were no state or federal laws governing their use. It must also be said that although Leary and Alpert flooded the academic community with research papers, memoranda, and descriptions, some of the tone of their written and verbal pronouncements had a quality of messianic overenthusiasm that turned a lot of people off.

The Harvard academic establishment put more and more restrictions on the conduct of the research, largely because of the mounting sensationalism of media accounts. The legitimate source of psilocybin for the research project dried up. Graduate students working on the project, like myself, were told that they would not be permitted to do their doctoral dissertation on research administering psilocybin. (Walter Pahnke's project was the last and only exception, and he was already an M.D., getting a Ph.D. in Religion.) With pressures mounting, we began to think of ways to carry on the work completely out of the

Timothy Leary, 1963, at the Millbrook, N.Y., psychedelic research center. (Photographer unknown; collection of Ralph Metzner)

University context. After two years of working exclusively with psilocybin in moderate dosages, LSD made its appearance, brought to Leary by a mysterious and unconventional Englishman named Michael Hollingshead. The depth and power of those experiences seemed several orders greater than psilocybin. We had referred to psilocybin as a "love drug" because of the interpersonal closeness that often developed among participants in a group session. LSD was never called that; with LSD, experiences of "ego-death" and "disintegration" became much more common.

Leary and Alpert felt that it was time to pursue psychedelic research under other than University auspices. Leary, with characteristic whimsy, said it was "as unfair to expect a university to sponsor research on visionary experience, as it would be to expect the Vatican to support research on effective aphrodisiacs." A nonprofit educational and research foundation was established in Cambridge, Massachusetts, for that purpose. It was called the International Federation for Internal Freedom, or IFIF for short. A summer program of guided psychedelic exploration was established in the little Mexican village of Zihuatanejo (which has since become a major resort). In the summer of 1962 a small group of colleagues and friends met there; in the following summer the program was advertised and offered to the general public. At that time uproar and sensationalistic news stories about LSD were escalating almost daily. After one month, the public summer program in Zihuatanejo was closed down by the Mexican authorities and the group expelled. Attempts were made to continue the program on the islands of Dominica and Antigua but were met with bitter resistance. Leary, Alpert, and their associates, my wife and myself included, retreated to a huge estate in the small upstate New York town of Millbrook, where an experimental community devoted to consciousness expansion by natural and traditional means was established and flourished for about ten years. For accounts of these projects and activities, the reader is referred to Leary's two autobiographical works, *High Priest* and *Flashbacks,* as well as to my account, "From Harvard to Zihuatanejo"(Metzner 1999).

The following year, 1964, LSD and all other psychedelics, including psilocybin, were placed on the FDA's Schedule I, the same category as heroin and cannabis, designated as having no accepted medical use with possession totally banned. The mushrooms containing psilocybin in natural form, like the ayahuasca plant concoction that contains DMT, remained in a legal limbo, since they were not specifically listed. Legitimate scientific research with psilocybin and other psychedelic research came to an almost complete halt in the United States. Nonetheless, underground exploration of heightened states of consciousness with entheogenic plants, fungi, and synthetic substances continued unabated, generating a vast literature of anthropological, literary, historical, and philosophical texts, as well as art works in painting, film, music, and the new arts of electronic digital imaging. Profound transformations of society and culture as well as expansions of collective consciousness occurred over the next several decades and continue to this day.

Some observers have blamed Tim Leary, with his admittedly passionate advocacy of psychedelic drug use, for the clamp down of government authority on scientific research. Some erstwhile colleagues and collaborators have said that federal agents told them that it was because of Leary and his provocative statements that their projects were being closed. Undoubtedly, this kind of conversation did occur. However, it is worth remembering that it was not the Harvard group that organized and produced mass events with thousands of psychedelic celebrants—this was a West Coast phenomenon associated with Ken Kesey and his group. The Harvard group's mission, if I may put it that way, was to find a way for the middle-class professional groups, of psychology, medicine, and religious ministry, as well as the artistic subcultures, to accommodate these astounding new substances. This attempt succeeded, to a point. After a critical mass of thousands of tripping youths and adults was reached, the establishment panicked. There was no way, in my opinion, that they were going to let these kinds of revolutionary activities continue. They *were* revolutionary expansions of consciousness, increasing the ability to think for oneself and take responsibility for one's own thoughts and behaviors.

I believe the proof of this assertion can be found in the exactly parallel process that happened in the 1980s with MDMA: for twelve years it was used in circles of a couple of dozen psychotherapists who found its empathogenic effects a wonderful aid to therapeutic insight. Then, because of the attractiveness of the experience, MDMA left the professional offices and became widely distributed, marketed, sold, used recreationally, ecstatically, in "rave" dances involving thousands. It was demonized (made to appear much more dangerous than it actually was) and, despite the sober and considered opposition of numerous doctors and therapists, prohibited.

TERENCE MCKENNA: MUSHROOMS, ALIENS, EVOLUTION, AND LANGUAGE

No account of the world of psilocybin mushrooms, or tryptamine hallucinogens in general for that matter, would be complete without an acknowledgement of the profound and far-reaching contributions of Terence McKenna. Before his death in the year 2000 of a brain tumor, at the age of fifty-three, he had become the most articulate, provocative, and inspiring spokesman for what could be called the "psychedelic movement," a loose nonorganized association of shamanistic consciousness explorers, pagan hippie revelers, techno-freaks, and advocates for global cultural evolution, who share a passionate interest in natural and synthetic mind-expanding technologies. Some have said he inherited the mantle of psychedelic prophet from Timothy Leary. Certainly he shared with Leary the Irishman's gift of eloquence and biting satirical wit, the intellectual brilliance and enthusiasm for radical innovation, as well as down-to-earth kindness and outrageous humor.

In 1971, Terence and his brother Dennis, young men in their twenties, went to the Amazon with some friends to search for ayahuasca, the legendary shamanic hallucinogen. What they found instead were large quantities of psilocybe mushrooms, with which they began what they called "the experiment at La Chorera." This was described in their book *The Invisible Landscape*. Basically, the experiment consisted of both of them repeatedly ingesting large quantities of the mushrooms, listening to a kind of interior, alien-sounding, buzzing or humming sound, and then reproducing that sound vocally to induce a lasting expanded state of consciousness. They had an elaborate and complex theory of how the psilocybin could activate endogenous tryptamines in the brain and create some kind of "holo-cybernetic unit of superconductive genetic material in which the entirety of the DNA memory bank would be at the command of the harmine readout mechanism, activated via tryptamine harmonic interference" (McKenna and McKenna 1975).

They later wrote that they experienced what psychologists would call a kind of shared psychotic break, with one of them becoming reactive and the other paranoid schizophrenic, a state that lasted for several weeks. Many unusual paranormal phenomena accompanied this state: synchronicities, telepathic communication between them, even sightings of what seemed like a UFO, and the apparent partial creation of some kind of hyperspatial communication device. One could say it was as much a shamanic madness initiation, a mythic journey to the outer reaches of the mind, as it was schizophrenia. The two intrepid explorers wrote a complex and difficult book on their experiences and theories, which also included a new mathematical theory of "time wave" based on the I Ching.

On first returning to the United States, the two brothers, more convinced than ever of the value of psilocybin mushrooms, wrote and published, under pseudonyms and with the collaboration of Kathleen Harrison as illustrator, the first Magic Mushroom Grower's Guide, which gave easy instructions for indoor cultivation and made the mushroom experience accessible to thousands (Oss and Oeric 1976). In it, Terence described a vision he received, perhaps the core and guiding vision of his life, of the interstellar origin of the mycelial nets, the true body of the mushrooms, which he believed maintain a "vast historical archive of the career of evolving intelligence on many worlds." The mycelial networks seek habitable planets, he was told, where they can enter into symbiotic communication and exchange with intelligent species, providing that species with access to the "community of galactic intelligence." The notion of the true form of the mushroom being the mycelial nets and the emphasis on symbiotic interactions of fungi with other species are points consistent with current scientific understanding of fungal evolution, as formulated in the work of Paul Stamets and Lynn Margulis. The idea of extraterrestrial origin is uniquely and provocatively Terence McKenna, emissary from the world of entheogenic fungi.

The McKenna brothers eventually took different career paths. Dennis went on to pursue graduate, doctoral, and postdoctoral studies in plant chemistry and pharmacology, published research in the pharmacology of Amazonian psychoactive plants, and worked as a research consultant for the pharmaceutical and herbal industry. Terence, more of an autodidact, devoted himself to ethnobotanical research and writing and became a much sought-after speaker on the lecture circuit.

The Mushroom Speaks

By Terence McKenna

"I am old, older than thought in your species, which is itself fifty times older than your history. Though I have been on earth for ages, I am from the stars. My home is no one planet, for many worlds scattered through the shining disc of the galaxy have conditions which allow my spores an opportunity for life. The mushroom which you see is the part of my body given to sex thrills and sun bathing, my true body is a fine network of fibers growing through the soil. These networks may cover acres and may have far more connections than the number in a human brain. My mycelial network is nearly immortal—only the sudden toxification of a planet or the explosion of its parent star can wipe me out. By means impossible to explain because of certain misconceptions in your model of reality all my mycelial networks are in hyperlight communication across space and time. The mycelial body is as fragile as a spider's web but the collective hypermind and memory is a vast and historical archive of the career of evolving intelligence on many worlds in our spiral star swarm. Space, you see, is a vast ocean to those hardy life forms that have the ability to reproduce from spores, for spores are covered with the hardest organic substance known. Across the aeons of time and space drift many spore-forming life-forms in suspended animation for millions of years until contact is made with a suitable environment. Few such species are minded, only myself and my recently evolved near relatives have achieved the hyper-communication mode and memory capacity that makes us leading members in the community of galactic intelligence. How the hyper-communication mode operates is a secret which will not be lightly given to man. But the means should be obvious: it is the occurrence of psilocybin and psilocin in the biosynthetic pathways of my living body that opens for me and my symbiots the vision screens to many worlds. You as an individual and man as a species are on the brink of the formation of a symbiotic relationship with my genetic material that will eventually carry humanity and earth into the galactic mainstream of the higher civilizations.

"Since it is not easy for you to recognize other varieties of intelligence around you, your most advanced theories of politics and society have advanced only as far as the notion of collectivism. But beyond the cohesion of the members of a species into a single organism there lie richer and even more baroque evolutionary possibilities. Symbiosis is one of these. Symbiosis is a relation of mutual dependence and positive benefits for both of the species involved. Symbiotic relationships between myself and civilized forms of higher animals have been established many times and in many places throughout the long ages of my development. These relationships have been mutually useful; within my memory is the knowledge of hyperlight drive ships and how to build them. I will trade this knowledge for a free ticket to new worlds around suns younger and more stable that your own. To secure an eternal existence down the long river of cosmic time I again and again offer this agreement to higher beings and thereby have spread throughout the galaxy over the long millenia. A mycelial network has no organs to move the world, no hands; but higher animals with manipulative abilities can become partners with the star knowledge within me and if they act in good faith, return both themselves and their humble mushroom teacher to the million worlds to which all citizens of our starswarm are heir. "

(FROM PSILOCYBIN—MAGIC MUSHROOM GROWER'S GUIDE BY O. T. OSS & O. N. OERIC, BERKELEY: AND/OR PRESS, 1976, PP. 8-9. REPRINTED BY PERMISSION OF LUX NATURA.)

In a later essay published in his book *The Archaic Revival*, Terence McKenna returns to this theory that:

the mushroom was a species that did not evolve on Earth. Within the mushroom trance I was informed that once a culture has complete understanding of its genetic information, it reengineers itself for survival. The *Stropharia cubensis* mushroom's version of reengineering is a mycelial network strategy when in contact with planetary surfaces and spore-dispersion strategy as a means of radiating throughout the galaxy . . . The other side does seem to be in possession of a huge body of information drawn from the history of the galaxy . . . The *Stropharia cubensis* mushroom, if one can believe what it says in one of its moods, is a symbiote, and it desires ever deeper symbiosis with the human species. It achieved symbiosis with human society early by associating itself with domesticated cattle and through them human nomads (McKenna 1991).

He cheerfully goes on to argue against his own thesis of extraterrestrial origin though, when he goes on to say: "I've recently come to suspect that the human soul is so alienated from our present culture that we treat it as an extraterrestrial. To us the most alien thing in the cosmos is the human soul." I personally find the thesis that extraterrestrial sources of vast intelligence might be communicating to the human species via entheogenic plants and mushrooms quite plausible and worthy of further investigation. It is consistent with the fact that interest in UFOs and extraterrestrial culture and contact has been growing tremendously in the second half of the twentieth century, in tandem with other movements of consciousness expansion, such as psychedelics, shamanism, spiritual practices, and higher states of consciousness. Harvard psychiatrist John Mack, who had made an intensive study of the UFO abduction experience, has shown, in his most recent book, *Passport to the Cosmos,* that reported contact and communication with alien intelligences is widespread and almost taken for granted in societies with living shamanic traditions (Mack 1999).

McKenna's thesis on the symbiotic role of entheogenic fungi was further extended in his major work, *The Food of the Gods,* in which he proposed that the discovery of consciousness-expanding mushrooms by our protohominid ancestors might have led to the development of language, greater intelligence, and culture (McKenna 1992). While this thesis has been generally treated with disdain, or else ignored, by the academic establishment, it is interesting that there isn't really a good alternative theory of the development of language or higher intelligence; furthermore, establishment academics are likely to be unfamiliar with the nature of psychedelic experience.

In favor of the idea that mind-expanding plants may have played some role (if not the only one) are (1) laboratory evidence that psilocybin and other psychedelics lower sensory thresholds, i.e., heighten acuity of sense perception, which would confer a direct adaptive advantage; (2) evidence from subjective experience accounts, as in this book and elsewhere, that psychedelic mushrooms heighten cognitive awareness and linguistic fluidity—as, for example, in the chants of Maria Sabina; (3) heightened problem-solving ability, with adaptive advantages, is also suggested by the effective use of psychedelic drugs in psychotherapy and shamanic divination; (4) studies of brain areas activated during psilocybin states that show major activity in the frontal cortex, the area most involved in processing complex perceptions and thoughts.

McKenna's book ranges far and wide through history, anthropology, and around the globe. He reexamines R. G. Wasson's hypothesis that soma was basically the fly agaric mushroom cult, imported from central Asia. Though historian of religion Mircea Eliade, who had written a masterful overview of shamanism, considered the use of psychoactive plants a degenerate form of religious practice, Wasson, on the basis of his experiences in Mexico with the psilocybe mushroom and his beliefs about soma, took the opposite view. Wasson held that all religious experience was

Terence McKenna, with *Banisteriopsis* vine, Hawaii, 1987. (Photo by Ralph Metzner)

originally induced by psychoactive plants and that the practices of yoga developed in India were substitute methods, created when the mushroom was no longer available to the ecstatic visionaries. McKenna comes down on the side of Wasson but thinks soma was the psilocybe mushroom, not the fly agaric, for the main reason that the latter is only mildly and ambiguously psychedelic; however, apart from some ambiguous mushroom-shaped stones, no evidence has been found for either mushroom species existing in India.

It may be impossible to ever settle this question in the history of religion completely. But that *some* psychedelic plants may have played a role in the origins of *some* religious traditions, as well as some aspects of language (for example, bardic poetry) seems both probable and plausible.

Central to the argument McKenna makes for a role of psilocybe mushrooms are the facts that *Stropharia cubensis* grows in cow dung and that cattle were the main source of wealth and livelihood in early Neolithic cultures in Asia and Africa. When McKenna came upon the

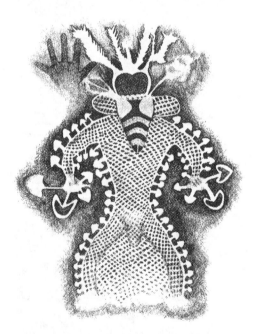

Cave painting of Bee-Head Mushroom Goddess, from the Round-Head Culture, ninth to sixth millennium B.C.E.; Tassili Plateau, southern Algeria. (Drawing by Kathleen Harrison)

cave paintings on the Tassili plateau in the Sahara Desert of southern Algeria, he found the most impressive piece of evidence for a mushroom cult in the Neolithic period, dating from the ninth to the seventh millennium B.C.E. Judging from cave paintings of giant female beings, these people worshipped the Great Goddess, as did other cultures during the Neolithic period in Old Europe and Anatolia. The people of the Tassili Plateau are described as the "Round Head" culture, because of cave paintings that show figures with rounded heads that could obviously be mushrooms. Among the surviving images there are running figures clutching fistfuls of mushrooms and a magnificent image of a giant anthropoid bee-faced goddess (the bee was often associated with the Goddess in Old Europe). The image is holding clusters of mushrooms in each hand and smaller mushrooms sprout from her arms, legs and trunk. Unmistakably, these people held mushrooms in very high regard. McKenna writes, "The contention here is that the rise of language, partnership society, and complex religious ideas may have occurred not far from the area where humans emerged—the game-filled, mushroom-dotted grasslands and savannahs of tropical and subtropical Africa. There the partnership society arose and flourished; there hunter-gatherer culture slowly gave way to domestication of animals and plants. In this milieu the psilocybin-containing mushrooms were encountered, consumed and deified. Language, poetry, ritual, and thought emerged from the darkness of the hominid mind" (McKenna 1992).

HYBRID NEO-SHAMANIC MUSHROOM RITUALS

In the ayahuasca book (Metzner 1999) I pointed out that one can distinguish four quite different approaches or frameworks to the use of the entheogenic ayahuasca: (1) the traditional shamanic healing framework, which works within a worldview completely different from the Western; (2) studies with tryptamine psychedelics as adjuvants to psychotherapy with a Western medical model; (3) the syncretic Brazilian churches (UDV, Santo Daime, Barquinia) that consider ayahuasca their sacrament and use it in a framework of worship and community building; and (4) shamanic-psychological hybrid rituals, conducted mostly in Europe and North America, that respect some of the basic forms of the shamanic traditions, but add psychological elements of preparation and integration.

In looking in a comparative way at the accounts of psilocybe mushroom experiences we have gathered for the present collection, several differences with the ayahuasca situation are immediately obvious. There are very few accounts of experiences with traditional healers using mushrooms, because mushroom curanderos like Maria Sabina are vanishing (unlike the situation with *ayahuasqueros*). We are fortunate to include two accounts of sessions with curanderos by Fred Swain and Bret Blosser, both of whom visited the Mazatec Indians in Oaxaca and encountered mushroom practitioners there.

Next, there are, to my knowledge, no mushroom "churches" using psilocybe mushrooms as their sacrament in religious ceremony. One could argue that the ecstatic musical events created by the Grateful Dead and their Dead Head followers, which involve the ingestion of psilocybin mushrooms ("shrooms") as well as cannabis and LSD, taken in a respectful, even reverential manner, constitute a novel kind of spiritual celebration, akin perhaps to Dionysian revels of ancient Greece.

Also, the use of psilocybin as an adjuvant to psychotherapy, prisoner rehabilitation, and the experimental induction of religious experience is described in review chapters and experiential accounts of the early days of the Harvard project. So, the majority of the accounts in this book are of experiences that took place in the context of what I call neo-shamanic hybrid rituals, which I shall describe in a bit more detail.

One variation of these contemporary neo-shamanic ritual forms, seldom if ever encountered with ayahuasca, is the use of mushrooms by individuals or small groups in an outdoor environment in the daytime. This is a marked departure from the traditional shamanic model in which any entheogen, including mushrooms, are always taken at night in almost total darkness. It is believed that reducing visual stimulation from the outer world enhances one's ability to see with the inner eyes of vision. Judging by the accounts of outdoor experiences in this book, such experiences, when carefully planned with conscious intention, often seem to produce a sense of profound connectedness to the spirit of the particular place, as well as the sacredness of the Earth as a whole and all her life forms.

These hybrid rituals preserve certain key elements from traditional shamanic healing and divination ceremonies. Participants sit, or sometimes lie, in a circle; there may be an altar in the center with objects representing the four elements (air, fire, water, earth), as well as ritual art objects or personal objects placed by the participants; there is an experienced guide or elder, with one or more assistants who don't take the mushroom medicine but take care of the material needs of the group and monitor the group energy flow; there may be drumming, rattling, and group chanting, as well as evocative recorded music; the ritual space is dedicated by prayers in the four directions and the invocations of spirits of animals and ancestors. A respectful attitude toward one another, toward Spirit, and to all life forms and Nature is key to a productive and illuminating experience. *Ritual is merely the conscious and intentional arrangement of set and setting*, which are the major determinants of any altered state of consciousness. Experienced entheogenic explorers understand the importance of setting and therefore devote attentive care to arranging a peaceful place and time, filled with natural beauty and free from outside distractions or interruptions.

Most of the participants in circles of this kind that I have witnessed were experienced in one or more psychospiritual practices, including shamanic drumming journeys, Buddhist *vipassana* meditation, tantric yoga, holotropic breathwork. Most participants have experienced and/or practiced various forms of psychotherapy and body-oriented therapy. The insights and learnings from these practices are woven by the participants into their work with the entheogenic mushrooms. Participants confirm that entheogenic mushroom or plant medicines combined with meditative or therapeutic insight processes amplify awareness and sensitize perception, particularly somatic, emotional, instinctual, and spiritual awareness.

The kinds of encounters with "alien intelligences" and "hyperspace communication" that Terence McKenna speaks about are probably more likely to be encountered in high dose sessions that the individual does alone. Such sessions do, however, carry a certain risk of temporary insanity and may often result in little more than prolonged states of dissociated awareness without any memory or understanding.

Some variation of the talking staff or singing staff is often used in group ceremonies. With this practice, also referred to as "council" or "wisdom circles," only the person who has the circulating staff speaks or sings and there is no discussion, questioning, or interpretation of what is spoken or sung, merely a respectful silence with a listening heart. In preparation for the circle, there is usually a sharing of intentions and purposes among the participants; after the circle ceremony often some time is given to sharing the experience for the purpose of integrating it more fully into one's life.

A common theme found repeatedly in experiences with entheogenic psilocybe mushrooms, as well as other entheogens, is a heightened awareness and concern for the protection of the Earth and its threatened habitats and wildlife, as well as of indigenous cultures. In that sense, it can be said that the growing interest in shamanism in general, and mushroom shamanism in particular, represents part of a worldwide movement toward a more direct experiential and spiritual connection to the natural world.

References

Estrada, Alvaro. 1981. *Maria Sabina—Her Life and Chants*. Santa Barbara: Ross-Erikson.

Gartz, Jochen. 1996. *Magic Mushrooms Around the World—A Scientific Journey Across Cultures and Time*. Los Angeles: Lis Publications.

Gershon, Michael. 1998. *The Second Brain*. New York: HarperCollins.

Gould, Stephen Jay. 1989. *Wonderful Life: The Burgess Shale and the Nature of History*. New York: W. W. Norton & Co.

Grob, Charles S. 1999. The Psychology of Ayahuasca. In *Ayahuasca—Human Consciousness and the Spirits of Nature,* ed. Ralph Metzner. New York: Thunder's Mouth Press.

Halpern, John. 1996. The Use of Hallucinogens in the Treatment of Addiction. Vol. 4, no. 2 of *Addiction Research,* 177–89.

Harner, Michael, ed. 1973. *Hallucinogens and Shamanism*. Oxford University Press.

Heinrich, Clark. 1982. *Strange Fruit—Alchemy, Religion and Magical Foods*. London: Bloomsbury Publishing.

Hofmann, Albert. 1990. Ride through the Sierra Mazateca in Search of the Magical Plant 'Ska Maria Pastora.' In *The Sacred Mushroom Seeker— Essays for Gordon Wasson,* ed. T. Riedlinger. Portland, Ore.: Dioscorides Press, 115–27.

James, William. 1912/1996. *Essays in Radical Empiricism*. Lincoln: University of Nebraska Press.

Leary, Timothy. 1968. *High Priest*. New York: New American Library; 1995 edition published by Ronin Publishing, Berkeley.

———. 1983. *Flashbacks—An Autobiography*. Los Angeles: J. P. Tarcher, Inc.

Mack, John, M.D. 1991. *Passport to the Cosmos—Human Transformation and Alien Encounters.* New York: Crown Publishers.

McKenna, Terence and Dennis McKenna. 1975/1993. *The Invisible Landscape—Mind, Hallucinogens and the I Ching.* San Francisco: HarperSanFrancisco.

McKenna, Terence. 1991. *The Archaic Revival.* San Francisco: HarperSanFrancisco.

———. 1992. *Food of the Gods—The Search for the Original Tree of Knowledge.* New York: Bantam Books.

Margulis, Lynn and Karlene Schwartz. 1982. *Five Kingdoms—An Illustrated Guide to the Phyla of Life on Earth.* New York: W. H. Freeman & Co.

Margulis, Lynn. 1998. *Symbiotic Planet—A New Look at Evolution.* New York: Basic Books.

Metzner, Ralph. 1968. On the evolutionary significance of psychedelic drugs. *Main Currents of Modern Thought* 25 (1):20–25.

Metzner, Ralph. 1994. Addiction and transcendence as altered states of consciousness. *Journal of Transpersonal Psychology* 26 (1):1–17.

——— ed. 1999a. *Ayahuasca—Human Consciousness and the Spirits of Nature.* New York: Thunder's Mouth Press.

———. 1999b. From Harvard to Zihuatanejo. In *Timothy Leary—Outside Looking In,* ed. Robert Forte. Rochester, Vt.: Park Street Press.

———. 1999c. *Green Psychology—Transforming Our Relationship to the Earth.* Rochester, Vt.: Park Street Press.

Murray, Michael. 1998. *5-HTP—The Natural Way to Overcome Depression, Obesity and Insomnia.* N.Y.: Bantam Books.

Oss, O. T. and Oeric, O. N. 1976. *Psilocybin—Magic Mushroom Growers Guide.* Berkeley, Calif.: Lux Natura.

Ott, Jonathan. 1976. *Hallucinogenic Plants of North America.* Berkeley, Calif.: Wingbow Press.

———. 1993. *Pharmacotheon—Entheogenic drugs, their plant sources and history.* Kennewick, Wash.: Natural Products Co.

———. 2001. *Shamanic Snuffs or Entheogenic Errhines.* Solothurn, Schweiz: Entheobotanica.

Ott, Jonathan and Jeremy Bigwood eds. 1978. *Teonanacatl—Hallucinogenic Mushrooms of North America.* Seattle, Wash.: Madrona Publishers.

Passie, Torsten, Juergen Seifert, Udo Schneider, Hinderk Emrich. 2002. The pharmacology of psilocybin. *Addiction Biology* 7:357–64.

Rätsch, Christian. 1996. Das Pilzritual der Mixe & Lol lu'um—Die Blüten der Erde: Entheogene Pilze bei den Tiefland Maya. In *Maria Sabina—Botin der heiligen Pilze* Liggenstorfer, R. and C. Rätsch, ed. Solothurn: Nachtschatten Verlag.

Schultes, Richard Evans and Albert Hofmann. 1979. *Plants of the Gods—Origins of Hallucinogenic Use.* New York: McGraw-Hill Book Co.

———. 1980. *The Botany and Chemistry of Hallucinogens.* Springfield, Ill.: Charles C. Thomas Publisher.

Shulgin, Alexander and Ann Shulgin. 1991. *PIHKAL—A Chemical Love Story.* Berkeley, Calif.: Transform Press.

———. 1997. *TIHKAL—The Continuation.* Berkeley, Calif.: Transform Press.

Stamets, Paul. 1996. *Psilocybin Mushrooms of the World—An Identification Guide.* Berkeley, Calif.: Ten Speed Press.

Strassman, Rick. 2001. *DMT—The Spirit Molecule.* Rochester, Vt.: Park Street Press.

Trout, K. 2002. *Some Simple Tryptamines—A brief overview & resource compendium.* Mydriatic Productions—Better Days Publication. Trout@yage.net.

Wasson, R. Gordon. 1963. The hallucinogenic fungi of Mexico: An inquiry into the origins of the religious idea among primitive peoples. *Psychedelic Review* 1(1):27–42.

———. 1968. *Soma—Divine Mushroom of Immortality.* New York: Harcourt, Brace, Jovanovich.

———. Gordon. 1980. *The Wondrous Mushroom—Mycolatry in Mesoamerica.* New York: McGraw-Hill.

Wasson, R. Gordon, Carl A. P. Ruck and Albert Hofmann. 1978. *The Road to Eleusis—Unveiling the Secret of the Mysteries.* New York: Harcourt, Brace, Jovanovich.

1

Ethnomycology and Distribution of the Psilocybian Mushrooms

John W. Allen and James Arthur

Throughout the ages, human beings have sought to alter their consciousness through the use of certain plants and fungi. The fascination of humans with dung-growing visionary mushrooms may go back to earliest times.

In their search for edible foods, early hunter-gatherers followed the trails of large migratory herds. When the weather conditions were right, they would find mushrooms growing from the manure left by ungulates. Being hungry and curious, early humans naturally consumed the small meaty mushrooms, some of which were psychoactive. These fungi presumably were valued not as food sources, but for the expansion of consciousness and perception they induced. Over the ages, a growing body of knowledge accumulated about which plants and fungi brought about what effects and how to prepare them. Archaeological records suggest

John W. Allen is an amateur ethnomycologist who has studied, photographed, and lectured on entheogenic fungi for more than twenty-five years. He is the author of many articles on field identification and nontraditional uses of psychoactive fungi around the world as well as books and CDs of mushroom data and mushroom-inspired art. See http://www.mushroomjohn.com and http://www.releasethereality.com/mjart.html.
James Arthur is an ethnomycologist, archaeoastronomer, mythologist, theologian, and shaman. He is the author of two books, *Mushrooms and Mankind* and the forthcoming *Mushrooms, Ayahuasca and DMT*. See: http://www.jamesarthur.yage.net.

that early humans knew about these mushrooms' special effects and consumed them intentionally for this very reason. Several writers have suggested that major religious ideas were inspired by the intake of the entheogenic mushrooms (Wasson 1968; Allegro 1970; Arthur 2000).

THE LIFE CYCLE OF MUSHROOMS

Approximately one hundred thousand species of fungi are known. Wild psychoactive mushrooms, known scientifically as *basidiomycetes* (club fungi), are the fruiting bodies of *saprophytes,* meaning they obtain their food by direct absorption of nutrients from the soil or other medium, such as the decomposing manure of ruminants or the decaying leaves, twigs, and wood of plants. The nutrients are dissolved by enzymes and then absorbed through the fungi's thin cell walls.

Most fungi reproduce by spores (fig. 1), tiny particles of protoplasm enclosed in sturdy cell walls. A common mushroom produces ten billion or more spores on its fruiting body, while giant puffballs may have as many as several trillion. Spores are found on the gill plates on the underside of the cap of a gilled mushroom. When the mushroom cap has fully opened and separated from its veil, the mature spores are dispersed by the wind or fall beneath the mushroom. Various small animals and insects, notably dung beetles and millipedes, feed on mushrooms and are instrumental in spore distribution. When the spores land on a habitable medium, they germinate and form *hyphae,* which grow and spread under the surface into many small fine silklike hairs that collectively form the mushroom *mycelium* (spawn). The mycelium grows, radiating outward into large, occasionally vast mats that permeate the material in which it is growing. When conditions are correct, the mycelium fruits and a mushroom appears above the ground (Encarta 2000).

WORLDWIDE DISTRIBUTION OF TRYPTAMINE-CONTAINING MUSHROOMS

The mushrooms under discussion here are those capable of producing altered states of consciousness brought on by the alkaloids psilocin and psilocybin. Mushrooms with these properties are referred to as *hallucinogenic, narcotic, magic, sacred, psychedelic, psychoactive, entheogenic,* and *neurotropic.* They have great diversity and worldwide distribution.

More than 180 species of fungi are recognized as containing the tryptamine alkaloids psilocin and/or psilocybin. They are Agaricales and include the general *Psilocybe* (117 species), *Gymnopilus* (13 species), *Panaeolus* (7 species), *Copelandia* (12 species), *Hypholoma* (6 species), *Pluteus* (6 species), *Inocybe* (6 species), *Conocybe* (4 species), and *Agrocybe, Galerina,* and *Mycena* (one each). Concerning the *Psilocybe,* the majority of species are found in subtropical humid forests. Mexico

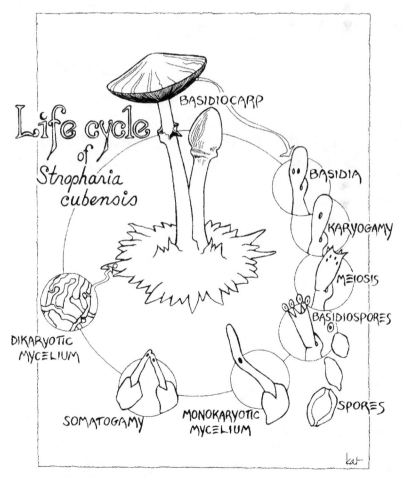

Figure 1. The lifecycle of a mushroom. (Drawn by Kathleen Harrison and reprinted with permission from *Magic Mushroom Grower's Guide*)

has the highest number of neurotropic fungi, with 76 species (39% of all known), of which 44 belong to the *Psilocybe* genus.

Neurotropic mushrooms have been identified as far north as Alaska and Siberia in the northern hemisphere and as far south as Chile, Australia, and New Zealand in the southern hemisphere. They grow wild from California in the western United States of North America to China and Japan, and from sea level up to 4,000 m elevation (e.g., *Psilocybe aztecorum* in high mountains of Mexico). As Gartz (1996) has pointed out, "The mushrooms occur in abundance wherever mycologists abound" (Guzmán, Allen, and Gartz 2000).

Although neurotropic fungi occur worldwide, knowledge of their distribution is still poorly developed. When they were first rediscovered and documented (Heim 1956; Singer 1949), for a time it was believed that they occurred only in Mexico. Later, numerous species were found in North and South America, Europe, Siberia, southwestern Asia, and Japan (Singer and Smith 1958). Guzmán, in his 1983 monograph on the genus *Psilocybe,* showed distribution in all the continents. Recently, Allen and Merlin (1992) and Guzmán (1995) described new species of *Psilocybe* in the United States, Mexico, Colombia, Puerto Rico, Spain, Thailand, and New Zealand. Gartz et al. (1995) and Stamets and Gartz (1995) reported new species in South Africa and the United States,

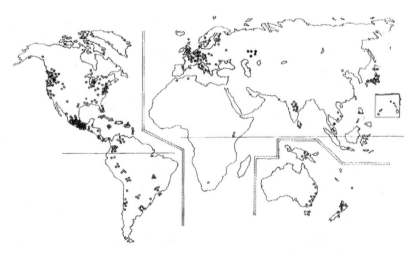

Figure 2. The worldwide distribution of psilocybian mushrooms. (Drawing courtesy of Gastón Guzmán, Instituto de Ecologia, Xalapa, Veracruz, Mexico)

respectively, confirming the broad distribution of these peculiar fungi. Guzmán, Allen, and Gartz (2000) have published a map of all the known species and their distribution throughout the world (fig. 2).

Today we lack records of neurotropic fungi from several parts of the world, including southern Russia, Mongolia, Arabia, and Turkey, and many regions of Africa and the Middle East, but this is not to say they don't exist. Magic mushrooms enjoy growing popularity amongst young people in Russia, Africa, and Israel, where Western influence brings knowledge of their existence. There are no presently known records of wild *Psilocybe* from Korea, Hawaii, Alaska, and Costa Rica. Even in the United States, mycological research is somewhat limited in several states, such as Arizona, Colorado, Illinois, Maryland, Vermont, Massachusetts, New Hampshire, and Pennsylvania, where there are no records of neurotropic species of *Psilocybe*. Most recently, two new species have been documented in Georgia, *Psilocybe weilii* and *Psilocybe atlantis,* and a new species is reported from Czechoslovakia (*Psilocybe arcana*).

ARCHAEOLOGICAL EVIDENCE OF HUMAN USE OF PSYCHOACTIVE MUSHROOMS

At an archaeological site in the Non Nak Tha region of northern Thailand, the bones of *Bos indicus* cattle were recently unearthed in conjunction with human remains. We know that *Psilocybe cubensis* flourishes in the manure of cattle in this region of Thailand. Terence McKenna has suggested that the temporal and physical relationship between the human bones and the bones of cattle is conclusive evidence that psychoactive mushrooms were known to the people who frequented this region around 15,000 B.C.E. (McKenna 1992). He suggested that the consumption of these types of mushrooms provided a certain impetus to humanity's intellectual evolution.

On the Tassili Plains in northern Algeria, cave paintings dating as far back as 9000 B.C.E. (Samorini 1992; Gartz 1996) portray anthropomorphic figures with mushroom images on their bodies, evidence that mushrooms were known and used in a mystic manner. Emboden (1979) describes, among traditional folk remedies from the second century Chin dynasty in China, a cure for "the laughing sickness," mushroom intoxication attributed to the accidental ingestion of psilo-cybian mushrooms. In eleventh century Japanese folklore there is a story of a group of woodcutters and nuns who became lost, hungry, and then quite inebriated after consuming what is believed to have been psilocybin-containing fungi. This exciting tale is recorded in the Japanese classic *Tales of Long Ago* (Sanford 1972).

HISTORICAL DOCUMENTATION OF FUNGAL SACRAMENTS

Amanita muscaria

The earliest record of the possible use of *Amanita muscaria* as an ine-briant is in the ancient Vedic hymns of India. Urine drinking associated with mushroom intoxication is mentioned in the *Rig Veda* (ninth and tenth mandalas).

Travelers and explorers in Siberia reported this practice during the late seventeenth and eighteenth century. In her books, *Windmills of the Mind* and *Hallucinogens: Cross Cultural Perspectives*, Marlene Dobkin de Rios (1976, 1984) discusses the custom of *Amanita*-related urine-drinking by the reindeer herdsmen of Siberia. It is likely that some psilo-cybian mushrooms were also historically used in Siberian shamanism (Wasson 1968). Recent research shows that certain isolated groups of Finn-Ugrian people, the Ostyak and the Vogul of western Siberia, today employ this mushroom shamanically, as do the Chukchee, Koryak, and Kamchadal people of northeastern Siberia (Heizer 1944; Brekham and Sam 1967; Wasson 1968; LaBarre 1975).

The contemporary use of *Amanita muscaria* is not restricted geo-graphically to Siberia (Arthur 2000; Ruck and Staples 2001). Graves (1960) and Schultes (1976) have revealed that some Finns, Lapps, and Afghanis use this species (Graves 1960; Schultes 1976). Its use is also well documented in Japan and the Philippines.

Among some groups of North American Indians (Wasson 1979), the Dogrib Athabascan (Schultes and Hofmann 1979) and the Ojibway of northern Michigan and Ontario (Keewaydinoquay 1978, 1979, 1998; Wasson 1979), use of *Amanita* species as a sacrament dates back over four hundred years. Several tribes (Ojibway, Chippewa, Iroquois, and others) have stories of little people associated with mushrooms, which imply a hidden widespread knowledge of entheogenic mushrooms among North American tribes.

The active ingredients isolated from *Amanita muscaria* include ibotenic acid and muscimol (Saleminck 1963; Eugster, Muller, and Good 1965). The same causative agents have also been isolated from a similar species, *Amanita pantherina* (Takemoto, Nakajima, and Sakuma 1964). Both species are sometimes employed recreationally in the Pacific Northwest region of North America (Ott 1978; Weil 1977, 1980) and in Europe (Fericgla 1992, 1993; Festi and Bianchi 1991). There are several other species of *Amanita*, which also contain these classical agents (Ott 1993; Guzmán, Allen, and Gartz 2000), but have no history of sacramental or recreational use.

Claviceps purpurea and LSD

A psychoactive fungus, *Claviceps purpurea,* is the most likely basis of another historically significant sacramental substance, the *kykeon* beverage of the ancient Greek rites of Demeter and Persephone, which were held annually for over two thousand years at Eleusis, outside of Athens. This ergot fungus is found on several wild grasses common in the Mediterranean region (Ott 1978; Wasson, Ruck, and Hofmann 1978; Schultes and Hofmann 1973, 1979), as well as on cultivated barley, rye, and wheat. Lysergic acid is a component of ergot, a small purple fungus that deforms the grains (Hofmann 1980, 1983). From this, Albert Hofmann derived LSD in the Sandoz laboratories in Basel, Switzerland, in 1938.

Boletus, Heimiella, and *Russula*

There is substantial evidence of the continuing use on the islands of New Guinea of several other families of fungi, *Boletus, Heimiella,* and *Russula* (Singer 1958; Reay 1959, 1960; Singer 1960; Heim and Wasson 1964, 1965; Nelson 1970; Heim 1972; Rios 1976, 1984). The Kuma people of the Western Highlands know these mushrooms as *nonda*. Tribes belonging to the Nangamp group call them *nong'n*. Effects attributed to these mushrooms include chronic states of hysteria and madness that may last for up to two days, for which the term *therogen* (becoming a beast) has been coined.

Copelandia cyanescens is a common species found in the manure of four-legged ruminants, with a worldwide distribution in the tropics and neotropics of both hemispheres. (Photo by John W. Allen)

PSILOCYBIAN MUSHROOM USE IN MESOAMERICA

Central and North American psychoactive and other mushrooms were first documented in the writings of early Spanish chroniclers, which included naturalists, botanists, and clergy. As the conquest spread through Central America to Mexico, they observed the Aztec priests and their followers being served the sacred fungi at festivals and other celebrations. The *Nahuatl*-speaking Aztec priests called the mushrooms *teonanácatl* (*teunamacatlth*), translatable as "Flesh of the Gods." The Spanish were a very mycophobic (mushroom-fearing) people and they deplored the Aztec rituals and the priests who employed mushrooms and other magical plants as divinatory substances (Sahagún 1956).

Various stages of the growth and development of *Psilocybe cubensis*, a species common in manure, with a worldwide distribution. (Photo by John W. Allen)

The magic mushroom was one of many fungi described in codices written by the Spanish in the fifteenth century. They relate that the mushrooms were often administered among the common people, merchants, and visiting dignitaries. The wealthy consumed them served with honey or chocolate. Botanists and historians, eager to please their masters back in Spain, reported the effects of the mushrooms in diabolical terms. They described the effects of these mushrooms and other plants as leaving their users in uncontrollable fits, claiming that when under the influence, native people would commit violent acts toward themselves and each other. They reported that many would fall into rages or into a stupor. To god-fearing Europeans of those days, this was reason enough for destroying devil-possessed natives.

Over the intervening centuries, the native people concealed their use of their sacred mushrooms from outsiders. Thus the sacred mushrooms remained a secret until the Wassons celebrated *velada* with Dona María Sabina in 1955. In the High Sierra region of the southern Mexican, indigenous Mazateca *curanderos* still use the sacred mushrooms today

Psilocybe semilanceata is known as the "liberty cap" mushroom. It is the most common
species sought after by psilophorian enthusiasts for its tranquil effects.
(Photo by John W. Allen)

as they have always done. The Nahua, who are direct descendants of
the Olmecs, Toltecs, and Aztecs, employ more than two dozen species
of entheogenic *Psilocybe* mushrooms for the purpose of healing and
curing (Wasson and Wasson 1957; Schultes 1939, 1940; Singer 1958).

Guzmán (1997) reported more than two hundred common names
that were used by various groups of Mexican Indians living in the Sierra
Mazateca of Oaxaca. The rare word *teonanácatl*, first reported by
Sahagún (1569–1582), is now used by Western scholars to refer to any
of the Mexican hallucinogenic fungi. However, no present day Indians
use this epithet. Among the most common Spanish names used to refer
to the sacred mushrooms are: *San Isidros* (a saint of agriculture), *pajaritos* ("little birds"), and *derrumbes* ("landslides") (Guzmán 1997;
Guzmán, Allen, and Gartz 2000; Allen 1997).

MUSHROOM CULTURE IN THE TWENTIETH CENTURY

The use of entheogenic fungi for laudable purposes first gained public recognition through research initiated by Timothy Leary, Richard Alpert, Ralph Metzner, and others at Harvard University in the early 1960s (Graves 1962; Weil 1963; Leary 1968). Timothy Leary had consumed seven sacred mushrooms while on vacation with friends in Cuernavaca, Mexico. He believed that the mushrooms could be a beneficial tool in psychiatric medicine. Ten years after Leary brought psilocybin to Harvard, mushroom use had spread from Mexico (Ott 1975; Sandford 1973; Pollock 1977–1978; Weil 1973, 1975–1976) to the northeast United States and Australia (Stocks 1963; McCarthy 1971; Southcott 1974), and then from Bali (Schultes and Hofmann 1980 [1973]) to Hawaii (Pollock 1974). Fifteen years after the announcement of the rediscovery of the ceremonial use of sacred mushrooms in Mexico, recreational use of psilocybian fungi had become widespread in the mainland United States. The recreational use of entheogenic mushrooms, *Psilocybe semilanceata* was reported in British Colombia by Heim et al. in 1966.

By the late 1960s, entheogenic mushroom awareness had arrived in the British Isles (Young et al. 1982; Harries and Evans 1981; Peden et al. 1982), spreading to Scandinavia (Christiansen et al. 1981, 1984; Ohenoja et al. 1987), and other European countries (Gartz 1993). In the early 1970s, psilocybian mushrooms gained large followings in Indonesia, South Asia, and Southeast Asia. Such use is now widespread amongst tourist populations in several third world countries (Allen and Gartz 1997). Liberty cap mushrooms (*Psilocybe semilanceata*) are common in Peru as is *Copelandia cyanescens*. Both *Psilocybe cubensis* and *Psilocybe subcubensis* are common in Colombia and other South American countries and several new species have recently been identified from Brazil.

Tourists with a desire to purchase magic mushrooms have influenced many poor Mexicans. Singer (1958, 1978) reported that Mexicans were debasing the mushroom rites of the Mazateca people of Oaxaca. For many poor people residing in undeveloped regions of Mexico, central and South America, the mushrooms were a welcome economic boon.

Predictably, by the early 1960s various scoundrels had learned the art of selling mushrooms that had no entheogenic properties, though this deception appeared to have subsided by the late 1970s.

As more people became aware of and experimented with hallucinogenic mushrooms, unenlightened governments of many countries proceeded to forbid their use and commerce. However, in the United States, Canada, Europe, and Australia, thousands of individuals continue using the mushrooms recreationally. Illicit cultivation of the tropical *Psilocybe cubensis* and the Pacific Northwest cold weather species *Psilocybe azurescens* is now reported in Europe. *Psilocybe cubensis*, *Copelandia (Panaeolus) cyanescens*, and *Psilocybe tampanensis* are legally cultivated and sold in "smart shops" in Holland. Fresh mushrooms are cultivated clandestinely and sold openly in shops in Denmark. Until 2002, fresh and dried mushrooms were sold in vending machines and shops in Japan. In the British Isles, possession and cultivation of fresh magic mushrooms is not illegal as long as the mushrooms are fresh. Additionally, possession of fresh specimens of *Psilocybe cubensis* is legal in the state of Florida.

Travelers became aware that entheogenic mushrooms were common on the island of Bali, they communicated this message to their friends, and eventually Balinese natives learned the economic value of the mushrooms. By the early 1980s, magic mushroom omelets and smoothies had become popular at several resort locations in Thailand, Nepal, and on both coasts of the Indian continent. It was recently reported that some species of magic mushrooms are now being served to tourists in the Philippine Islands.

Acknowledgments

The authors would like to thank Dr. Gastón Guzmán of the Instituto de Ecologia, Xalapa, Veracruz, Mexico for the use of the map of the worldwide distribution of species and Kathleen Harrison for her rendition of the lifecycle of a mushroom. All photographs are by John W. Allen.

References

Allen, John W. 1997 [1976]. *Magic Mushrooms of the Pacific Northwest.* Seattle: Psilly Publications.

———. 1997. Teonanácatl: Ancient and contemporary shamanic mushroom names of Mesoamerica and other regions of the world. *Ethnomycological Journals Sacred Mushroom Studies* 3:1–48. Seattle: Psilly Publications and RaverBooks.

———. 1998. Magic mushrooms of the Hawaiian Islands. *Ethnomycological Journals Sacred Mushroom Studies* 4:1–52. Seattle: Psilly Publications and RaverBooks.

———. 2000. Magic mushrooms of Australia and New Zealand. Online: www.erowid.org/library/books_online/magic_mushrooms_aunz/ magic_mushrooms_aunz.shtml/.

———. 2001. Mushroom pioneers: R. Gordon Wasson, Richard Evans Schultes, Albert Hofmann, Timothy Francis Leary and others. *Ethnomycological Journals Sacred Mushroom Studies* 7. Seattle: Psilly Publications and Raverbooks.

Allen, J. W. and J. Gartz. 1997. Magic mushrooms in some Third World countries: Part I: The symbiosis of entheogenic fungi, illicit drug use, and tourist influence on third world indigenous peoples. Part II: The ethnobotanical distribution, use, and users of entheogenic fungi in Indonesia, South Asia and Southeast Asia. *Ethnomycological Journals Sacred Mushroom Studies* 4:1–52. Seattle: Psilly Publications and RaverBooks. Also in Lyttle, Thomas, ed. 2000. *Psychedelics Reimagined.*

———. 2001. Psilocybian mushroom cultivation: A brief history regarding the contemporary use, cultivation and marketing of psilocybian fungi. *Ethnomycological Journals Sacred Mushroom Studies* 5. Seattle: CD-Rom Products.

———. 2001. *Teonanácatl: A Bibliography of Entheogenic Mushrooms.* Seattle: CD-Rom Products.

Allen, J. W. and M. D. Merlin. 1992. Psychoactive fungi use in Koh Samui and Koh Pha-Ngan, Thailand. *Journal of Ethnopharmacology* 35 (3):205–28.

Arthur, James. 2000. *Mushrooms and Mankind, The Impact of Mushrooms on Human Consciousness and Religion.* Glendale, Calif.: The Book Tree.

———. (Not yet published). *Mushrooms, Ayahuasca and DMT: The Keys to the Doorways of Eternity.* Glendale, Calif.: The Book Tree.

Brekman, I. and Y. A. Sam. 1967. Ethnopharmacological investigation of some psychoactive drugs used by Siberians and far Eastern minor nationalities of the USSR. In *Ethnopharmacological Search for Psychoactive Drugs,* ed. David H. Efron, 415. United States Public Health Services no. 1645.

Christiansen, A. L., K. E. Rasmussen, and Klaus Høiland. 1981. The content of psilocybin in Norwegian *P. semilanceata. Planta Medica* 42 (3):299–35.

———. 1984. Detection of psilocybin and psilocin in Norwegian species of *Pluteus* and *Conocybe. Planta Medica* 50 (4):341–43.

Dobkin de Rios, Marlene. 1976. *The Wilderness of Mind: Sacred Plants in Cross-Cultural Perspective.* Beverly Hills: Sage Publications.

———. 1984. *Hallucinogens: Cross-Cultural Perspectives. The Aztecs of Mexico.* Albuquerque: University of New Mexico Press.

Doniger, Wendy, trans. 1982. *The Rig Veda:* An Anthology of One Hundred Eight Hymns. Middlesex: Penguin Classics.

Eugster, C. H., G. F. R. Muller, and R. Good. 1965. Wirkstoffe aus *Amanita muscaria:* Ibotensauere und Muscazoni. *Tetrahedron Letters* 25:1813–15.

Fericgla, J. M. 1992. *Amanita muscaria* usage in Cataluña. *Integration: The Journal for Mind Moving Plants and Kultur* 2–3:63–65.

———. 1993. Las supervivencias culturales y el consumo actual de *Amanita muscaria* en Cataluña. *Atti 2 Convegno Nazionale Sugli Avvelenamenti da Funghi Rovereto Suppl.* 8 (3–4):245–56. 1992.

Festi, F. and A. Bianchi. 1991. *Amanita muscaria*, myco-pharmacological outline and personal experiences. *Psychedelic Monographs & Essays* 5:209–50.

Gartz, J. 1993. *Narrenschwämme: Psychotrope Pilze in Europa.* Herausforderung an Forschung und Wertsystem. Editions Heuwinkel. In German.

———. 1996. *Magic Mushrooms Around the World: A Scientific Journey Across Cultures and Time. The Case for Challenging Research and Value Systems,* trans. Claudia Taake. Los Angeles: Lis Publications.

Gartz, Jochen, Derek A. Reid, Michael T. Smith, and Albert Eicker. 1995. *Psilocybe natalensis* sp. nov.—The first indigenous bluing member of the Agaricales of South Africa. *Integration: The Journal for Mind Moving Plants and Kultur* 6:29–32.

Graves, R. 1960. What food the centaurs ate. *Food for centaurs.* 257–82. New York: Doubleday, Garden City.

————. 1962. A journey to paradise: Of toadstools and toxins, and a vivid tour of the Heaven (and Hell) that lies within us all. *Holiday* 32 (2):36–37, 110–11.

Guzmán, G. 1983. The genus Psilocybe: A systematic revision of the known species including the history, distribution and chemistry of the hallucinogenic species. *Beihefte zur Nova Hedwigia* 74. J. Germany: Cramer.

————. 1995. Supplement to the monograph of the genus *Psilocybe*. In *Taxonomic Monographs of Agaricales,* O. Petrini and E. Horak. *Bibliotheca Mycologica* 159:91–141. Berlin-Stuttgart: Cramer.

————. 1997. *Los Nombres de Los Hongos y lo Relaconado con ellos en América Latina. (Introdución a la Etnomicobiota y Micología aplicada de la Región. Sinonimia Vulgar y Científica).* Xalapa, Veracruz: CONABIO & Instituto de Ecologia.

Guzmán, G., J. W. Allen, and J. Gartz. 2000. A worldwide geographical distribution of the neurotropic fungi, analysis and discussion. Anali dei Civ. Mus. *Rovereto* 14:189–270. Italia. In English.

Harries, A. D. and V. Evans. 1981. Sequelae of a "magic mushroom banquet." *Postgraduate Medical Journal* 57 (671):571–72.

Heim, Roger. 1956. Les champignons divinatoires utileses dans let rites des Indiens Mazatiques, recueilles au cours de leur premier voyage au Mexique, en 1953, par Mme Valentina Pavlovna Wasson et M. R. Gordon Wasson. *Comptes Rendus Hebdomadaries des Séances de l'Académie des Sciences* 242:965–68 and 1389–95.

————. 1957. *Les Champignons D'Europe,* 162–63. Paris: Boubee and Cie.

————. 1972. Mushroom madness in the Kuma. *Human Biology in Oceana* 1 (3):170–78.

Heim, Roger and R. Gordon Wasson. 1958. Les champignons hallucinogènes du Mexique: Etude ethnologiques, taxonomique, biologiques, physiologiques et chemiques. With the collaboration of Albert Hofmann, Roger Cailleux, A. Cerletti, Arthur Brack, Hans Kobel, Jean DeLay, Pierre Pichot, Th. Lempiere and J. Nicolas-Charles. *Archives Du Museum National d'Histoire Naturalle* 6 (7).

————. 1964. Note préliminaire sur la folie fongique des Kuma. *Comptes Rendus Hebdomadaries des Séances de l'Académie des Sciences* 258:1593–98.

————. 1965. The mushroom madness of Kuma. *Botanical Museum Leaflets of Harvard* 21 (1):1–36.

Heim, R., R. Cailleux, R. G. Wasson, and P. Thevenard. 1967. *Nouvelle Investigations sur les Champignons Hallucinogènes,* ed. Du Mus. Paris: Nat. d'Hist. Nat.

Heizer, Robert F. 1944. Mixtum Compositum: The use of narcotic mushrooms by primitive peoples. *Ciba Symposium* 5 (2):1713–16.

Hofmann, A. 1980. The Mexican relatives of LSD—The sacred mushroom Teonanácatl. *LSD My Problem Child*, trans. Jonathan Ott, 101–44. New York: McGraw-Hill.

Hofmann, A. 1983. *LSD My Problem Child.* New York: McGraw-Hill.

Jenkins, John Major. 1998. *Maya Cosmogenesis 2012: The True Meaning of the Maya Calendar End Date.* Santa Fe: Bear & Company.

Keewaydinoquay. 1978. Puhpohwee for the people: A narrative account of some uses among the Anishinaubeg. *Ethnomycological Studies No. 5.* Cambridge, Mass.: Botanical Museum of Harvard.

———. 1979. The legend of Wiskwedo. *Journal of Psychedelic Drugs* 11 (1–2):29–32. Proceedings from the Conference on Hallucinogens and Shamanism in Native American Life. San Francisco, Calif.

Keewaydinoquay et al. 1990. The people of the Miniss Kitigan who were and are honor the spirit of Waussungnaabe who was and is. In *The Sacred Mushroom Seeker: Essays for R. Gordon Wasson,* ed. Thomas J. Reidlinger, 141–46. Portland: Dioscorides Press.

LaBarre, W. 1975. Anthropological perspectives on hallucination and hallu-cinogens. In *Hallucinations: Behavior, Experience and Theory,* eds. Ronald K. Siegel and Louis Jolyon West, 9–52. New York: John Wiley & Sons.

Leary, T. F. 1968. *High Priest.* New York: The World Publishing Co.

Lowy, B. 1977. Hallucinogenic mushrooms of Guatemala. *Journal of Psychedelic Drugs* 9 (2):123–25.

McCarthy, J. P. 1971. Some familiar drugs of abuse. *Medical Journal of Australia* 2 (21):1078–81.

McKenna, T. 1992. *Food of the Gods: The Search for the Original Tree of Life. A Radical History of Plants, Drugs, and Human Evolution.* New York: Bantam Books.

Nelson, H. 1976. On the etiology of mushroom madness in highland New Guinea. *Kaimbi Culture and Psychotropism.*

Oakenbough, W. 1975. A guide to the Psilocybin mushrooms of British Columbia. *Georgia Straight.* September 18.

Ohenoja, E., J. Jokiranta, T. Makinen, A. Kaikkonen, and M. M. Airaksinen. 1987. Occurrence of psilocybin and psilocin in Finnish fungi. *Journal of Natural Products (Lloydia)* 50 (4):741–44.

Oldridge, S. G., D. N. Pegler, and B. M. Spooner. 1989. *Wild Mushrooms and Toadstool Poisoning.* Kew, U.K.: Royal Botanic Gardens Publications.

Ott, J. 1975. *Amanita muscaria:* usos y química. *Cuadernos Científicos* 4:203–21.

———. 1978. Recreational use of hallucinogenic mushrooms in the United States. In *Mushroom Poisoning: Diagnosis and Treatment,* eds. Barry H. Rumack and Emanuell Saltzman, 231–43.

———. 1993. *Amanita muscaria. Pharmacotheon: Entheogenic Drugs, their plant sources and History.* Kenniwick, Wash.: Natural Products.

Padmore, T. 1980. Magic mushrooms pose few risks. *Vancouver Sun,* 20. October 17. British Colombia.

———. 1980. Magic of mushrooms charms science sleuth. *The Vancouver Sun,* A3. October 31. British Columbia.

Peden, N. R., S. D. Pringle, and J. Crooks. 1982. The problem of psilocybin mushroom abuse. *Human Toxicology* 1:417–24.

Pollock, Steven H. 1974. A novel experience with *Panaeolus:* A case study from Hawaii. *Journal of Psychedelic Drugs* 6 (1):85–89.

———. 1975–1976. Liberty caps: Recreational hallucinogenic mushrooms. *Drug and Alcohol Dependence* 1 (6):445–47.

———. 1975. The psilocybin mushroom pandemic. *Journal of Psychedelic Drugs* 7 (1):73–84.

———. 1976. Psilocybian mycetismus with special reference to *Panaeolus. Journal of Psychedelic Drugs* 8 (1):43–57.

———. 1977–1978. Psychotropic mushrooms and the alteration of consciousness, I: The ascent of psilocybin mushroom consciousness. *Journal of Altered States of Consciousness* 3 (1):15–35.

Reay, Marie. 1959. *The Kuma: Conformity in the New Guinea Highlands.* Melbourne: Melbourne University Press.

———. 1960. Mushroom madness in the New Guinea Highlands. *Oceana* 31 (3):137–39.

Rumack, Barry and Emanuell Saltzman, eds. 1978. *Mushroom Poisoning: Diagnosis and Treatment.* West Palm Beach: CRC Press.

Sahagún, Bernardino de. 1956 [Sixteenth century]. *The Florentine Codex.* Sahagún's Spanish text and the Florentine Codex text translated by Angel Maria Garibay K. Porrua, Mexico.

———. 1950–1969. *Florentine Codex: General History of the Things of New Spain.* English translation by C. E. Dibble and A. J. O. Anderson. 12 vols. Salt Lake City: University of Utah Press.

Saleminck, C. A., J. W. ten Broeke, P. L. Schuller, and E. Veen. 1963. Über die basischen Inhaltssetoffe des Fliegenpilzes XII. Mitteilung: Über die Anwesenheit von l-Hyoscyamin. *Planta Medica* 11:139–44.

Samorini, G. 1992. The oldest representations of hallucinogenic mushrooms in the world (Sahara desert. 9000–7000 B.P.). *Integration: The Journal for Mind-Moving Plants and Kultur* 2–3:69–78.

Sandford, Jeremy. 1973. *In Search of the Magic Mushroom.* New York: Clarkson N. Porter.

Sanford, J. H. 1972. Japan's laughing mushrooms. *Economic Botany* 26:174–81.

Schultes, R. E. 1939. The identification of Teonanácatl, a narcotic basidiomycete of the Aztecs. *Botanical Museum Leaflets of Harvard* 7 (3):37–54.

———. 1940. Teonanácatl: The narcotic mushroom of the Aztecs. *American Anthropologist* 42:429–43.

———. 1976. Mushrooms. *Hallucinogenic Plants,* 58–71. A Golden Garden Guide. N.Y.: Golden Press.

Schultes, R. E. and A. Hofmann. 1973. *The Botany and Chemistry of the Hallucinogens.* Springfield: Charles E. Thomas. 2nd ed. 1980.

———. 1979. *Plants of the Gods: Origins of Hallucinogenic Use.* New York: McGraw-Hill Book Co.

Singer, R. 1949. *The Agaricales (Mushrooms) in Modern Taxonomy. Lilloa* 22:472, 506. 2nd ed. from University of Tucuman, Argentina, August 1962.

———. 1958. Mycological investigations on Teonanácatl, the Mexican hallucinogenic mushrooms part one: The history of Teonanácatl, field work and culture. *Mycologia* 50 (2):239–61.

———. 1958. A *Russula* provoking hysteria in New Guinea. *Mycopathologia et Mycología Applicata* 9 (4):275–79.

———. 1960. Sobre algunas especies de hongos presumiblemente psicotrópicos. *Lilloa* 30:117–29.

————. 1978. Hallucinogenic mushrooms. In *Mushroom Poisoning: Diagnosis and Treatment,* eds. Barry H. Rumack and Emanuell Saltzman, 201–14.

Singer, R. and A. H. Smith. 1958. Mycological investigations on Teonanácatl, the Mexican Hallucinogenic mushrooms part two: A taxonomic monograph of *Psilocybe* section *Caerulescens. Mycologia* 50 (2):262–303.

Southcott, R. V. 1974. Notes on some poisoning and other clinical effects following the ingestion of Australian fungi. *South Australian Clinics* 6 (5):441–78.

Stamets, P. 1978. *Psilocybe Mushrooms and their Allies.* Seattle: Homestead Book Co.

————. 1996. *Psilocybin Mushrooms of the World.* An Identification Guide. Berkeley, Calif.: Ten Speed Press.

Stamets, P. and J. Gartz. 1995. A new caerulescent Psilocybe from the Pacific Coast of Northwestern America. *Integration: Journal for Mind-Moving Plants and Kultur* 6:21–28.

Stocks, A. E. 1963. Mushroom poisoning in Brisbane. *Journal of Princess Alexandria Hospital* 1:21–24.

Takemoto, T., T. Nakajima, and R. Sakuma. 1964. Isolation of a flyicidal constituent: Ibotenic acid from *Amanita muscaria* and *Amanita pantherina. Yakugaku Zasshi* 84 (12):1233–34.

Unsigned. 2002. Japan bans magic mushrooms. AP Wire Service. May 29.

Wasson, R. G. 1957. Seeking the magic mushroom. *Life,* 100–102, 109–120.

————. 1959a. The hallucinogenic mushrooms of Mexico: An adventure in ethnomycological exploration. *Transactions of the NY Academy of Science* Series II, 21 (4):325–39

————. 1959b. Wild mushrooms: A world of wonder and adventure. *Herbarist* 24:13–28. Boston.

————. 1968. *Soma: Divine Mushroom of Immortality.* Ethno-Mycological Studies No. 1. The Hague: Mouton and Co. N.Y.: Harcourt Brace Jovanovich.

————. 1979. Foreword. In *Phantastica: Rare and Important Psychoactive Drug Literature from 1700 to the present.* Privately published by William and Victoria Dailey. Antiquarian Books and Fine Prints. 8216 Melrose Avenue, Los Angeles, California 90046.

————. 1980. *The Wondrous Mushroom: Mycolatry in Mesoamerica.* Ethnomycological Studies No. 7. New York: McGraw-Hill Book Co.

Wasson, R. Gordon., Albert Hofmann, and Carl A. P. Ruck. 1978. *The Road to Eleusis: Unveiling the Secret of the Mysteries*. Ethnomycological Studies No. 4. New York and London: Harcourt Brace Jovanovich.

Wasson, Valentina P. 1958. I ate the sacred mushroom. *This Week*, 8–10, 36. May 19.

Wasson, Valentina P. and R. Gordon Wasson. 1957. *Mushrooms, Russia, and History*. 2 vols. New York: Pantheon Books.

———. 1958. The hallucinogenic mushrooms. *Garden Journal* 1–5, 31.

Weil, Andrew. 1963. Drugs and the mind. *Harvard Review* 1 (4):1–3.

———. 1972. *The Natural Mind: A New Way of Looking at Drugs and the Higher Consciousness*. Boston: Houghton Mifflin.

———. 1973. Stalking the wild mushroom high. *Boston After Dark*, 18. August 14.

———. 1975. Mushroom hunting in Oregon: Part 1–4. *Journal of Psychedelic Drugs* 7 (1):89–102.

———. 1975–1976. A mushroom omelette. *Journal of Altered States of Consciousness* 2 (2):123–32. Bayview Publishing Co., Inc.

———. 1977. The use of psychoactive mushrooms in the Pacific Northwest. *Botanical Museum Leaflets of Harvard* 25 (5):131–48.

———. 1978. Reflections on psychedelic mycophagy. In *Teonanácatl: Hallucinogenic Mushrooms*, eds. Jonathan Ott and Jeremy Bigwood, 149–55.

———. 1980. Mushroom Hunting in Oregon. Mushrooms I–IV. *Marriage of the Sun and Moon*, 43–57. Boston: Houghton Mifflin Company.

Young, R., R. Milroy, S. Hutchinson, and C. Mikessen. 1982. The rising price of mushrooms. *Lancet* no. 8265:213–15.

2

GLOBAL ECOLOGIES, WORLD DISTRIBUTION, AND RELATIVE POTENCY OF PSILOCYBIN MUSHROOMS

PAUL STAMETS

Psilocybin mushrooms grow throughout most of the world and can be found in both fields and forests. Psilocybin mushrooms are *saprophytes*—they grow on dead plant material. Before the impact of human civilization, psilocybin species were largely restricted to narrowly defined ecosystems. Many thrive after ecological catastrophes. Landslides, floods, hurricanes, and volcanoes all create supportive habitats for many *Psilocybe* mushrooms. This peculiar affection for disturbed habitats enables them to travel, following streams of debris.

As humans destroy woodlands and engage in artificial construction, *Psilocybes* and other litter saprophytes proliferate, feeding on the surrounding plus of wood chips and refuse, especially in interface environments where humans, forests and grasslands struggle to coexist. Since human development seems inextricably associated with ecological

Paul Stamets has been studying mushrooms for over twenty years and has discovered and coauthored four new psilocybin species. He runs a mail-order business, Fungi Perfecti (www.fungi.com), which grows and distributes gourmet and medicinal (no psilocybin) species. Paul Stamets also conducts workshops on mushroom cultivation and is the author of the definitive guide *Growing Gourmet and Medicinal Mushrooms*.

disturbance, *Psilocybe* mushrooms and civilization continue to co-evolve. Today, many *Psilocybes* are concentrated wherever people congregate—around parks, housing developments, schools, churches, golf courses, industrial complexes, nurseries, gardens, freeway rest areas, and government buildings—including county and state courthouses and jails! This successful adaptation is a comparatively recent phenomenon; in the not-too-distant past, these species were competing in a different environmental arena. Many of the *Psilocybes* are now evolving in a decidedly advantageous direction, parallel to human development. The way these mushrooms have evolved in close association with humans suggests an innate intelligence on the part of the mushrooms.

At the end of the last major ice age, about twelve thousand years ago, melting glaciers etched exposed lands with rivers. As climates shifted, new ecosystems appeared and continued to be transformed. Through millennia, either from natural or from man-made causes, jungles evolved into savannas and in many cases became deserts. Coincident with the retreat of the glaciers, the human species became less nomadic and more dependent upon planted crops. Many believe this marked the beginning of the path leading to civilization as we know it today.

Northern Algeria is one example. Today, the region is in stark contrast to its water-rich past. Once filled with rivers and lined with riparian woodlands, the Tassili plateau has now been engulfed by the expanding Sahara Desert.

In the 1930s and 1940s, hundreds of Paleolithic drawings were discovered in this region, painted on the walls of caves and on rock faces. Ethno-archaeologist Henri Lhote and photographer Kazuyoshi Nomachi were the first to systematically catalogue the thousands of cave art drawings. While searching for water, they accidentally encountered "a figure wearing a mask in a deep recess that may have been a sanctuary." The original artist lived seven thousand years ago, at a time when glaciers were rapidly receding. The glacial waters fueled the life cycles of many mushroom species.

Time has erased much of the original detail, which showed many mushrooms outlining the shamanic figure. Fortunately, early photographs clearly communicate the intent of the artist: that mushrooms were revered in a magico-spiritual context and were a powerful influence on the artist's vision of the world. The beelike face may relate to the pre-serving of the mushrooms in honey. For the Paleolithic human, the effects from ingesting psilocybin mushrooms would have precipitated one of the most phenomenal events they would ever experience: a cascade of con-sciousness, the awakening of the spiritual and intellectual self, the intro-duction to complex fractal mathematics and to other dimensions. Such experiences continue to inspire artists, computer geniuses, and some of the greatest thinkers in history.

One *Psilocybe* species is documented from northern Algeria: *P. mairei*, resembling the potent *Psilocybe cyanescens*. This group thrives in riparian habitats—open areas with sandy soils seasonally littered with wood debris. *P. mairei* is relatively rare, having been collected only a few times this century. Do these few collections represent the end of a bygone era when mushrooms were more prevalent? Perhaps *P. mairei* is the same species that inspired the artist who drew the mushroom fig-ures in the Tassili cave.

Other reports of presumably psilocybin varieties from northern Africa occasionally surface. Reports of a *tamu* (mushroom of knowl-edge) from the Ivory Coast are teasing but not sufficiently docu-mented. The Italian researcher Giorgio Samorini noted that there are mushroom-based churches in southern Nigeria. Over the years, I have heard similar reports of Christian churches from Mexico, Brazil, and Russia that feature crosses whose centerpieces contain mysterious, encapsulate dried mushrooms of unknown identities and origins.

With the domestication of cattle, the dung-dwelling *Psilocybes* were brought within a defined geographical sphere of daily human experi-ence. Pasture species such as *Psilocybe semilanceata*, the liberty cap, proliferated. Some researchers have suggested that *Psilocybe cubensis* (golden top of the Old World) was imported into the Western Hemisphere with the Spanish missionaries and slave traders via the cat-tle they brought with them from islands off West Africa. *P. cubensis* soon became the most prominent dung mushroom throughout the trop-ics. Today, several hundred years later, *P. cubensis* can be collected from the dung of cattle in subtropical pastures around the globe.

Non-native mushrooms have also spread with the importation of exotic plants. Many species in the Pacific Northwest were undoubtedly brought from Europe, probably in the soil around the bases of exotic trees and ornamentals such as rhododendrons, roses, and azaleas. *Psilocybe cyanescens*, the wavy capped *Psilocybe*, is a good example. Every fall, when there are few visitors, I go searching for *Psilocybes* at rhododendron or rose gardens. Rarely am I disappointed.

Today, *P. cubensis* is the most commonly cultivated psilocybin mushroom in the world. Underground centers of cultivation, where large crops are grown, function as invisible spore geysers, gushing germ plasm into their immediate surroundings. Uplifted into the airstreams, spore clouds have spread across the continents. With the emission of so much spore mass, the range of distribution is likely to continue to expand. It seems that new strains could evolve in our lifetime, with tolerances for cooler and/or drier environments. And, with modern means of travel, spores can be carried thousands of miles in the course of a day—they can simply hitchhike upon unknowing airline passengers. I know of some people who have publicly opposed the spread of information about *Psilocybe*, but have unwittingly spread spores through casual contact with it.

Psilocybes have propelled themselves to the front lines of the evolutionary race precisely because of their psilocybin content. The production of psilocybin has proven to be a competitive evolutionary advantage. Psilocybin mushrooms carry with them a message from nature about the health of the planet. At a time of planetary crisis brought on by human abuse, the Earth calls out through these mushrooms—sacraments that lead directly to a deeper ecological consciousness and motivate people to take action.

Throughout the world at least thirty thousand mushroom species have been documented. About a hundred are known or suspected active species and varieties. By active, I mean they produce psilocybin, psilocin, baeocystin, or nor-baeocystin. The species producing psilocybin analogues are concentrated in the species *Psilocybe*, which has more than eighty species. A few psilocybin mushrooms belong to other genera, including *Panaeolus*, *Pluteus*, *Gymnopilus*, *Conocybe*, and *Inocybe*. Although the vast majority of the species in these genera are not active, more than half the species in the genus *Psilocybe* are psilocybin-producing.

Psilocybin mushrooms from the genera *Psilocybe* and *Panaeolus* are fairly safe to identify, in that there are no known poisonous species in these two genera. There are, however, several nasty species in the genera *Conocybe* and *Inocybe* that could be damaging or lethal. Because of the danger of misidentification, I recommend that you avoid the genera *Conocybe* and *Inocybe* until you become sufficiently skilled at identification.

I spent hundreds of hours hunting in woods and fields before finding my first *Psilocybe*. I did run across many small brown mushrooms and hoped they might contain psilocybin but subsequently learned that the ones I had collected were poisonous! Today I am grateful that my eagerness in finding these mushrooms was tempered by a prevailing concern for self-preservation. Knowing that many people are not as cautious as I has convinced me that a good guide is urgently needed.

In the Pacific Northwest, at least four thousand mushroom species have been identified, with more than a dozen of these containing psilocybin. About three-quarters as many have been reported in Europe thus far. Mexico is the richest in psilocybin mycoflora. In fact, I have yet to find a single temperate or tropical habitat with high annual rainfall that lacks psilocybin mushrooms. But without some form of guidance, the random discovery of a psilocybin mushroom is, frankly, remote. In any region of the world, psilocybin mushrooms are greatly outnumbered by toxic mushrooms.

In some parts of the world, psilocybin mushrooms have not been reported at all. But just because they have not been reported does not mean they do not exist. Perhaps the indigenous population is simply unaware of them. Or, perhaps those who are knowledgeable are reluctant to discuss the subject.

RELATIVE POTENCY OF PSILOCYBIN MUSHROOM SPECIES

The following analyses are derived from research conducted over the past twenty years. Considerable variation in the content of psilocybin and psilocin had been found within each species. For the purpose here and with but one exception, I am listing the maximum concentrations detected in twelve *Psilocybe* species. [For more complete information, please consult the references in *Psilocybin Mushrooms of the World*—

eds.] Other indole alkaloids have been found in these mushrooms besides psilocybin and psilocin. Baeocystin, nor-baeocystin and/or aeruginacine are closely related to psilocin and may be active (Gartz 1992). In general, these related indoles are present in lesser concentrations than psilocybin and psilocin. The actual potency of the mushrooms you collect is likely to be less rather than more potent than the table indicates.

SPECIES	% PSILOCYBIN	% PSILOCIN	% BAEOCYSTIN	REFERENCE
P. azurescens	1.78	.38	.35	Stamets and Gartz 1995
P. bohemica	1.34	11	.02	Gartz & Muller 1989; Gartz 1994
P. semilanceata	.98	.02	.36	Gartz 1994
P. baeocystis	.85	.59	.10	Repke et al. 1977; Beug and Bigwood 1982 (b)
P. cyanescens	.85	.36	.03	Stijve and Kuyper 1985; Repke et al. 1977
P. tampanensis	.68	.32	n/a	Gartz 1994
P. cubensis	.63	.60	.025	Gartz 1994; Stijve and de Meijer 1993
P. weilii (nom. prov.)	.61	.27	.05	
P. hoogshagenii	.60	.10	n/a	Heim and Hofmann 1958
P. stuntzii	.36	.12	.02	Beug and Bigwood 1982(b); Repke et al. 1977
P. cyanofibrillosa	.21	.04	n/a	Stamets et al. 1980
P. liniformans	.16	n/d	.005	Stijve and Kuyper 1985

The percentage figures are always based on dry weight. For instance, a one-gram mushroom containing 1% psilocybin would have .01 grams or 10 mg psilocybin. The threshold dose, the amount where pharmacological effects can first be noticed, is 2–4 mg. Stronger but still moderate effects, which Jonathan Ott (1993) describes as "entheogenic," are inspired above 6 mg for psilocin or 10 mg for psilocybin. Since psilocybin is degraded into psilocin during digestion, one is feeling the effects only of psilocin, a dephosphorylated form of psilocybin.

Readers should note that within any one species there can be a tenfold or more range in psilocybin and psilocin production from one collection to the next!

The "Wondrous Mushroom" Legacy of R. Gordon Wasson

Thomas Riedlinger

Many events helped transform the American cultural landscape during the 1950s, but perhaps none more profoundly than a little-noticed event that transpired on June 29, 1955. In Huautla de Jiménez, a village in south central Mexico, a middle-aged white man from New York City found himself taking possession of an ancient mystical secret that a tribe of local Indians, the Mazatecs, had guarded for thousands of years. Though some would later say he stole this secret, others believe that he acted as an agent or courier charged with transmitting a gift from the Indian culture to ours: a gift of sacred medicine for Western seekers.

The medicine—the gift—was a variety of psychoactive mushrooms that the Indians in ancient times called *teonanácatl*. The man from New York, a Wall Street banker by the name of R. Gordon Wasson, had come to Mexico to confirm his belief that the legend of teonanácatl was

Thomas J. Riedlinger has degrees in psychology and theological studies. He has been an Associate in Ethnomycology at Harvard Botanical Museum and currently is a Fellow of the Linnean Society of London. In addition to writing and lecturing, he works as a Licensed Mental Health Counselor in Olympia, Washington. He has published several essays and book chapters on entheogens and edited *The Sacred Mushroom Seeker: Essays for R. Gordon Wasson* (1990). He can be reached via e-mail at: tom@sunbreak.org.

no fabricated myth. Other researchers had found a few years earlier that Mazatecs ate psychoactive mushrooms in their sacred healing ceremonies, which were always held at night behind closed doors in private homes. Wasson intended to prove that ingesting these mushrooms could trigger spectacular visions and spiritual insights, something no "white outsider" before him and his traveling companion, a professional New York photographer named Allan Richardson, had ever before, until that night, been invited to experience firsthand.

The success of Wasson's enterprise itself remained a secret for the next two years. Then, in a widely-read article published in *LIFE* magazine on May 13, 1957, he introduced Western society to teonanácatl with these captivating words:

On the night of June 29–30, 1955, in a Mexican Indian village so remote from the world that most of the people speak no Spanish, my friend Allan Richardson and I shared with a family of Indian friends a celebration of "holy communion" where "divine" mushrooms were first adored and then consumed. The Indians mingled Christian and pre-Christian elements in their religious practices in a way disconcerting for Christians but natural for them. The rite was led by two women, mother and daughter, both of them *curanderas*, or shamans . . . The mushrooms were of a species with hallucinogenic powers; that is, they cause the eater to see visions. We chewed and swallowed these acrid mushrooms, saw visions, and emerged from the experience awestruck. We had come from afar to attend a mushroom rite but had expected nothing so staggering as the virtuosity of the performing *curanderas* and the astonishing effects of the mushrooms.

"For the first time," Wasson added, "the word ecstasy took on real meaning. For the first time it did not mean someone else's state of mind."

That many others in the West had a similar, unfulfilled longing for ecstasy soon become evident. Suddenly, sacred mushrooms could be found growing everywhere, it seemed, and thousands of spiritual seekers rushed forth to consume them. Not everyone who did so was prepared for a mushroom epiphany; many failed to anticipate what Wasson really meant by "awestruck." Most, however, weathered the experience just fine. The mushrooms fortified their souls, they said, by helping them perceive a basic truth about existence: God and nature are not separate; the universe around us is suffused with the divine; it is an animistic world that we live in, as most pagans have historically (and no doubt prehistorically) professed.

If Western mushroom eaters found the revelation shocking, it was mainly because they'd been raised in a christianized culture that preaches the view that God cannot, by definition, be part of nature, because nature is what God created; everything in nature is God's creation and, as such, can't be its own creator. That makes sense from a limited, earthbound perspective; less so when one's soul, "untrammeled and free, is sent soaring by mushrooms to bask in the dazzling light of God's revealed presence." That's how Wasson described his own mushroom experience, adding that "the mushroom holds the key to a mystical union with God, whereas only rare souls can attain similar ecstasy and divine communion by intensive contemplation" of the Eucharist in mainstream Christian services (Wasson 1957).

Not surprisingly, therefore, many sacred mushroom-eaters in the West have been converted by the evidence of personal experience to switch their allegiance from Christian to pagan religious beliefs, often with a corresponding anti-Christian bias. It is frequently assumed from Wasson's writings that he likewise renounced Christianity. The following brief account of Wasson's mushroom quest will show that he remained, in fact, a Christian—though a Christian with a difference. What he learned from his Mazatec hosts and their wondrous mushrooms helped him become what I propose to call a *Gaian Christian*.

Robert Gordon Wasson was born in Great Falls, Montana, in 1898 and moved with his family several years later to Newark, New Jersey. His mother, Mary, and his father, Edmund, a somewhat free-thinking Episcopalian priest, both impressed upon Wasson a respect for rigorous scholarship. His father had written and published a book called

Religion and Drink (1914) that refuted prohibitionists with passages from the Bible. At home, Edmund drilled his sons in "higher criticism" of the Bible, requiring that they read it through entirely three times and analyze everything in it from different perspectives. Consequently, Wasson came away with a far deeper understanding of the Bible's flaws and virtues than most Christians. Many years later, when Wasson was in his sixties and had eaten sacred mushrooms several times, he still openly admired what he called the Bible's "wealth of illuminating episodes both fictional and veridical."

After serving in the U.S. Army during World War I as a radio operator based in France, Wasson moved to New York and completed a bachelor's degree in English literature from Columbia University. On a subsequent visit to London, he met a Russian pediatrician, Valentina Pavlovna Guercken, who, in 1926, became his wife. Two years later, after having worked first as a college English teacher at Columbia and then as a business journalist, Wasson started his career as an investment banker at the Guaranty Company of New York. In 1934 he transferred to J. P. Morgan and Company on Wall Street, where he remained until his retirement in 1963.

Wasson's involvement with mushrooms began on his honeymoon, in late summer 1927. He and his wife, Tina, had taken a cabin in the Catskill Mountains. While out for a walk one day, Tina shouted with joy upon noticing some mushrooms in the forest. As she gathered them for dinner, Wasson begged her to stop. Like many people of English extraction, Wasson regarded all mushrooms as probably poisonous. Tina, on the other hand, loved mushrooms with a passion that is typical of people raised in Russia. "That evening she ate them, alone," recalled Wasson. "I thought to wake up the next morning a widower." Later he wrote that the episode impressed them both so deeply that "from then on, as circumstances permitted, we gathered all the information that we could about the attitude of various peoples toward mushrooms: what kinds they know, their names for them, the etymology of those names, the folklore and legends in which mushrooms figure, references to them in proverbs and literature and mythology" (Wasson 1959). In doing so, the Wassons launched a field of research they called *ethnomycology*—the study of cultural uses of mushrooms.

Their serious work in this field began with a chapter for a book they were writing on Russian cuisine. By the time it was published in 1957, the chapter had become the entire book, a two-volume treatise called *Mushrooms, Russia and History*. The Wassons developed their theory that mushrooms played a role in the religious rites of ancient Europeans. That would help explain, they said, why some Europeans today, such as Russians and Czechs, are *mycophilic*, regarding mushrooms with open delight, while others, such as the English, are *mycophobic*, regarding mushrooms with distrust and even horror. In their view, both reactions are degraded forms of what had been experienced in ancient times as epiphanic awe.

But what kind of mushrooms could generate such an experience? The only psychoactivity then attributed to mushrooms was delirium, a side effect of poisoning. The earliest historical accounts of the Mexican psychoactive mushroom's existence were recorded in the early 1500s by Catholic friars who accompanied Spanish soldiers into Mexico during the Conquest. According to the friars, local Indians were found consuming mushrooms they called *teonanácatl* that reportedly caused visions. The meaning of this Aztec word has never been conclusively determined, but most likely it translates to "wondrous mushroom." The friars, however, construed it to mean "god's flesh" or "divine flesh." Its use in Indian ceremonies seemed to them a kind of profane parody of Catholic Holy Communion. As Wasson later wrote:

> One can imagine the many trembling confabulations of the friars as they would whisper together on how to meet this Satanic enemy. The *teonanácatl* struck at the heart of the Christian religion. I need hardly remind my readers of the parallel, the designation of the elements of our Eucharist: "Take, eat, this is my Body . . . " and again, "Grant us therefore, gracious Lord, so to eat the flesh of thy dear Son . . . and to drink His blood . . . " But the truth was even worse. The orthodox Christian must accept on faith the miracle of the conversion of the bread and wine into God's flesh and blood: that is what is meant by the Doctrine of Transubstantiation. By contrast the sacred mushroom of the Aztecs carries its own conviction: every communicant will testify to the miracle that he has experienced (Wasson 1980).

The Spaniards, appalled, made an effort to suppress the mushroom ceremony and believed that they had succeeded. So completely did the practice disappear from light of day that over time Western scholars concluded that the friars had made a mistake: that teonanácatl never had been mind-altering mushrooms, which were doubted to exist, but instead were dried peyote cactus buttons.

Meanwhile, mushroom ceremonies continued in secret for hundreds of years in remote mountain villages scattered throughout central and south Mexico. Over time, Christian concepts were mixed in with the pagan ones. The mushrooms themselves, for example, came to be viewed as a manifestation of Jesus that sprang from the ground where his blood fell at the time he was tortured and crucified. Since the mushroom *veladas* were secret, this conflation does not reflect a strategic concession by the Indians to please the authorities. Rather, it was spontaneous and sincere syncretism, such as marked the original spread of Christianity through pagan Europe.

In 1936, a Mexican ethnobotanist named Blas Pablo Reko rebelled against the prevailing scientific view that teonanácatl was peyote. He began to consult with indigenous peoples in the mountains of Oaxaca in south central Mexico about the possible existence of mind-altering mushrooms. They confirmed for him not only their existence, but also that the mushrooms still were used in secret. In 1938, Reko was joined in his field research by a young ethnobotany student from Harvard named Richard Evans Schultes, who secured and identified samples of mind-altering mushrooms in the Mazatec village of Huautla de Jiménez. One year later, a Mexico City anthropologist named Jean Bassett Johnson and his wife, Irmgard Weitlaner, became the first white outsiders to attend a mushroom velada, though their hosts did not offer them mushrooms; they participated only as observers. Also that year, Schultes (1939) published a paper identifying teonanácatl as a specific mushroom. The onset of World War II ensured that this was overlooked for more than a decade.

That is where things stood when Tina Wasson, in the early 1950s, told her friend, the poet Robert Graves, about their research for *Mushrooms, Russia and History*. Graves called her attention to Schultes' paper on teonanácatl, which was referenced in an article he'd recently read in a pharmaceutical company's newsletter. The Wassons then contacted Schultes, who by then was a faculty member at Harvard, and Schultes referred them to his contacts in Huautla.

Thus it was that Wasson, beginning in 1953, made the first of ten annual visits to the Oaxaca region, sometimes accompanied by Tina and their teenage daughter, Masha. In 1953 they sat in on a mushroom velada but were not invited to participate by eating mushrooms. The male shaman who presided said the mushrooms had the power to take those who ingest them "*ahí donde Dios está*"—there where God is. Wasson noted at the time that the mushrooms are treated with reverence by the Indians, so he always made it a point to do likewise. "After all," he wrote, "it was a bold thing we were doing, strangers probing the innermost secrets of this remote people. How would a Christian priest receive a pagan's request for samples of the Host?" (Wasson and Wasson 1957).

Beginning in 1954, Wasson hired New York society photographer Allan Richardson to accompany him on the next few expeditions to take photographs. These were difficult journeys by foot and by mule on deplorable roads winding over the mountains to villages such as Mazatlán and Huautla at elevations up to a mile and a half. At first they succeeded only in compiling information about the velada—for example, that it is not a regularly scheduled event like Christian worship services, but rather is convened for healing purposes, broadly defined. Therefore the shaman who conducts it holds the title *curandera* if a woman, *curandero* if a man; both words mean "healer."

Wasson's breakthrough came on June 29, 1955, when he and Richardson met Cayetano and Guadelupe García, a married couple living at the edge of town in Huautla. That afternoon, the Garcías and some of their friends took Wasson and Richardson down the mountainside to gather mind-altering mushrooms growing on sugar cane refuse. The mushrooms they gathered, *Psilocybe caerulescens*, were one of several kinds of psychoactive mushrooms that the Indians use in veladas and that have been identified as teonanácatl.

Cayetano then sent his brother, an interpreter, along with Wasson and Richardson to meet a curandera named María Sabina who lived in Huautla. Believing that she had no choice because Wasson had been authorized, apparently, by Cayetano, an official of the village, she agreed to conduct a velada that evening with her daughter, Apollonia, at the home of the Garcías. Guadelupe Garcia described her to him as *"una Señora sin mancha,"* Wasson later recalled—"a lady without blemish, immaculate, one who had never dishonored her calling by using her personal powers for evil" (Wasson and Wasson 1957). To Wasson she seemed "the hierophant, the thaumaturge, the psychopompos, in whom the troubles and aspirations of countless generations of mankind had found, were still finding, their relief" (Wasson 1980). He later reported, in *Mushrooms, Russia and History:*

On that last Wednesday of June, after nightfall, we gathered [at about 8:15] in the lower chamber . . . In all, at one time or another, there must have been twenty-five persons present . . . Both Allan . . . [and I] were deeply impressed by the mood of the gathering. We were received and the night's events unrolled in an atmosphere of simple friendliness that reminded us of the agape [love feast] of early Christian times . . . We were mindful of the drama of the situation. We were attending as participants a mushroomic Supper of unique anthropological interest, which was being held pursuant to a tradition of unfathomed age, possibly going back to the time when the remote ancestors of our hosts were living in Asia, back perhaps to the dawn of man's cultural history, when he was discovering the idea of God (Wasson and Wasson 1957).

The ceremony started at about 10:30 when María and her daughter took their positions before a small table that served as their altar. On this table, Wasson reported, were two "holy pictures"—one depicting Jesus as a child, the other his baptism in the Jordan River. This confirmed, if further proof were needed, that the Mazatecs viewed their ritual as linked in some basic way with Christianity. Furthermore, Wasson noted: "The Señora had asked us to take care not to invade the corner of the room on the left of the altar table, for down that corner would descend the Holy Ghost" (Wasson and Wasson 1957).

Wasson noted during this and later veladas he attended that the Mazatecs normally follow a certain procedure with ritual overtones. The healer first praises the mushrooms while passing them through the

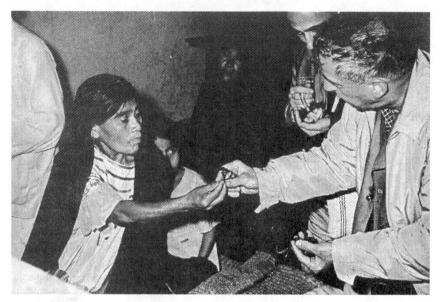

The historic encounter, 1956: Maria Sabina hands R. Gordon Wasson his portion of mushrooms for the velada with *los santos niños*. (*LIFE* magazine photo by Allan Richardson; reproduced courtesy of the R. G. Wasson Estate)

smoke of burning copal incense to purify them, before handing them out to the other participants. Wasson and Richardson each ate six pairs of mushrooms, which in a velada are always distributed in pairs (representing a male and a female) and eaten reverently with one's face turned toward the altar. María's dose as *curandera* was twice as much—twelve pairs.

After the mushrooms were eaten, all the candles were extinguished (veladas always are conducted in the evening), followed by silence for about twenty minutes. The healer then started humming and the humming eventually modulates into a chant that continues at intervals throughout the night. María's songs put Wasson in mind of "age's-old chants" which sometimes seemed "soaked in weary melancholy." They were punctuated by percussive sounds produced when María and her daughter clapped their hands or thumped their chests. As the mushrooms took effect, Maria talked "as though invoking the Spirits or as though the Holy Ghost was speaking through the mushrooms" (Wasson and Wasson 1957). At times she declared her credentials with words such as these from a later velada that Wasson translated:

Woman of space am I,
Woman of day am I,
Woman of light am I, . . .
Lawyer woman am I, woman of affairs am I,
I give account to the judge,
I give account to the government,
And I give account to the Father Jesus Christ,
And mother princess, my patron mother, oh Jesus,
Father Jesus Christ,
Woman of danger am I, woman of beauty am I . . .
I am going to the sky [heaven], Jesus Christ . . .
Whirling woman of the whirlwind am I,
Woman of a sacred, enchanted place am I,
Eagle woman am I, and clock woman am I . . .
The world can be cheered up, let's cheer up, let's be
enlightened,
Let our Father come out to us, let Christ come out to us,
We wait for our Father, we wait for our Father, we
wait for Christ . . .

In *Mushrooms, Russia and History*, Wasson described what transpired that evening in words of great beauty and piety. Speaking for
both Richardson and himself, he reports that they first saw:

> geometric patterns, angular not circular, in richest colors, such as might
> adorn textiles or carpets. Then the patterns grew into architectural
> structures, with colonnades and architraves, patios of regal splendor,
> the stone-work all in brilliant colors, gold and onyx and ebony, all most
> harmoniously and ingeniously contrived, in richest magnificence
> extending beyond the reach of sight, in vistas measureless to man . . .
> They seemed to belong . . . to the imaginary architecture described by
> the visionaries of the Bible (Wasson and Wasson 1957).

Included in these visions, Wasson said, were "resplendent palaces
all laid over with semiprecious stones . . . mountains rising tier above
tier to the very heavens . . . gardens of ineffable beauty" and "river

The historic encounter, 1956: Gordon Wasson ingests the mushrooms while Maria Sabina prays at the household altar. (*LIFE* magazine photo by Allan Richardson; reproduced courtesy of the R. G. Wasson Estate)

estuaries, pellucid waters flowing through an endless expanse of reeds down to a measureless sea, all by the pastel light of a horizontal sun." Of the objects he saw in these visions, Wasson marveled that:

> No patina of age hung on them. They were all fresh from God's workshop, pristine in their finish . . . They seemed the very archetypes of beautiful form and color. We felt ourselves in the presence of the Ideas that Plato had talked about. In saying this let not the reader think that we are indulging in rhetoric, straining to command his attention by an extravagant figure of speech. For the world our visions were and must remain *hallucinations*. But for us they were not false or shadowy suggestions of real things, figments of an unhinged imagination. What we were seeing was, we knew, the only reality, of which the counterparts of every day are mere imperfect adumbrations (Wasson and Wasson 1957).

As the visions increased in intensity Wasson and Richardson experienced firsthand what the Indians mean when they say that the mushrooms have the power to take users "there where God is."

> There is no better way to describe the sensation than to say it was as though our very soul had been scooped out of our body and translated to a point floating in space, leaving behind the husk of clay, our body . . . We had the sensation that the walls of our humble house had vanished, that our untrammeled souls were floating in the universe, stroked by divine breezes, possessed of a divine mobility that would transport us anywhere on the wings of a thought . . . There came a moment when it seemed as though the visions themselves were about to be transcended, and dark gates reaching upward beyond sight were about to part, and we were to find ourselves in the presence of the Ultimate. We seemed to be flying at the dark gates as a swallow at a dazzling lighthouse, and the gates were to part and admit us. But they did not open, and with a thud we fell back, gasping. We felt disappointed, but also frightened and half relieved, that we had not entered into the presence of the Ineffable, whence, it seemed to us at the time, we might not have returned, for we had sensed that a willing extinction in the divine radiance had been awaiting us (Wasson and Wasson 1957).

When Wasson later asked Cayetano what he could pay him for having arranged the velada, the Indian turned to his wife and let her speak: "*No hicimos esto por dinero,*" she said: "We did not do this for money."

Upon returning to New York, the Wassons focused their attention on completing the long-delayed *Mushrooms, Russia and History,* adding detailed accounts of their discoveries in Mexico. It finally was published two years later in a lavishly-produced, two-volume limited edition of 512 copies released the same day as the *LIFE* magazine article. Though Wasson made an effort to disguise the true identities of

Huautla and María in his article (giving her a pseudonym), it wasn't long before the curandera found herself besieged by a variety of sacred mushroom seekers from the West, including beatniks, hippies, rock stars, and journalists. Many came respectfully in search of religious enlightenment. Others, it seemed, wanted only to find a good high. Their sometimes inappropriate behavior made life difficult for people in Huautla, especially when Mexico's federal government, under pressure from the U.S. Drug Enforcement Administration, declared sacred mushrooms an illegal drug and threatened to prosecute anyone found using them for any purpose. At one point angry villagers, upset with María for having revealed the secret of their teonanácatl, burned her house down. Eventually, however, they forgave her. By the time she died in 1985, María's reputation as a wise and holy woman was established for the ages in Huautla, throughout Mexico and worldwide.

Wasson's research and writings contributed much to this outcome. After Tina died of cancer in 1958, Wasson pressed on with what he called "our work," publishing numerous groundbreaking articles, papers, and books on sacred mushroom use in Mexico, Guatemala, and other Mesoamerican countries. The first of these books, *María Sabina and her Mazatec Mushroom Velada* (1974), includes an audio recording of an all-night velada conducted by María in 1958, plus a written transcription and musical score of her chanting. Wasson often remarked he was prouder of this than any of his other publications, and indeed it represents a unique milestone in anthropological studies. A later book, titled *The Wondrous Mushroom: Mycolatry in Mesoamerica* (1980), is Wasson's *summa theologica* on teonanácatl. In addition to providing a review of all the relevant historical accounts by Spanish friars during the Conquest, it cites evidence from disciplines as varied as linguistics, archeology, ethnobotany, musicology, architecture, graphic arts, and literature to buttress his and Tina's claim that sacred mushrooms played a crucial role in the religious life of central American Indians and their ancestors. Wasson also, in this book, endorses teonanácatl's viability for any man or woman—not just Indians—with courage enough to risk going "there where God is."

In the lives of us all, even those who are most earthbound, there are moments when the world stops, when the most humdrum things suddenly and unaccountably clothe themselves with beauty, haunting and ravishing beauty. It now seems to me that such flashes must emerge from our subconscious well where our visions have all this time been stored, for the mushroomic visions are an endless sequence of those flashes . . . What an amazing thing that we should all be carrying this inventory of wonders around with us, ready to be tripped into our conscious world by mushrooms! Are the Indians far wrong in calling these divine? We suspect that, in its fullest sense, the creative faculty, whether in the humanities or science or industry, that most precious of man's distinctive possessions and the one most clearly partaking of the divine, is linked in some way with the area of the mind that the mushrooms unlock (Wasson 1980).

Wasson still firmly maintained this belief when I met him in 1985, about a year before he died. That visit and another one year later are described in *The Sacred Mushroom Seeker* (1990), a book of memorial essays about Wasson that I compiled and edited after his death in 1986. It was my privilege to hear him tell the story of the night he first took teonanácatl, his enthusiasm for the mushroom experience clearly undiminished. We also discussed U.S. laws that make it a felony to eat or possess sacred mushrooms. It was clear, he agreed, that these laws had done much to curtail their use in the West, but he thought that complacency too was a factor. "Entheogens will be appreciated in fifteen of twenty years—thirty years at most," he told me. "People don't want to be awed these days."

Wasson's writings about sacred mushrooms will inspire and instruct new generations seeking spiritual enlightenment. His legacy will endure partly because the information he added to the scientific record will be just as valid years in the future as it is today, but also because his discoveries have lasting implications for spiritual seekers. Gordon Wasson was a level-headed scientist whose scholarly writings, while grounded in fact, inspire many to regard the sacred mushrooms with religious awe and reverence.

Gordon Wasson chose as his final resting place the Chapel of St. Joseph of Arimathea in the Washington Cathedral in Washington, D.C., where his ashes are interred. Joseph of Arimathea is said to be the first to take possession of the Holy Grail after the Last Supper, and to have brought Christianity to England. Wasson may have considered him a spiritual patron, in light of his own pioneering, almost missionary, efforts to establish the field of ethnomycology and entheogens.

Wasson's work and writings are profoundly religious as well as scientific. I believe that Wasson knew this and expected to be honored sooner or later by people who use sacred mushrooms to help them know the divine by direct experience. "When we first went down to Mexico we felt certain, my wife and I, that we were on the trail of an ancient and holy mystery, and we went as pilgrims seeking the Grail" (Wasson 1961). In effect, they found the Grail when they found the sacred mushrooms, making Wasson's final resting place especially significant. By having his ashes interred in a room that is accessed from the chapel of a saint who is associated with the Grail—a chapel that lies at the heart of a cathedral built to last thousands of years—he has established a *de facto* shrine commemorating his and Tina's quest.

Certain writers who admire Wasson's work are far less tolerant than he toward the Christian religion. They fail to notice that, however much Wasson respected the spiritual power of pagan religions, he also believed that the Christian religion is basically good and deserving of equal respect. Of course he deplored the horrific abuses committed by people professing to be Christians; but he did not blame the Bible any more than he blamed Jesus for the criminal behavior perpetrated in his name. In *The Wondrous Mushroom,* Wasson wrote: "I suppose most persons would call us deeply religious, though we did not really adhere to any creed. She [Tina] was a member of the Russian Orthodox Church and I am an Episcopalian, my father having been a minister" (Wasson 1980). Wasson did not valorize Christian spiritual values over pagan beliefs. Neither did he elevate the pagan point of view above the Christian. Instead, like the Mazatecs, he perceived that the two belief systems are not necessarily antagonistic. In Alexander Shulgin's essay published in *The Sacred Mushroom Seeker,* Shulgin recalls that Wasson told him that he:

thought his most lasting contribution was allowing that article in *LIFE* to appear, and to appear in the form it took. It was, for many devout and curious readers of the magazine, their first exposure to the concept of a union between nature and God. And that there are many different ways to be in the presence of God. And that a lowly mushroom, like ordinary bread and wine, can allow, can insist, that you identify with and acknowledge the divine . . . It was this article that caught the attention of the populace. It was this article that served as the single most important "trigger" to initiate the psychedelic revolution of the '60s. It was this article, he felt, that resulted in what proved to be an irreversible change in human awareness (Shulgin 1990).

References

Riedlinger, T. J., ed. 1990. *The Sacred Mushroom Seeker: Essays for R. Gordon Wasson*. Portland, Ore.: Dioscorides Press.

———. 1990a. Preface. In *The Sacred Mushroom Seeker: Essays for R. Gordon Wasson*, ed. Thomas J. Riedlinger. Portland, Ore.: Dioscorides Press.

———. 1990b. A latecomer's view of R. Gordon Wasson. In *The Sacred Mushroom Seeker: Essays for R. Gordon Wasson*, ed. Thomas J. Riedlinger. Portland, Ore.: Dioscorides Press.

Schultes, R. E. 1939. The identification of a narcotic Basidiomycete of the Aztecs. *Botanical Museum Leaflets*. Cambridge, Mass.: Harvard University 7 (3):37–54.

Shulgin, A. T. 1990. Celebrating Gordon Wasson. In *The Sacred Mushroom Seeker: Essays for R. Gordon Wasson*, ed. Thomas J. Riedlinger. Portland, Ore.: Dioscorides Press.

Wasson, E. A. 1914. *Religion and Drink*. New York: Burr Printing House.

Wasson, R. G. 1957. Seeking the magic mushroom Teonanácatl. *LIFE* 42 (19):100–120. May 13.

———. 1959. The hallucinogenic mushrooms of Mexico: An adventure in eth-nomycological exploration. *Transactions of the New York Academy of Sciences Series II*, 24 (4):325–39.

———. 1961. The hallucinogenic fungi of Mexico; an inquiry into the origins of the religious idea among primitive peoples. *Harvard University Botanical Museum Leaflets* 1 (7):137–62. (Reprinted in *Psychedelic Review* 1 (1), June 1963, 27–42).

———. 1974. *Maria Sabina and her Mazatec Mushroom Velada*. New York and London: Harcourt Brace Jovanovich.

———. 1980. *The Wondrous Mushroom: Mycolatry in Mesoamerica*. New York: McGraw-Hill.

———. 1990. Gordon Wasson's account of his childhood. In *The Sacred Mushroom Seeker: Essays for R. Gordon Wasson,* ed. Thomas J. Riedlinger. Portland, Ore.: Dioscorides Press.

Wasson, V. P. and R. G. Wasson. 1957. *Mushrooms, Russia and History*. New York: Pantheon Books.

4

BIOCHEMISTRY AND NEUROPHARMACOLOGY OF PSILOCYBIN MUSHROOMS

DAVID E. PRESTI, PH.D., AND DAVID E. NICHOLS, PH.D.

This chapter will present a discussion of the chemistry of a particular type of psychoactive mushroom, of the genus *Psilocybe*, often known collectively as psilocybin mushrooms, and sometimes referred to as "magic mushrooms."

The history of the ritual use of these mushrooms spans millennia, from the contemporary Mazatec Indians of southern Mexico, to the Mayan and Aztec cultures of Mexico and central America six hundred years ago, to the cultures that came many centuries before them. In the sixteenth century the Spanish chronicler de Sahagún described teonanácatl, an Aztec word that can be translated as "sacred mushroom" or

David E. Presti, Ph.D., is a neurobiologist and clinical psychologist who teaches in the Department of Molecular and Cell Biology at the University of California in Berkeley. He has doctorates in molecular biology and biophysics from the California Institute of Technology and in clinical psychology from the University of Oregon. He can be contacted at: presti@socrates.berkeley.edu.

David E. Nichols, Ph.D., is Professor of Medicinal Chemistry and Molecular Pharmacology at Purdue University. He has over 230 published research reports, book chapters, and symposia proceedings, and six U.S. patents. In 1993, he was the lead founder of the Heffter Research Institute (www.heffter.org), a nonprofit institute to support research into the scientific and medical value of hallucinogens. He can be contacted at: drdave@pharmacy.purdue.edu.

"God's flesh." We know from Sahagún's writings that teonanácatl was used for social occasions, festivals, and by the Aztec shamans (Hofmann 1971).

When used in a ritual context by the shaman, teonanácatl provided a bridge between everyday consensus reality and extraordinary states of consciousness that allowed perception of events and situations that were not ordinarily accessible: the weather was forecast, illness was diagnosed, aspects of the future might be seen, such as whether or not the harvest would be good. Thus, his ingestion of the "God's flesh" made the Aztec shaman seem like a god, able to transcend time and space.

Teonanácatl is classified as an entheogen, a substance that can manifest the god within. Certainly, for the Aztec shaman, the connection with the gods that arose in his mind through the ritual use of teonanácatl was the central purpose of the substance. Within this context, and for the purposes of the discussion, we shall use the term entheogenic to describe the effects produced by psilocybin fungi. This convention seems particularly appropriate because, of all the similar types of psychoactive substances of which we know today, these mushrooms have one of the clearest historical justifications for applying this term. Those readers who are more formally inclined should consider it to be synonymous with the terms psychedelic and hallucinogenic.

The chemical makeup of psychoactive mushrooms is extraordinarily complex, with hundreds of chemicals created by the organism's metabolic biochemistry. Though any number of these may have effects on human physiology, the psychoactive effects of various entheogenic fungi and plants are usually attributable to a small number of identified compounds. The psychoactive chemicals identified in entheogenic fungi are generally secondary metabolites of the organism's biosynthetic processes. That is, they are not believed to function as part of the mushroom's energy-generating or structural biochemistry, their primary metabolism, but are instead products of biochemical syntheses.

Recently it has become increasingly appreciated that so-called secondary metabolites may play any number of important roles for the organism. For some plants, certain secondary metabolites that have psychoactive effects in humans have been demonstrated to function as chemical defenses against insect predators. This observation is usually hypothesized to be the reason why they are present, having been selected over the course of biological evolution for their defensive properties. Examples include noxious effects on insects from cocaine in coca plants, caffeine in coffee and tea plants, and nicotine in tobacco plants. Moreover, the psychoactive effects produced by these plants in humans have resulted in an additional evolutionary advantage for the plants in that they have been spread throughout the world by people who cultivate them to maintain ready availability.

The psychoactive chemicals synthesized by entheogenic fungi have not thus far been demonstrated to play chemical defensive roles for the organism. No experiments have been conducted, for example, to investigate whether entheogenic fungi avoid predation by invertebrates such as slugs and snails because of their peculiar chemical content. The notion that entheogenic substances are present in fungi and plants primarily to foster their consumption by humans is a speculative and interesting hypothesis (McKenna 1992), but one for which there is absolutely no scientific evidence.

PSILOCYBIN AND ITS CHEMICAL RELATIVES

The primary effects of the entheogenic psilocybin mushrooms on human physiology are due to several tryptamine alkaloids synthesized and accumulated by these fungi. The categorical name "tryptamine alkaloids" (or "tryptamines") designates molecules whose molecular structure contains 3-(2-aminoethyl)indole as a central feature (fig. 1).

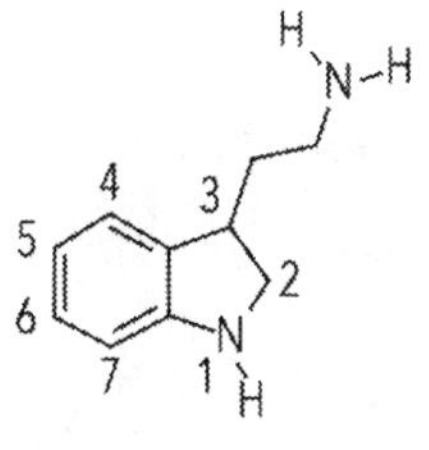

Figure 1. Tryptamine, showing numbering of
the indole ring.

The identified psychoactive chemical components of psilocybin mushrooms are psilocybin, psilocin, baeocystin, and norbaeocystin (figs. 2–5).

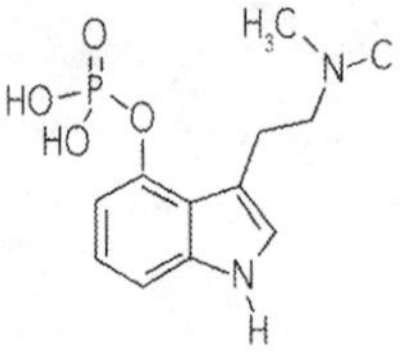

Figure 2. Psilocybin or 4-phosphoryloxy-
N,N-dimethyltryptamine.

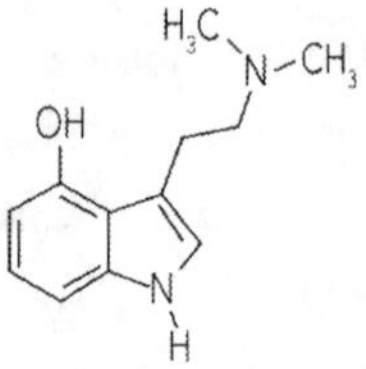

Figure 3. Psilocin or 4-hydroxy-
N,N-dimethyltryptamine.

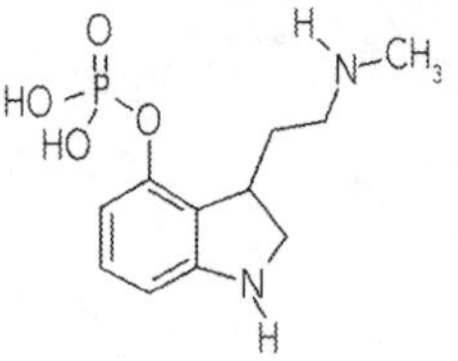

Figure 4. Baeocystin or 4-phosphoryloxy-
N-methyltryptamine.

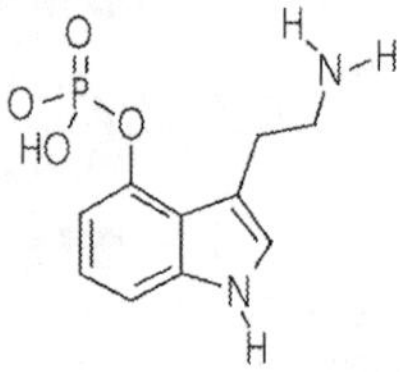

Figure 5. Norbaeocystin or
4-phosphoryloxytryptamine.

Psilocybin and psilocin were identified as the primary psychoactive components of *Psilocybe* mushrooms by the renowned Swiss chemist Albert Hofmann in 1958. Hofmann isolated and identified the compounds from samples of *Psilocybe mexicana* mushrooms collected in Mexico. To identify the compounds that produced the effects on consciousness, he and several of his coworkers ingested fractions obtained from the paper chromatographic separation of the fungal extracts (Hofmann et al. 1958, 1959).

Psilocybin can produce significant psychoactive effects in humans following oral doses of approximately 10 to 20 mg (Shulgin and Shulgin 1997). Taken orally, psilocybin and psilocin produce identical effects when given at equivalent molar doses. That is because following oral ingestion, the phosphoryl group of psilocybin is rapidly lost to generate psilocin, which is the actual active molecule. Alkaline phosphatases located in the digestive system, kidney, and perhaps in the blood probably carry out this enzymatic transformation (Horita and Weber 1961). Early animal studies showed that the behavioral effects of psilocybin paralleled the increase in brain level of psilocin (Horita 1963). After administration of psilocybin, only psilocin is detectable in the blood (Hasler et al. 1997). These same workers found that following oral administration of 10–20 mg of pure psilocybin, peak levels of psilocin in the blood (about 8 ng/ml) occur approximately 105 minutes after ingestion. Effects on the psyche appear when a blood concentration of between 2–6 ng/ml is achieved, about 20–90 minutes after oral administration of pure psilocybin. After intravenous administration of 1 mg of pure psilocybin, the conversion to psilocin occurs rapidly, and peak blood concentrations of psilocin (about 13 ng/ml) are achieved within 2 minutes of injection (Hasler et al. 1997).

In the mushroom, the phosphoryl group of psilocybin confers protection against oxidation. Indeed, crystalline samples of psilocybin have been stored at room temperature for decades with no appreciable degradation. Furthermore, psilocybin can even be recrystallized from boiling water, a treatment that would destroy psilocin itself (Nichols and Frescas 1999). Thus, psilocybin is a remarkably stable molecule, particularly when compared with other tryptamines. This stability provides the basis for the extraction of psilocybin mushrooms with hot water for the preparation of ritual teas.

Psilocin, by contrast, is a fairly unstable molecule. The pure material slowly darkens in air, whereas solutions, particularly at basic pH, decompose rapidly. Many psilocin-containing mushrooms turn a bluish color when bruised. This effect is believed to be due to degradation products of psilocin that have yet to be chemically identified (Stamets 1996). Hydroxyindoles in general are readily oxidized, leading to highly colored products, and it is likely that bruising the mushrooms releases psilocin from a protective matrix so that it is exposed to air oxidation or to the action of enzymes that use oxygen to oxidize aromatic substrates. Although the nature of these colored products has not been elucidated, no doubt some of them are quinoid-type species, which typically have dark colors. Although 5-hydroxytryptamines such as bufotenin also oxidize very readily, they do not generate the blue colors that occur with 4-hydroxytryptamines.

Baeocystin and norbaeocystin were first identified from *Psilocybe baeocystis* (Leung and Paul 1968). Baeocystin has since been found in at least twenty-six species of mushrooms and there is one report that it is psychoactive in humans at doses of approximately 10 mg, ingested orally (Ott 1993). Unfortunately, sufficient data are not available for these two compounds to assess their clinical properties, but it is very likely that they produce qualitatively different psychopharmacological effects. Based on current neurochemical knowledge, one could reasonably speculate that these two compounds would have different affinities and abilities to activate the various brain receptors relevant to the actions of entheogens. Therefore, the relative proportions of psilocybin and baeocystin in a particular species of mushroom are probably relevant to its effects after ingestion. This idea would be consistent with anecdotal reports that some species of mushroom, for example *P. cubensis* and *P. azurescens*, can induce qualitatively different effects.

Several related psychoactive tryptamine molecules, which, although synthesized by a variety of plants, have not yet been detected in fungi, include: N,N-dimethyltryptamine or DMT (fig. 6); 5-hydroxy-N,N-dimethyltryptamine or bufotenin; and 5-methoxy-N,N-dimethyltryptamine or 5-MeO-DMT (fig. 7). Conversely, psilocin and psilocybin have not thus far been found in plants.

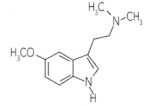

Figure 6. N,N-dimethyltryptamine or DMT.   Figure 7. 5-methoxy-N,N-dimethyltryptamine or 5-MeO-DMT.

LEGAL STATUS

The legal status of several of these molecules has been specified by the Federal Controlled Substance Act, passed into law by the United States Congress in 1970. Psilocybin, psilocin, DMT, and bufotenin have been classified as Schedule 1 substances by the U.S. Controlled Substances Act. Psilocybin and psilocin are essentially nontoxic to body organs and do not cause physiological dependence or addictive behaviors (presumably the basis for the dangers of drugs of abuse as this term is used in the Controlled

Substances Act). The classification of psilocybin, psilocin, and many other entheogens as dangerous drugs is primarily based on socio-political reasons rather than clinical-scientific evidence. Psilocybin, psilocin, and DMT are also internationally classified as Schedule 1 substances by the 1971 United Nations Convention on Psychotropic Substances.

TRYPTAMINES IN THE HUMAN BODY

Some tryptamine molecules found naturally in the human body include *tryptophan, 5-hydroxytryptophan, serotonin, melatonin,* and *N,N-dimethyltryptamine.*

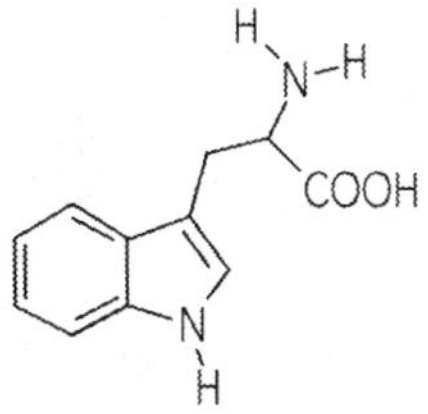

Figure 8. Tryptophan.

Tryptophan (fig. 8) is one of the twenty amino acids used by all of life on Earth to build proteins. Although plants, fungi, bacteria, and some other organisms can biosynthesize tryptophan from smaller carbon molecules, humans cannot and must ingest tryptophan as part of their diet. That is, tryptophan is one of the "essential" amino acids. In fungi and plants, tryptophan is the chemical precursor for the biosynthesis of tryptamines such as DMT and psilocybin. In humans and other animals, tryptophan is the precursor for the synthesis of the neurotransmitter serotonin, 5-hydroxytryptamine (5-HT; fig. 9).

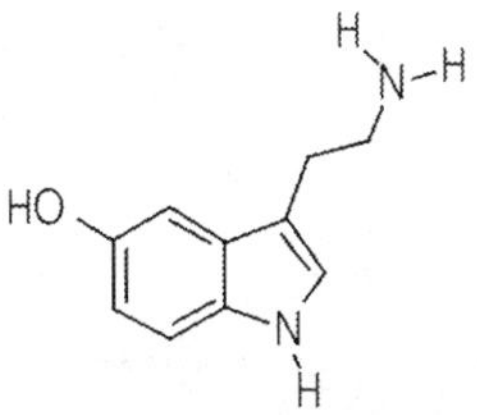

Figure 9. Serotonin or 5-hydroxytryptamine.

The synthesis of 5-HT from tryptophan in serotonergic neurons occurs in two steps. First, the enzyme tryptophan hydroxylase catalyzes the conversion of tryptophan to 5-hydroxytryptophan (5-HTP). Then, the enzyme aromatic amino acid decarboxylase catalyzes the conversion of 5-HTP to serotonin.

In the brain, serotonergic neurons are located in the brainstem in clusters of cells called the *raphe nuclei*, within which is the *reticular network*. These serotonergic neurons send their axonal projections throughout the entire brain. As a neurotransmitter, serotonin is involved in the regulation of numerous behavioral and physiological processes, including mood, appetite, sleep, sexual function, blood flow, body temperature, and more. The fact that both tryptophan and 5-HTP are chemical precursors for the synthesis of serotonin is presumably the reason for the claim of their efficacy in the treatment of problems related to mood, sleep, and appetite (Murray 1999).

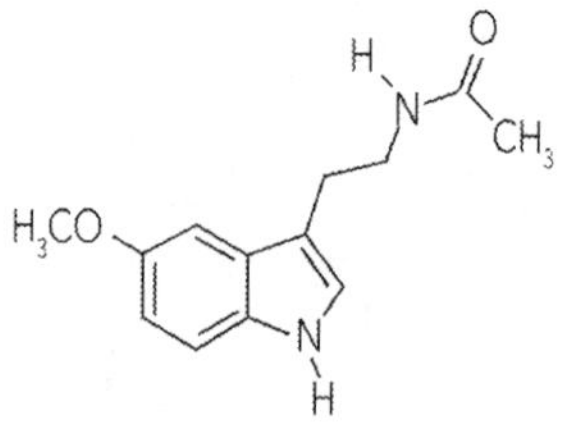

Figure 10. Melatonin.

Melatonin (fig. 10) is a hormone produced from serotonin in the pineal gland, which is embedded within the brain. It is released into the brain and general blood circulation and is involved in the regulation of the sleep-wake cycle and other circadian biological clock processes.

N,N-dimethyltryptamine (DMT) (fig. 6) has been found to occur endogenously at very low concentrations within the human brain, cerebrospinal fluid, and blood. Its function is unknown, but some have speculated that it plays neurotransmitter-like roles in psychotic mental states and dream-sleep imagery (Barker et al. 1981; Callaway 1988; Strassman 2001). Thus, all humans are, presumably at all times, in possession of a Schedule 1 substance and therefore in violation of United States and international law!

METABOLISM OF TRYPTAMINES BY MONOAMINE OXIDASE

Most tryptamine molecules are metabolized by the enzyme *monoamine oxidase* (MAO). MAO actually occurs in two different forms, MAO-A and MAO-B, which have preferences for different neurotransmitter molecules. MAO-A oxidizes the terminal amine of the tryptamines to an imine. This imine then undergoes nonenzymatic hydrolysis to an aldehyde that is subsequently converted to a carboxylic acid by a second enzyme, aldehyde dehydrogenase. The result is the conversion of the tryptamine into an acidic molecule, called an indole-3-acetic acid, which lacks psychoactivity. DMT is converted into indole acetic acid, whereas serotonin is converted into 5-hydroxyindole acetic acid (5-HIAA), and psilocin is converted into 4-hydroxyindole acetic acid.

The two forms of MAO are found throughout the body, including in the nervous system, where they function to inactivate monoamine neurotransmitters such as serotonin, dopamine, and norepinephrine. MAO is also found in the liver, where it is involved in the metabolism of amines taken in through the digestive system. MAO in the liver will limit the bioavailability of some tryptamines that are orally ingested. For example, DMT lacks significant oral activity due to breakdown by MAO in the liver. However, psilocybin, psilocin, and baeocystin are orally active. Apparently the presence of the 4-oxygen substituent on these latter tryptamines confers resistance to MAO because tryptamines lacking this substituent, or those with the oxygen moved to the 5-indole position, are readily degraded by MAO.

There may be some unique chemical interaction between the tryptamine side chain and the 4-oxygen substituent. A study by Migliaccio et al. (1981) found that psilocin had much greater lipid solubility than bufotenin (5-hydroxy-DMT), and that the amino group of psilocin was also less basic. The decreased basicity of psilocin results in a larger fraction of this molecule being in an uncharged (unionized) form in the body, which leads to enhanced intestinal absorption and enhanced penetration into the brain, relative to a tryptamine such as bufotenin. Those workers speculated that hydrogen bonding could occur between the 4-hydroxy group and the amine side chain, as illustrated in figures 11A and 11B. It was noted that such a hydrogen bond, if it indeed formed, need only be a weak one to explain their results on basicity and lipid solubility. Computer modeling shows that because of the particular geometry of the indole ring, the illustrated structure has almost ideal geometry for hydrogen bonding.

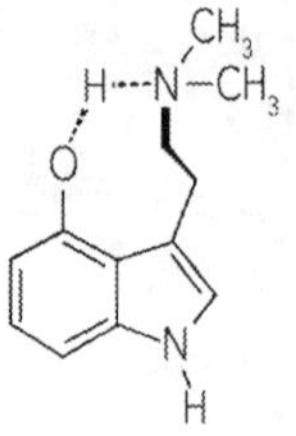

Figure 11A. Possible hydrogen bonding interaction in psilocin.

It is not unreasonable to speculate that the interaction between the 4-hydroxy and the side chain amino group also lies at the heart of the resistance of 4-oxygenated tryptamines to attack by MAO. Although still controversial, MAO catalysis is generally thought to proceed by what is called a single-electron-transfer pathway. According to this mechanism, the initial step of this catalytic process involves transfer of one electron from the nitrogen lone pair of the amine group to oxidized flavin adenine dinucleotide (FAD), a necessary cofactor for the reaction, to generate an aminyl radical cation and reduced FAD. The important point to be made here is that the type of intramolecular interaction illustrated between the 4-hydroxy and the side chain amine group (figs. 11A and 11B) would make the nitrogen lone pair of electrons less available for this initial step of the MAO degradation process. Hence, by making the first step of the MAO mechanism less efficient, the whole degradation process is blocked.

The oral activity of tryptamines that are degraded by MAO can be enhanced by chemicals called *monoamine oxidase inhibitors* (MAOI). This synergism serves as the basis for the Amazonian entheogenic brew, ayahuasca (which means "vine of the souls"), where DMT is rendered orally active by the presence of MAOI harmala alkaloids from the plant *Banisteriopsis caapi* (Metzner 1999). Another botanical source of the MAOI harmala alkaloids *harmaline* and *harmine* is the seed of the Syrian rue, *Peganum harmala*, a bush related to the creosote, native to Asia and Africa. There are anecdotal reports that the potency of psilocybin

Figure 11B. A space-filling representation of the framework drawing of psilocin depicted in Figure 11A. The molecular structures depicted in the figures in this chapter are two-dimensional, line-drawing representations of the molecules that show how the atoms are connected and allow for ready comparison of similarity between molecules. Molecules actually have three-dimensional shapes in which each of the constituent atoms occupies a volume defined by its cloud of electrons. Linus Pauling and two of his colleagues, Robert Corey and Walter Koltun, first developed a form of molecular models to depict the 3-dimensional space-filling aspect of molecules in the way shown in this figure.

mushrooms can be increased by perhaps a factor of two by ingestion of 1 to 3 grams of ground *Peganum harmala* seeds 30 minutes prior to ingestion of the mushrooms (DeKorne 1994).

Note: MAO inhibitors can have a profound impact on the metabolism of the monoamine neurotransmitters, serotonin, dopamine, and norepinephrine. Phenethylamines such as amphetamine and MDMA (3,4-methylenedioxymethamphetamine, "ecstasy") cause the release from axon terminals of monoamine neurotransmitters. Normally these amines are rapidly degraded by MAO and have little physiological effect. In the presence of an MAOI, however, these transmitters can accumulate and lead to severe and potentially fatal consequences. Thus, it is essential to avoid using MAOIs together with any amine that might stress the cardiovascular system (such as amphetamine or MDMA). One must also avoid the ingestion of MAOIs if one is using any of the antidepressant medications that block the uptake of serotonin into neurons, such as SSRIs (like Prozac, Paxil, Zoloft, or celexa) and certain tricyclic antidepressants. Such a combination could result in toxic overactivity of serotonergic neurotransmission and produce what is called a serotonin syndrome. This potentially life-threatening condition may include symptoms such as mental confusion, anxiety, hypomania, hallucinations, hyperthermia, tachycardia, muscle rigidity, and tremor. Your physician will counsel you that it is best (and sometimes essential) to avoid MAOIs whenever any antidepressant medications are being used.

CROSSING THE BLOOD-BRAIN BARRIER

The particular way in which the walls of the blood vessels in the central nervous system are constructed results in their being impermeable to many substances, thereby limiting the ability of molecules to pass from the blood into the brain. This phenomenon is called the "blood-brain barrier." Molecules may cross the blood-brain barrier by mechanisms of active transport, or by being sufficiently lipid soluble that they can diffuse through the hydrophobic core of the lipid membranes that form the boundaries of the cells composing the blood-brain barrier. Most psychoactive drugs are sufficiently lipid soluble that they can pass from the blood into the brain by passive diffusion.

It was noted earlier that psilocin is less basic than bufotenin by a factor of more than ten-fold. The consequence of this is that there is less of the protonated form of psilocin in the blood, and therefore more of the free base, which is the more lipid-soluble species that actually crosses the blood-brain barrier. In that earlier cited study (Migliaccio et al. 1981), it was shown that even after one considers the reduced ionization of psilocin, this molecule still has greater lipid solubility than would be predicted. Again, it appears that some interaction between the 4-hydroxy and the amino group of the side chain may be responsible, perhaps a hydrogen bond between the 4-hydroxy and the amine (fig. 11A). The same effects are not seen in bufotenin, 5-hydroxy-DMT, which has much lower lipid solubility than psilocin, and also is a substrate for MAO. The atomic distances would preclude such an intramolecular hydrogen bond in bufotenin. Thus, not only does the 4-oxygen substituent of psilocin appear to confer resistance to degradation by MAO, but it also enhances lipid solubility, making the molecule enter the brain more readily.

NEUROCHEMISTRY

Entheogens pharmacologically related to psilocin produce profound changes in thought, feeling, perception, and conscious awareness. They produce alterations in some very basic brain neurochemical processes and many entheogenic chemicals share at least some common neuro-chemical mechanisms. Interaction with brain circuitry employing the neurotransmitter serotonin is believed to be central to the brain mechanism of entheogens, including the tryptamine entheogens found in psilocybin mushrooms.

Serotonin has many different types of receptors, characterized by differences in the amino-acid sequences of the protein that folds across the nerve cell membrane to form the receptor. All known serotonin receptors except one belong to a large family of receptors called G-protein (GTP-binding protein) coupled receptors. (The exception is the 5-HT3 receptor, which is a cation channel.) G-protein coupled receptor proteins are thought to be comprised of seven alpha-helical segments that span the neuronal membrane, with external and inter-nal connecting loops. Different types of G-protein coupled receptors have certain key amino acids that appear in all such receptors, but also have differences that give them their unique properties of recognizing a specific neurotransmitter and producing a particular type of intra-cellular signaling message (fig. 12).

Molecules that activate G-protein coupled receptors and cause an intracellular signal to be generated are called *agonists*. Other molecules can occupy the receptor binding site and prevent the neurotransmitter from gaining access and generating a signal. Those drugs are called *antagonists*. Interaction of the neurotransmitter with a specific extra-cellular binding site on the receptor causes a change in the shape of the receptor that leads to the binding and activation of a G-protein on the side of the receptor that is within the neuronal cell. The activated G-protein then goes on to initiate various intracellular biochemical processes that may result in alterations of the activities of various enzymes, changes in cyclic nucleotide levels, and cleavage of membrane phospholipids. Such processes may cause the opening or closing of ion channels, which will alter membrane electric potential with resulting excitation or inhibition of neuronal activity.

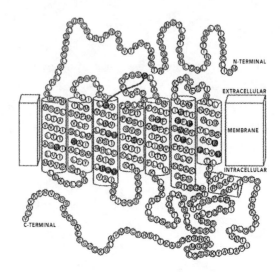

Figure 12. Schematic representation of the human serotonin 5-HT2A receptor. Each small circle represents one of the 471 amino acids that comprise the receptor and the alphabetic characters are the standard abbreviations for amino acids (e.g., alanine=A, glycine=G, tyrosine=Y, etc.). The protein structure is believed to be comprised of seven alpha-helices packed together and spanning the neuronal cell membrane; these are represented by the cylindrical segments. Although these helical segments are shown here arranged in a linear fashion for ease of visualization, in the actual receptor they adopt a more barrel-like packing arrangement, with a central cavity for binding serotonin. The connecting loops between the helical segments inside the cell membrane (at the bottom of the figure) also are arranged in specific shapes but are less well understood. Activating ligands (e.g., serotonin or psilocin) approach the receptor from the extracellular side of the receptor, which is at the top of the figure. After the agonist binds to the receptor, the bundle of helical segments rearranges, causing the connecting chains on the interior of the cell membrane (at the bottom in the figure) to change their 3-dimensional shape. This latter effect leads to the generation of a signal inside the cell by way of the association of the intracellular loops with the binding of a G-protein. When the intracellular loops change shape, a process is initiated within the associated G-protein that leads it to bind GTP (guanosine triphosphate), dissociate from the receptor, and become "activated." These activated G-proteins then interact with other enzymes within the cell that, in turn, increase or decrease in activity, leading to various changes in the cellular biochemistry that constitute the intracellular "signal" that ultimately derives from the agonist molecule. Amino acids of importance for maintaining structure/function are shown in black, and those thought necessary to recognize and interact with the agonist ligand are shown in gray. (Figure provided courtesy of Dr. James Chambers)

Still other changes may be induced by activating transcription factors within the cell nucleus, leading to alterations in gene expression and subsequent protein synthesis. In short, many things may happen following the activation of a G-protein coupled receptor by a neurotransmitter or other agonist, some things relatively quickly, and some over longer periods of time.

Although serotonin activates all subtypes of serotonin receptors, tryptamine entheogens interact predominantly with the type-2 serotonin receptors. In this subfamily, comprised of three members: 5-HT2A, 5-HT2B, and 5-HT2C, it is currently believed that the key receptor is the one designated as the 5-HT2A (Aghajanian and Marek 1999). Although other receptors could be involved, this is the one site that has been consistently implicated as most important. Antagonists that block this receptor appear to block the major psychoactive effects of psilocybin in humans (Vollenweider et al. 1998).

The 5-HT2A receptor has been the focus of increased interest in recent years for a variety of reasons. It has been implicated in a number of psychiatric disorders, consistent with its important role in the regulation of cognition and mood states. Furthermore, it is found in highest density throughout the cerebral cortex of the mammalian brain (Willins et al. 1997; Jakab and Goldman-Rakic 1998). This finding is significant because the cerebral cortex is the most recent and largest evolutionary addition to the brain. The frontal cortex of the human brain is very involved in judgment, planning, and complex reasoning (so-called "executive functions"), emotional processing, and language, while more posterior regions of the cortex (temporal, parietal, and occipital lobes) are responsible for the analysis and interpretation of sensory information. Jakab and Goldman-Rakic (1998) indicate that 5-HT2A receptors are highest in density in regions of the frontal cortex, temporal cortex, and occipital cortex, as well as the cingulate cortex of the limbic system. These workers also note that 5-HT2A receptors are often located on promixal dendritic regions rather than on more distal dendritic spines, the former location resulting in a greater impact on modulation of cell activity. More recently, Williams et al. (2002) have found that prefrontal cortical 5-HT2A receptors have a previously unrecognized role in the cognitive function of working memory.

These studies all indicate that the site that is believed to be essential to the action of entheogens, the serotonin 5-HT2A receptor, is located in key areas of the brain that are responsible for memory, sensory processing, and a variety of functions that make us uniquely human. There is great research interest today in the neuroscience community in these receptors. As they are studied further, we shall no doubt learn more about how they modulate our awareness, and how they are affected by entheogens. Indeed, one might suppose that continued study along these lines will result in increasing understanding of the cellular and molecular aspects of entheogenic experiences!

OTHER PSYCHOACTIVE FUNGI, BRIEFLY NOTED

Although psilocybin-containing fungi are the most well understood, there are other fungi with psychoactive properties, although their neurochemistry is completely different. *Amanita muscaria* is found throughout the world and is known as a picturesque mushroom with a bright red cap. In the decade following his work with the *Psilocybe* mushrooms of Mexico, R. Gordon Wasson (1968, 1971) proposed that *Amanita muscaria* might be the sacred intoxicant "Soma" mentioned in the ancient Asian texts of the *Rig Veda*. Ott (1993) reviews many reports of psychoactive and entheogenic effects from ingestion of *Amanita muscaria*. Physiologically active chemicals in this mushroom include *muscarine*, isolated from *Amanita muscaria* in 1869 by German chemists. Muscarine affects the peripheral nervous system by activating muscarinic acetylcholine receptors in the parasympathetic branch of the autonomic nervous system. It is a quaternary amine carrying a fixed positive charge and, as such, does not cross the blood-brain barrier. Thus, there are no effects of muscarine on the brain. In addition, it is found only in small quantities in the mushroom.

The psychoactive effects of *Amanita muscaria* are believed to be due to the chemicals *ibotenic acid* (fig. 13) and *muscimol* (fig. 14). Ott (1993) summarizes reports that there are entheogenic (hallucinogenic) effects in humans following oral doses of 50–100 mg of ibotenic acid or 10–15 mg of muscimol. Once in the blood circulation, muscimol would cross the blood-brain barrier by inefficient diffusion. Ibotenic acid would cross the blood-brain barrier using the transporter protein for certain amino acids. Ibotenic acid can be decarboxylated by the enzyme aromatic amino acid decarboxylase, found both within the brain and in the periphery, to form muscimol. Ibotenic acid is known to be an agonist at the NMDA-type glutamate receptor, one of the primary excitatory neurotransmitter receptors in the brain, and can lead to the so-called excitotoxic cell death of neurons. Muscimol is an agonist at the GABA-A receptor, the primary inhibitory neurotransmitter receptor in the brain. How these various receptor interactions may lead to hallucinogenic effects is unknown. What is clear, however, is that these effects are behaviorally and neurochemically very different from those of the tryptamine entheogens that occur in *Psilocybe* mushrooms.

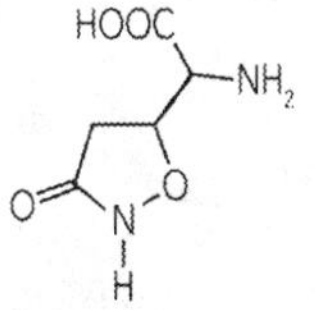

Figure 13. Ibotenic Acid. 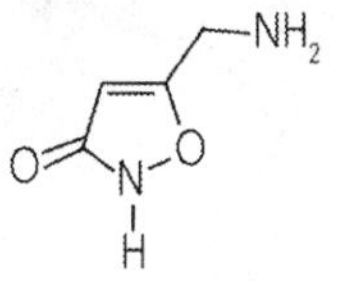   Figure 14. Muscimol.

It also should be noted that within the genus *Amanita* there exist several species of deadly mushrooms. They are among the small number of mushroom species the ingestion of which can prove fatal. These species include *Amanita phalloides* and *Amanita viA*, both of which contain small peptides called amanitins that inactivate RNA polymerase and cause irreversible damage to liver function.

A final example of a psychoactive fungus is the ergot *Claviceps purpurea*, which grows on grains such as rye and wheat, and from which Hofmann isolated the ergot-alkaloid precursor for his synthesis of LSD (lysergic acid diethylamide) (Hofmann 1980). Hofmann (in Wasson et al. 1998) has also established that the *Claviceps purpurea* fungus itself contains pharmacologically-active alkaloids in the form of ergonovine (lysergic acid propanolamide) and lysergic acid amide (fig. 15). The ergot alkaloids, in general, act at many different types of receptors, and the overall alkaloidal composition of ergot fungus makes it quite toxic. Nevertheless, there are a variety of strains of *Claviceps,* with differing alkaloid content, some of which likely are more toxic than others. Wasson, Hofmann, and Ruck (1998) further proposed that ingestion of *Claviceps purpurea* or related fungi growing on cultivated grains or wild grasses may have been the basis for an entheogenic ritual of ancient Greece called the Eleusinian Mysteries. The neurochemistry of these molecules, closely related to LSD in structure, would largely be through serotonin-receptor mechanisms similar to those described above for psilocin.

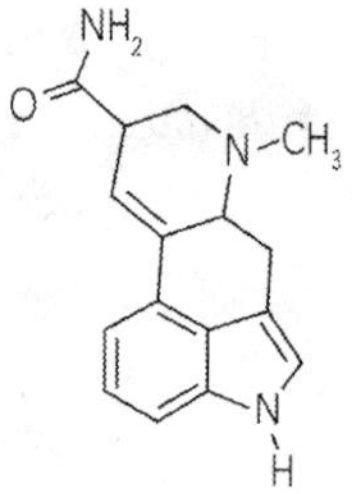

Figure 15. Lysergic Acid Amide.

CODA

The serotonergic neurons of the raphe nuclei in the brainstem innervate the entire brain and likely exert substantial modulatory effects on our perceptions, emotions, thought processes, and conscious awareness— the mental states that may collectively be called "the mind." Psilocybin and related tryptamines from *Psilocybe* fungi are believed to produce their profound effects on the brain and mind by way of interacting with 5-HT2A receptors in the cerebral cortex, limbic system, and elsewhere. As chemical probes that might lead to a better understanding of how the neural circuitry of the brain is related to the nature of mind, they offer unprecedented opportunities!

References

Aghajanian, G. K. and G. J. Marek. 1999. Serotonin and hallucinogens. *Neuropsychopharmacology* 21:16S–23S.

Barker, S. A., J. A. Monti, and S. T. Christian. 1981. N,N-dimethyltryptamine: An endogenous hallucinogen. *International Review of Neurobiology* 22:83–110.

Callaway, J. C. 1988. A proposed mechanism for the visions of dream sleep. *Medical Hypotheses* 26:119–24.

DeKorne, J. 1994. *Psychedelic Shamanisn*. Port Townsend, Wash.: Loompanics Unlimited.

Hasler, F., D. Bourquin, R. Brenneisen, T. Baer, and F. X. Vollenweider. 1997. Determination of psilocin and 4-hydroxyindole-3-acetic acid in plasma by HPLC-ECD and pharmacokinetic profiles of oral and intravenous psilocybin in man. *Pharmaceutica Acta Helvetiae* 72:175–84.

Hofmann, A. 1971. Teonanácatl and Ololuiqui, two ancient magic drugs of Mexico. *Bulletin on Narcotics* 23:3–14.

Hofmann, A. 1983. *LSD: My Problem Child*. Los Angeles, Calif.: Tarcher. (Originally published in 1979).

Hofmann, A., R. Heim, A. Brack, and H. Kobel. 1958. Psilocybin, ein psychotroper Wirkstoff aus dem mexikanischen Rauschpilz *Psilocybe mexicana*—Heim. *Experientia* 14:107–9.

Hofmann, A., R. Heim, A. Brack, H. Kobel, A. Frey, H. Ott, T. Petrzilka, and F. Troxler. 1959. Psilocybin und psilocin, zwei psychotrope Wirkstoffe aus dem mexikanischen Rauschpilz. *Helvetica Chimica Acta* 42:1557–72.

Horita, A. 1963. Some biochemical studies on psilocybin and psilocin. *Journal of Neuropsychiatry* 4:270.

Horita, A. and L. J. Weber. 1961. The enzymatic dephosphorylation and oxidation of psilocybin and psilocin by mammalian tissue homogenates. *Biochemical Pharmacology* 7:47–54.

Jakab, R. L. and P. S. Goldman-Rakic. 1998. 5-Hydroxytryptamine-2A serotonin receptors in the primate cerebral cortex: Possible site of action of hallucinogenic and antipsychotic drugs in pyramidal cell apical dendrites. *Proceedings of the National Academy of Sciences USA* 95:735–40.

Leung, A. Y. and A. G. Paul. 1968. Baeocystin and nor-baeocystin: new analogs of psilocybin from *Psilocybe baeocystis*. *Journal of Pharmaceutical Sciences* 57:1667–71.

McKenna, T. 1992. *Food of the Gods*. New York, N.Y.: Bantam Books.

Metzner, R., ed. 1999. *Ayahuasca: Hallucinogens, Consciousness, and the Spirit of Nature*. New York: Thunder's Mouth Press.

Migliaccio, G. P., T. L. N. Shieh, S. R. Byrn, B. A. Hathaway, and D. E. Nichols. 1981. Comparison of solution conformational preferences for the

hallucinogens bufotenin and psilocin using 360 MHz proton NMR spec-
troscopy. *Journal of Medicinal Chemistry* 24:206–9.

Murray, M. T. 1999. *5-HTP: The Natural Way to Overcome Depression,
Obesity, and Insomnia.* New York, N.Y.: Bantam Books.

Nichols, D. E., and S. Frescas. 1999. Improvements to the synthesis of psilocybin and a facile method for preparing the O-acetyl prodrug of psilocin.
Synthesis (6):935–38.

Ott, J. 1993. *Pharmacotheon: Entheogenic Drugs, their Plant Sources and
History.* Kennewick, Wash.: Natural Products Company.

Shulgin, A. and A. Shulgin. 1997. *TiHKAL (Tryptamines I Have Known and
Loved): The Continuation.* Berkeley, Calif.: Transform Press.

Stamets, P. 1996. *Psilocybin Mushrooms of the World.* Berkeley, Calif.: Ten
Speed Press.

Strassman, R. 2001. *DMT: The Spirit Molecule.* Rochester, Vt.: Park Street
Press.

Vollenweider, F. X., M. F. Vollenweider-Scherpenhuyzen, A. Babler, H. Vogel,
and D. Hell. 1998. Psilocybin induces schizophrenia-like psychosis in
humans via a serotonin-2 agonist action. *Neuroreport* 9:3897–3902.

Wasson, R. G. 1968. *Soma: Divine Mushroom of Immortality.* New York,
N.Y.: Harcourt Brace Jovanovich.

———. 1971. The Soma of the Rig Veda: What was it? *Journal of the
American Oriental Society* 91:169–87.

Wasson, R. G., A. Hofmann, and C. A. P. Ruck. 1998. *The Road to Eleusis:
Unveiling the Secrets of the Mysteries.* Los Angeles, Calif.: William Dailey
Rare Books. (Originally published in 1978).

Williams, G. V., S. G. Rao, and P. S. Goldman-Rakic. 2002. The physiological
role of 5-HT2A receptors in working memory. *Journal of Neuroscience*
22:2843–54.

Willins, D. L., A. Y. Deutch, and B. L. Roth. 1997. Serotonin 5-HT2A receptors are expressed on pyramidal cells and interneurons in the rat cortex.
Synapse 27:79–82.

5

A HISTORY OF THE USE OF PSILOCYBIN IN PSYCHOTHERAPY

TORSTEN PASSIE, M.D.

INTRODUCTION

The Application of hallucinogens in modern psychotherapeutic methods can be traced back to the 1950s. At first, lysergic acid diethylamide (LSD) was the most commonly used of the *psycholytics*, as LSD and mescaline were then categorized (Abramson 1960, 1967; Passie 1997). In the early 1960s, psilocybin (4-phosphoryloxy-N, N-dimethyl-tryptamin) was discovered in Mexican mushrooms (Hofmann et al. 1958; 1959). Shortly thereafter it was synthesized and applied in psychotherapy under the name *Indocybin* by Sandoz.

Psilocybin was used almost exclusively in Europe as an agent to help activate unconscious material in depth psychology *(psycholysis)*.

Torsten Passie, M.D., obtained his medical degree at the Hannover University Medical School and also has an M.A. in philosophy and sociology from Hannover University, Germany. He worked for some years with psycholytic pioneer Professor Hanscarl Leuner and is now at the Dept. of Clinical Psychiatry of the Medical School Hannover where he is doing research with psychedelics and other altered states of consciousness. He is a member of the European College for the Study of Consciousness (ECSC) and the Swiss Physicians Society for Psycholytic Therapy (SÄPT). He is the author of *Psycholytic and Psychedelic Therapy Research 1931–1995: A Complete International Bibilography.*

This procedure utilizes the properties of hallucinogenic substances to stimulate the emotions and promote a fluid, dreamlike state that is experienced in clear consciousness and with good recollection of what is occurring. In this manner, subconscious conflicts and memories can be re-created and made accessible to psychotherapy. It is understood that it is not the pharmacological effect that causes the therapeutic result, but the long-term therapeutic processing of material that has been exposed.

In utilizing this pharmacologically-aided method, many previously therapy-resistant patients could be treated. Psilocybin, as well as its quick-acting derivative, CZ 74 (4-hydroxy-N-diethyltryptamine), distinguishes itself by its unique properties of short duration of effects, mild neurovegetative side effects, few instances of depersonalization or anxiety provocation, as well as a stable and positive influence on the emotional experience (Hofmann 1959; Leuner et al. 1965; Baer 1967). Since it offers a more gentle and direct control of the altered state than LSD, it appears to be a substance of choice for future applications in psychotherapy (Leuner 1968, 1981).

In regard to its use in psychotherapy, I will introduce four types of treatment that have been studied on approximately fifteen hundred patients. To start, the following discussion will elaborate on differences and similarities between traditional and modern applications.

EARLY HISTORY OF PSILOCYBIN USE

In the monumental work *Historia General de las Cosas de Nueva España* (1598) by the Franciscan monk Berhardino de Sahagún, we find descriptions of natives in the New World who ingested certain intoxicating mushrooms during religious ceremonies. The clergy of the Inquisition deemed these rituals the work of the devil, whereas the natives regarded the effect of the mushrooms as the direct work of god and consequently named the mushroom *teonanácatl*, which means "divine mushroom" (Wasson 1958). In the same source there are further references to the fact that these mushrooms are not only used during religious ceremonies, but also for healing purposes by a medicine man. Reportedly, ingesting these mushrooms gave the medicine man certain visionary powers that enabled him to not only recognize the cause of an illness but also guided him in its treatment.

In the framework of such shamanistic treatment, psychological as well as social conflicts of the patient are addressed. The therapeutic sessions usually take place in the presence of relatives, who selectively will be involved in the ceremonial treatment. Frequently, only the healer actually will ingest the mushrooms for diagnostic purposes, or on other occasions the patient, the healer, and the attending relatives will ingest the mushrooms. This procedure is applied to diagnose not only the character and cause of the illness, but to simultaneously utilize the sensitization in the altered state of consciousness for healing catharsis and its manipulation (Wasson 1980; Passie 1985, 1987). By including direct family members and relatives, a positive healing outcome is made much more likely.

The first modern psychopharmacological research with psilocybin was presented between 1958 and 1960 (Dealay et al. 1995; Ruemmele 1959; Quetin 1960). Reports included dreamlike experiences that approximate the effect of other well-known hallucinogens such as LSD and mescaline, namely the intensification of the senses, illusions, pseudohallucinations, extreme tendency toward introversion, synaesthesia, changes in the experience of time, space, and the body, symptoms of depersonalization and the nonspecific increase in emotional qualities. Special attention was given to the frequent reliving of vivid memories with pronounced emotional undertones. This patient profile was observed particularly among neurotic subjects (Delay et al. 1959, 1961, 1963; Quetin 1960).

During the 1960s, other research that addressed different aspects was conducted by scientists of various nationalities, occasionally with a substantial number of subjects (Leary 1961; Salgueiro 1964). These studies confirmed the above-described psychopharmacological effects, the controllability of the state of inebriation and the physiological harmlessness of psilocybin (Malitz et al. 1960; Hollister 1961; Heimann 1961; Sercl et al. 1961; Rinkel et al. 1961; Nieto Gomez 1962; Leuner 1962; Aguilar 1963; Perez de Francisco 1964; Reda et al. 1964; Keeler 1965; Metzner et al. 1963; Da Fonseca et al. 1965; Steinegger et al. 1966; Flores 1966; Dubansky et al. 1967; Fisher et al. 1970).

APPLICATIONS IN PSYCHOLYTIC THERAPY

The longstanding traditions of healing rituals using hallucinogenic substances, particularly mescaline (Passie 1995), in central and South American societies was reported from extensive research conducted during the first half of the twentieth century (Beringer 1927; LaBarre 1938). Experiments with the extremely potent hallucinogen LSD (Stoll 1947) led Busch et al. (1950) to conduct the first trials including these substances in psychotherapy for neurotic patients. Later research was conducted in the context of psychoanalytical methods by Frederking (1953–1954). The English scientists working with Sandison et al. (1954) were particularly interested in the potential use of these substances as adjuncts to psychotherapeutic treatment. They reported improvements among their neurotic patients after a single treatment with LSD.

Initially, some scientists thought that the drug was responsible for the therapeutic effect. However, it quickly became evident that because of the unproductive structure and short-lived nature of experiences induced by the drugs, lasting benefits could only be realized with long-term therapy. The substances served as supporting agents in revealing unconscious material and gaining a more profound understanding of the self.

Psycholytic agents, such as LSD and psilocybin, possess the capability to aid in psychotherapy because they cause a fluid, dreamlike state experienced in clear consciousness with good recollection of what is occurring. Thus, unconscious conflicts and memories that have been suppressed can be activated and vividly recalled. Additionally, psychological defense mechanisms are relaxed and psychotherapeutically valuable types of regressive experience, such as age regression, can be evoked. Stimulating affectivity allows the recollection of long-past emotional experiences as well as recent ones. The transference relationship between the therapist and the patient is intensified and is sometimes accompanied by illusionary distortion of the therapist's features and identity. Hence, the patient clearly experiences the projective character, possibly that of infantile transference.

Under the influence of low dosages of psycholytic agents, a peculiar distancing enables the patient, or the reflective core of the self, to observe the altered state. This assures continuous understanding by the patient of the artificial cause of his altered state of experience.

Furthermore, the patient focuses on and associates separate emotional facts and reminiscences, personal relationships or wrongful evaluations of character, differently from an enlarged perspective. In this process, several areas of consciousness are addressed simultaneously and a broad integration of unconscious matter is achieved. The patient gains wide introspective access into delusional neurotic behavior. Due to the extraordinary emotional involvement, this process is particularly convincing, all the while intensifying and accelerating the therapy.

With the above-mentioned effects in mind, a considerable number of therapists thought it possible to expand the spectrum of psychotherapy by including patients who were formerly thought to be untreatable, due to their serious and chronic neuroses. These patients were characterized by their rigid defense and displacement mechanisms, lack of ability to form interpersonal relationships, and inability to process unconscious material through regular channels such as free association and dreams. Most psychotherapeutic treatments were ineffective for these patients. Psychotherapists recognized the potential of psycholytics to treat these difficult patients by stimulating a dreamlike alteration of experiences (Arendsen Hein 1963).

During the following ten years, the application of hallucinogens in psychotherapy treatment of extremely disturbed neurotic patients was tested internationally, improved, and established as clinical procedure (Sandison et al. 1954; Leuner 1962; Ling et al. 1963; Hausner et al. 1963; Grof 1967; also Abramson 1960, 1967; Passie 1995, 1997). Initially, LSD was the agent in these experiments, but very shortly after the discovery and synthesis of psilocybin, experiments were conducted with it as a psychotherapeutic drug (1958–1961). The basic psychopharmacological effect on individual neurotic patients was studied without psychotherapeutic preparation and postanalysis of the experience (Delay et al. 1959; Vernet 1960; Quetin 1960; David et al. 1961; Duche 1961; Sercl et al. 1961). Leuner described early treatments with psilocybin in a psycholytic setting (Barolin 1961; Leuner 1962). Until the 1980s, Leuner and his group of scientists treated more than 150 neurotic patients with psilocybin or its short-acting derivative, CZ 74, in a longitudinal study at the University Clinic of Goettingen, Germany (Leuner 1981, 1987, 1995; Fernandez-ceredeno et al. 1967).

The advantages of psilocybin in comparison to LSD were: short-term effectiveness, fewer neurovegetative side effects, less tendency to experience depersonalization, a stable, positive experience, and little distress while reliving conflicts and traumatic material. The entire experience under the influence of psilocybin was found to be altogether gentler and less confrontational than with LSD.

PROCEDURES IN PSYCHOTHERAPY WITH PSILOCYBIN

Psilocybin psychotherapy can be categorized in the following four types:

A. *Individual psychoanalytic therapy* including out-patient or residential psycholytic treatment and follow-up visits in psychoanalytic one-on-one sessions.

This method concerns the application of psycholytic substances in the course of psychotherapeutic individual treatment. It was developed and perfected for clinical application by various teams (Sandison et al. 1954; Leuner 1959; Hausner et al. 1963; Ling et al. 1963; Grof 1967). The first psycholytic session is almost always preceded by psychoanalytic treatment that has lasted for months. Psychoanalytic individual treatment with additional weekly or monthly psycholytic sessions sets the framework for the procedure that Sandison was the first to call "psycholysis" in 1960 (Barolin 1961). Experiences gained in psycholytic sessions are subsequently analyzed during intervening sessions without the use of drugs and with the help of documentation and memories.

The setting is arranged in such manner that the patient is able to surrender to his experiences uninhibitedly. All authors recommend a darkened room and quiet music to subtly stimulate the experience. The continuous presence of the therapist or a specifically trained assistant offers the patient protective support during the sessions. Occasional visits by the treating physician complement the care. These professionals do not intervene with interpretation during the course of the experience.

During the early sessions, the dosage is gradually increased from low dosages of LSD (50–150 mcg) or psilocybin (3–15 mg) up to the level at which the patient produces the most productive experiences. Psychodynamic encounters as well as the intensification of the transference relationship are deemed the most important indicators of adequate dosage.

Interpretation and integration take place during drug-free intermediate sessions. During the 1960s, much success was reported in treating more than a hundred neurotic patients with psilocybin (Fontana 1961; Heimann 1962; Leuner 1962; Alhadeff 1963, 1963; Hausner et al. 1963; Stevenin et al. 1962; Gnirss 1963, 1965; Kristensen 1963; Geert-Jörgensen et al. 1964, 1968; Massoni et al. 1964; Cwynar et al. 1966; Derbolowsky 1966; Johnson 1967; Fernandez-cerdeno et al. 1967; Clark 1967–1968; Berendes 1979–1980). Major indications for treatment were character neuroses, fear and compulsion, neurotic and reactive depressions, perversions and sexual neurosis. Counter indications would include hysterical neurosis, psychosis, and borderline cases, as well as patients that exhibit constitutionally infantile and weak-self properties.

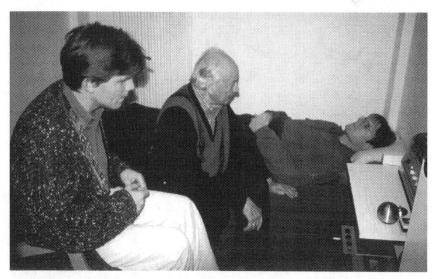

Early classic psycholytic setting, with attending nurses and physician in the background. (See: Bierer et al. 1961)

B. *Individual psychoanalytic therapy with psycholytic one-on-one sessions and follow up meetings in group therapy.*

First developed by Sandison et al. (1954) and tested with LSD on a great number of patients during the 1960s, this same methodology but using psilocybin was established by therapists using psychoanalysis (Fontana 1961; Derbolowsky 1966; Hausner et al. 1963; Geert Joergensn et al. 1964; Gnirss 1965; Johnsen 1967; Alnaes 1965; and particularly Leuner 1962).

This procedure followed the same premises as described in section A. The psycholytic one-on-one sessions were conducted at weekly or monthly intervals with the help of the therapist or an assistant. Patients were admitted to a clinic for several days to conduct each session. Before and after the psycholytic sessions in private rooms, the patients were brought together in a group to interpret and analyze the material through depth psychology. Their sensitized psychic condition could be utilized in the postsession analysis, while the effects of the drug were abating and the openness to discussion under the influence of the experience remained. In the next step, the patients had the opportunity to engage in artistic activities, such as painting or modeling with clay, to express their experiences. The following day, more single and group therapy sessions were conducted to further integrate the experience.

A reliable alternative to this procedure was stationary interval treatment used by Leuner (1964), Derbolowski (1966), Fontana (1961, 1963), Geert-Jörgensen et al. (1964), Alnaes (1965), and Johnsen (1967). Here five to six patients being treated in ambulatory psychoanalytic one-on-one sessions were admitted for two to three days and treated according to the procedure outlined above. This combined the advantages of a long-term ambulatory psychotherapy with the possibility of intensification and deepening through psycholytic sessions. Additionally, the safety of the procedure was increased through constant monitoring during and after the sessions.

C. *Group therapy interspersed with psycholytic group sessions.*

Fontana (1961, 1963) studied the use of psilocybin and LSD in depth psychological group sessions on more than 240 patients. A group of 7 to 8 patients that had consistently met once or twice a week over a period of several months was offered the opportunity to participate in psycholytic group sessions. The participants met in suitable rooms within the clinic and received low dosages of psilocybin (8–12 mg) or LSD (50–150 mcg). Without asking for interaction within the group, participants were expected to surrender to their own experience uninhibitedly. According to their individual needs, participants were also encouraged to communicate with other group members. The group therapist in charge and the co-therapist acted as chaperones and would only interfere when problems occurred.

Recently, Swiss psycholytic therapists (Benz 1989; Styk 1994; Gasser 1995) have worked utilizing a similar method. Scientists see particular advantages of this method in the activation of the group dynamic and intensification of transference-phenomena, as well as in the individual patient's ability to understand and visualize his/her own defense mechanisms. Here, the group also supports the individual who thus experiences fewer fears and feelings of isolation.

Fontana (1963) describes the dynamic of a carefully planned group session as "comparable with that of a musical group, in that the melodies and rhythms of each one serve to form a collective rhythm and a complete melody not interfering with the individual melodies." In spite of particularly intensified transference reactions within the group, due to careful preparation no difficulties in supervising the meeting were observed (Fontana 1963; Styk 1994; Gasser 1995). Johnson (1964), however, reported difficulties with group application of psycholytic agents. He found increased confusion within the group dynamic and that individuals encountered interference with their personal experience. These problems can probably be traced back to the change from group therapy to interaction demands in psycholytic sessions. Follow-up analysis of the experiences is conducted in groups and, when necessary, in one-on-one sessions.

Fontana (1963) recognized the special indications for group treatment to be useful in cases of character neurosis (clarification of otherwise ego-syntonic defense mechanisms), hypochondriacs (a dissociation between psychic and somatic entities is experienced under the influence of psycholytic agents and often helps the patient to recognize their interactive effect), adolescents (intense confrontation with specific patterns of conflict during this particular phase in life: relationship with the outside world and severance from the maternal influence). Otherwise, the indications described under A and B apply.

D. *Preparation in group therapy and high dosage (psychedelic) in a supportive group setting.*

This is the practice of administration of high dose psilocybin in group sessions for the purpose of inducing religious experiences that effect personality changes. The group associated with Leary (Leary 1961; Leary et al. 1963; Metzner et al. 1963, 1965; and also Pahnke 1962) researched the effect of high dosage psilocybin with over one hundred healthy volunteers in natural settings (nature, private homes, churches). Based on the observations of these normal subjects, therapists began to work with subjects with behavior problems (prison inmates). They utilized the deep changes in the experience of the self and the world while under the influence of psilocybin to improve therapeutically-effective self-realization in their subjects. This was based on the hypothesis that, with a given supportive setting and satisfactory agreement of the subjects: "(psilocybin) produces a state of dissociation or detachment from the roles and games of everyday interaction . . . This can provide insight and perspective about repetitive behavior or thought patterns and open up the way for the construction of alternatives." (Leary et al. 1965). The project at Concord Prison in Massachusetts, initiated by Leary et al., was laid out as a six-week program for behavioral changes. Each subject underwent regular group therapy sessions (under the premises of transaction analysis) as well as two psilocybin sessions in small groups characterized as improving self confrontation. The subjects were informed about the scope and purpose of the program as well as the effects of psilocybin. Following a few organized group sessions, the subjects received 20–30 mg of psilocybin in the first session and 50–70 mg in the second one. These latter sessions took place in specially prepared rooms within the infirmary of the prison. They were initially conducted with 5–10 subjects and later reduced to only four subjects and one psychologist. The sessions were marked by intense experiences and self-confrontation that were subsequently discussed in groups. Despite careful postanalysis, instances of depressive aftereffects and difficulties in the emotional integration of the psychedelic experiences were sometimes observed (Leary et al. 1965). The authors also documented a reduced number of repeat offenders, particularly in respect to recurring criminal acts among participants of the study (Leary et al. 1968; see Doblin, chapter 6 this volume).

The Norwegian scientist Alnaes (1965) closely followed the group therapeutic approach developed by Leary et al. He worked with a group of twenty psychoneurotic patients to help them gain deep insight into their own experience and behavior. He utilized a depth psychology group process that was interspersed with high dosage psilocybin (20–50 mg) sessions to achieve experiences of self-transcendence. After preparation in psychotherapeutic one-on-one sessions, the patient would receive psilocybin or the derivative CZ 74 in group session in supportive surroundings (cozy treatment rooms with pictures, candle light, and music). In the afternoon, immediately following the session, the experiences were discussed and interpreted in a group setting. Alnaes reported improvement of his patients but did not provide detailed evaluation.

The Mexican psychiatrist Roquet used psilocybin and other psycholytic substances in a different way. After initially following Leuner's (1962) guidelines for treatment, in 1967 Roquet developed his own methodology by incrementally integrating certain practices of Native American healers and combining them with modern audiovisual instruments (Roquet et al. 1975, 1981). In the beginning, the patient is carefully prepared through depth psychology in group or individual therapy. The patients are then subjected to a sequence of experiences involving hallucinogenic plants or substances in a group setting of six to thirty-five patients (Villoldo 1977).

The day of the session the participants gathered in the morning for relaxation exercise. Later they met in special rooms that featured modern lighting and pictures of existential meaning. Once the effect of the drug took hold, the participants, who were in a sensitized psychic state, were subjected to strong sensory stimuli (sounds, music, movies, slides), which produced distinct emotional reactions. The sensory bombardment was produced deliberately to cause a severe psychic irritation with a concurrent breakdown of inner emotional defense mechanisms and mental concepts. The confrontational nature of this procedure aimed to evoke and stimulate personal and transpersonal emotional conflicts that were subsequently integrated into consciousness with the help of follow-up psychotherapy.

Roquet et al. (1981) used this procedure to treat patients with character neuroses, sexual neuroses, and drug addiction. Nine hundred fifty patients were treated in this manner and, according to a scientific follow-up study, approximately 80% of those treated showed distinct improvements (Roquet et al. 1981). Table I summarizes the information on these studies.

In addition to psilocybin, two related tryptamines have been used in psycholytic therapy. CZ 74, which has been clinically tested and applied in psychotherapy by Leuner (1967), Johnson (1967), and Alnaes (1965), should be of great interest for future research in psycholytic therapy. This derivative of psilocybin remains effective for only three hours and is entirely free of somatic side effects. Another related tryptamine derivative with an effective duration of 2–4 hours named DPT (dipropyltryptamine) was studied as an alternative to LSD in context of a research project of the Baltimore group led by Grof (1972–1973), Grof et al. (1973) and Soskin (1975; Soskin et al. 1973). The authors thought the short-term effectiveness of these substances also to be suitable for ambulatory psycholytic treatment (Leuner et al. 1965).

COMPARISON OF PSYCHOLYTIC THERAPY WITH TRADITIONAL SHAMANIC PRACTICES

The methods of psychoanalytic therapy described above are strongly influenced by the premises and procedures of Freudian and Jungian psychoanalysis. Psychoanalysis employs methods that are suitable for the exposure of traumatic experiences and hidden conflicts in personality development. Methods include hypnosis, dream evaluations, active imagination, free association, and guided visualizations, what Leuner calls "katathymic imagery." The use of psycholytic agents, which enhance introspective experience and activate subconscious material, thus produces fruitful results in the hands of psychoanalytically-oriented

AUTHOR(S)	TYPE OF STUDY	PRESENCE OF RITUAL ELEMENTS	INTENDED EXPERIENCES	# OF SESSIONS	PSILOCYBIN DOSAGE	# OF PATIENTS	OTHER SUBSTANCES
Leuner (1962 et seq.)	A/B	+	Activation of unconsious memories and conflicts	10–30	5–15 mg	150	LSD/CZ 74
Gnirss (1963 et seq.)	A	+	"	10–30	5–12 mg	25	---
Aldhadeff (1963)	A	+	"	1–5	5–15 mg	15	LSD
Hausner et al. (1963 et seq.)	B	+	"	1–35	3–10 mg	100s	LSD
Massoni et al. (1964)	A	+	"	Some	9–23 mg	92	LSD
Derbolowski (1966)	B	+	"	1–15	5–15 mg	65	LSD
Fernandez-cerdeno (1967)	A	+	"	7–30	5–15 mg	?	LSD
Berendes (1979/80)	A	+	"	?	?	?	LSD/DPT
Johnsen (1967)	B	+	"	1–3	20–30 mg	12	LSD/CZ 74
Kristensen (1963)	B	+	"	5–10	4–5 mg	20	---
Geert-Jörgensen (1968)	A/B	+	"	5–15	5–15 mg	150	LSD
Cwynar (1966)	?	+	"	9–12	9 mg	11	---
Clark (1967/68)	A	+	"	2–5	4–20 mg	20	LSD
Rydzynski et al. (1978)	A/B	+	"	12–15	6–30 mg	31	LSD
Hollister et al. (1962)	A (?)	+	"	?	5–10 mg	18	LSD/Mescaline
Fontana	C	++	"	1–10	?	250	LSD/Mescaline
Alnaes (1965)	D	+++	Psychedelic ego transcendence	2–5	20–30 mg	20	LSD/CZ 74
Leary et al. (1965 et seq.)	D	++	"	2–3	20–70 mg	40	---
Roquet et al. (1981)	D	+++	" and self-confrontation	5–10	10–30 mg	950	LSD/Mescaline/Ketamine

therapists and was quickly established as an experimental procedure among researchers. The activation of unconscious conflicts and the recollection of dreams achieved greater depth in psycholytic sessions than with conventional treatments. It was observed that recollection with psycholytic agents could reach childhood memories as early as the first year of the patient's life, producing a vivid and realistic recollection of events and making them available for therapeutic analysis.

In shamanistic healing, unconscious conflicts and illness-related memories are equally stimulated, recognized as root causes of the illness, and subsequently interpreted by the shaman. Classical psychotherapists encourage the patient to surrender to emerging material and to try not to interfere with the state of inebriation, while some indigenous healers exploit the sensitized state of their patients to make specific suggested cathartic interventions. The European psycholytic method puts more emphasis on the activation and analysis of unconscious conflicts and memories.

In traditional applications of very low dosages, suitable material appears mostly in the form of dream fragments. These fragments have been shown to possess personality-related characteristics; therefore it makes sense to integrate them into the therapy process of depth psychology. Missing from depth psychology is the psycho-dramatic momentum, as the stimulation/manipulation of the experience is limited to the playing of quiet music in a darkened room. The awareness of the self remains intact and allows the patient to observe from the perspective of a spectator.

A further difference from traditional applications is the repeated administration of psycholytic drugs, where the patients are subjected to a series of ten to seventy weekly or monthly sessions. In traditional settings, singular sessions centered around conflict and including psycho-dramatic elements are customary. Indigenous healers frequently make use of follow-up sessions, but they focus on acutely-occurring illnesses. To achieve a strong impact with these short-term interventions, suggestive, psycho-dramatic, and religious aspects of the induced altered experiences are utilized. Shamans will interfere in the process of the session much more decisively than modern therapists will in psycholysis. The latter offer help with interpretation and therapeutic analysis solely during drug-free intervening sessions.

The fact that the shamans include family members and relatives probably intensifies the impact of occasional interventions. Due to less frequent but higher dosages in shamanistic treatment, the awareness of the self is subject to greater fluctuation. In contrast, psycholytic therapists concentrate on the treatment of chronic neurotic diseases in the course of serial sessions. These chronic problems are usually based on structural distortions of the personality, so long-term treatment in psychotherapy promises success.

The time of day that sessions take place is another difference. The indigenous healers exclusively hold sessions at night, whereas classical psycholytic therapists administer substances in the morning to utilize the afternoons for follow-up sessions. The procedures described above in section D (psychedelic), however, more directly follow various aspects of the religious cultural applications of hallucinogenic substances. Therapists were aiming at religiously ecstatic experiences for participants who were specifically prepared and received higher dosages of these agents. Such experiences often entail conversion experiences with personality-changing effect.

This effect was scientifically proven by Pahnke (1962) and suggested the concept of "psychedelic therapy," as developed by American LSD therapists (Chewelos et al. 1959; Savage 1962; Sherwood et al. 1962). Here the setting resembles that of the practices and rituals among traditional indigenous cults: dimly lighted, specially prepared rooms, semi-religious preparation, music, and other circumstances favorable to absorption of the experiences. These create a feeling of security and set the mood for the participants. Also, in contrast to the psycholytic method, no psychodynamic interpretation and analysis of the experiences takes place.

Further differences include the fact that psychedelic therapy sessions only take place with individuals or in very small groups. On the other hand, traditional healings that are inspired by religious traditions are always performed in group settings with a ritual structure (LaBarre 1938; Myerhoff 1980). While in single settings the course of the experience is largely determined by the relationship between the therapist and the patient, in traditional group rituals the patient's experience is dependent on the structure of the entire group and the follow-up work

consists of a joint discussion of the pertaining experiences. In psychedelic therapy, just as in traditional applications, a small number of sessions over a period of time utilize higher dosages of the drug.

Both groups offer professional observation of the participants, necessary because of possible fluctuations after the treatment. The traditional healers hold nightly sessions and meetings on the following day
and the psycholytic therapists utilize an in-patient setting.

Combining the several advantages found in psycholytic and psychedelic approaches was suggested by Grof (1967) and applied by
Alnaes (1963) and Roquet et al. (1981), as well as by the Swiss psycholytic therapists Styk (1994) and Gasser (1995). These authors
favored psychedelic/mystical forms of experience, adhering to the traditional setting (group sessions with higher dosage, ingestion at night,
ritualistic structure, natural surroundings, etc.), as well as long-term
therapeutic analysis of the psycho-dynamic biographical experience.

SUMMARY

In summarizing the historic development in the use of psycholytic substances in modern psychotherapy, I observed two lines of development.
One direction is outlined in the psycholytic method in Europe, which inte-
grates evocation of unconscious materials through psycholytic agents with
the methods of classic depth psychology. The other direction is depicted in
the development of the psychedelic method, which provides the base for
therapeutic treatment by closely adhering to the traditional settings and
procedures with semireligious experiences of mystical self-transcendence.

In regard to results of treatments with psilocybin in modern psychotherapy, I will only point toward the research by Mascher (1966),
Schulz-Wittner (1989), Leuner (1994), and the studies of the
Baltimore-group (Yensen et al. 1995). These authors could (in agreement with many others) document a significant improvement in
approximately 65% of the patients with serious and chronic neuroses.
However, part of the evaluation seems problematic because it was conducted during the 1960s, when psycholytic substances were still being
researched, and could only satisfy the standards of psychotherapy evaluation at that time.

According to current standards, these evaluations seem to be lacking important data (Pletscher et al. 1994). Further research and examination of the promising treatment successes of those days are desirable under the following guidelines: 1. Specification of the diagnoses according to DSM IV/ICD-10; 2. The use of standardized instruments in understanding the psychopathology of the patient; 3. Specification of variables concerning the therapists and the environment; 4. Operational standardization of outcome variables; 5. The use of control groups. Some studies following these guidelines are in process now, in the United States and elsewhere, as described in a following chapter "A Note on Current Psilocybin Research" by Rick Doblin.

Translation of this essay from the German by Cordelia Ballent and Ralph Metzner.

References

Abramson, H. A., ed. 1960. *The Use of LSD in Psychotherapy*. New York: Josiah Macy Foundation.

Abramson, H. A., ed. 1967. *The Use of LSD in Psychotherapy and Alcoholism*. New York, Kansas City: Bobbs Merrill.

Aguilar, T. M. 1963. La Psilocybine: perspectives d'utilisation en psychiatrie clinique. *Acta Neurologica et Psychiatrica Belgica* 63:114–31.

Aldhadeff, B. W. 1963. Aspects cliniques de l'emploi du delyside et de l'indocybine en psychiatrie. *Schweizer Apotheker-Zeitung* 101:245–50.

———. 1963. Les effets psychotomimetiques du LSD et de a psilocybine dans l'exploration clinique de a personnalite. *Schweizer Archiv für Neurologie, Neurochirurgie und Psychiatrie* 92:238–42.

Alnaes, R. 1965. Therapeutic application of the change in consciousness produced by psycholytica (LSD, Psilocybin, etc.). *Acta Psychiatrica Scandinavica* 40:397–409. Suppl. 180.

Arendsen Hein, G. W. 1963. Psychotherapeutische Möglichkeiten zur Überwindung einer Behandlungsresistenz unter besonderer Berücksichtigung der psycholytischen methode. *Zeitschrift für Psychotherapie und medizinische Psychologie* 13:81–87.

Baer, G. 1967. Statistical results on reactions of normal subjects to the Psilocybin derivates ceY 19 and CZ 74. In *Neuro-Psycho-Pharmacology*, ed. H. Brill, 400–404. Amsterdam, New York, London: Excerpta Medica.

————. 1967. *Über die psychopathologische Wirkung zweier neuer Halluzinogene der Psilocybingruppe.* Göttingen: Medical dissertation.

Barolin, G. S. 1961. Erstes Europäisches Symposion für Psychotherapie unter LSD-25, Göttingen, November 1960. *Wiener Medizinische Wochenschrift* 111:466–68.

Benz, E. 1989. *Halluzinogen-unterstützte Psychotherapie.* Zürich: Medical dissertation.

Berendes, M. 1979–1980. Formation of typical dynamic stages in psychotherapy before and after psychedelic drug intervention. *Journal of Altered States of Consciousness* 5:325–38.

Beringer, K. 1927. *Der Meskalinrausch.* Berlin: Springer.

Busch, A. and W. Johnson. 1950. LSD 25 as an aid in psychotherapy. *Diseases of the Nervous System* 11:241–43.

Chwelos, N., D. B. Blewett, C. M. Smith, and A. Hoffer. 1959. Use of d-Lysergic Acid Diethylamide in the treatment of alcoholism. *Quarterly Journal of Studies on Alcohol* 20:577–90.

Clark, B. 1967–1968. Some early observations on the use of Psilocybin in psychiatric patients. *British Journal of Social Psychiatry* 2:21–26.

Clark, J. 1970. The use of Psilocybin in a prison setting. In *Psychedelics,* eds. B. Aaronson and H. Osmond, 40–44. London: Hogarth Press.

Clark, W. H. 1977. Art and psychotherapy in Mexico. *Art of Psychotherapy* 4:41–44.

Cwynar, S. and Z. Rydzynski. 1966. Psilocybin in der Behandlung von persönlichkeitsstörungen. *Activitas Nervosa Superior* 8:424.

Da Fonseca, J. S., C. Cardoso, P. Salguiero and M. L. Fialho. 1965. Neurophysiological and psychological study of Psilocybin-induced modifications of visual information processing in man. In *Neuro-Psychopharmacology Vol. 4,* eds. D. Bente & P. B. Bradley, 315–19. Amsterdam, London, New York: Elsevier.

David, A. E. and J. David. 1961. La psilocibina, un nuevo alucinogeno, y sus posibilidades terapeuticas en psicoterapia. *Acta Neuropsiquatrica Argentina* 7:143–44.

Delay, J., P. Pichot and P. Nicolas-Charles. 1959. Premiers essais de la psilocybine en psychiatrie. In *Neuro-Psychopharmacology,* eds. P. Bradley, P. Deniker and C. Radouco-Thomas, 528–31. Amsterdam, London, New York, Princeton: Elsevier.

Delay, J., P. Pichot, T. Lemperiere and A. M. Quetin. 1959. Effet therapeutique de la psilocybine sur une nevrose convulsive. *Annales medico-psychologiques* 117:509–15.

Delay, J., P. Pichot, T. Lemperiere, P. Nicolas-Charles and A. M. Quetin. 1959. Les effets psychiques de la psilocybine et les perspectives therapeutiques. *Annales medico-psychologiques* 117:899–907.

Delay, J., P. Pichot, and T. Lemperiere. 1961. La Psilocybine—Ses implications therapeutiques. *Le Sud Medical et Chirurgical* 97:9217–24.

———. 1963. The therapeutic implications of Psilocybine. In *Hallucinogenic drugs and their Psychotherapeutic Use,* eds. R. Crocket, R. A. Sandison, A. Walk, 37–41. London: Lewis.

Derbolowsky, G. 1967–1968. Dealing and working with materials in group-analysis and with "LSD-25." *British Journal of Social Psychiatry* 2:67–72.

Derbolowsky, U. 1966. Psycholytische intervalltherapie mit LSD 25 oder ambulante analytische psychotherapie? *Zeitschrift für Psychotherapie und medizinische Psychologie* 16:33–38.

Doblin, R. 1998. Dr. Leary′s Concord Prison Experiment: A 34-year follow-up study. *Journal of Psychoactive Drugs* 30:419–26

Dubansky, B., M. Vyhnankova and L. Setlik. 1967a. Veränderungen der ausseroptischen Sinneswahrnehmung nach Psilocybin. *Activitas Nervosa Superior* 9:378–79.

———. 1967b. Gleichzeitiges Vorkommen von propriozeptiven S innestäuschungen und neurologischer symptomatologie nach Psilocybin. *Activitas Nervosa Superior* 9:376–77.

Duche, D. 1961. Les effets de la psilocybine dans une cas d'hysterie. *Semaine des hospitaux de Paris* 37:3061–62.

Fernandez-cerdeno, A., A. Brugmann and A. Suarez. 1967. Besonderheiten der psycholytischen Technik im Vergleich mit der psychoanalytischen. *Jahrbuch für Psychologie, Psychotherapie und medizinische Anthropologie* 15:274–79.

Fernandez-cerdeno, A. and H. Leuner. 1967. Das Erleben der oralen regression unter Einfluss von halluzinogenen (LSD-25 und Psilocybin). *Zeitschrift für psychosomatische Medizin* 11:45–54.

Fischer, R., R. M. Hill, K. Thatcher, and J. Scheib. 1970. Psilocybin-induced contraction of nearby visual space. *Agents and Actions* 1:190–97.

Fisher, G. 1963. Some comments concerning dosage levels of psychedelic compounds for psychotherapeutic experiences. *Psychedelic Review* 1:208–18.

Flores, J. R. 1966. Psicosindrome experimental con psilocybina. *Revista de Neuropsiquiatria* 29:45–70.

Fontana, A. E. 1961. El uso clinico de las drogas alucinogenas. *Acta Neuropsiqiatrica Argentina* 7:94–98.

———. Clinical use of hallucinogenic drugs. In *Proceedings of the Third World Congress of Psychiatry Vol. 2.*, 942–44. Toronto: University of Toronto Press.

Fortes, J. R. A. 1964. Psilocibina e alcoolismo cronico: contribuciao para los estudo des efeitos somaticos e psiquicos em 30 casos. Sao Paulo: Medical dissertation.

Fortes, J. R. A., F. O. Bastos, and R. V. Arruda. 1968. Estudio comparativa de la accion psicopharmacologico del LSD-25 y de la psilocybina en los alocoholicos cronicos. In *Proceedings Fourth World Congress of Psychiatry 1966 Vol. 3*, ed. J. Lopez Ibor, 2010–13. Amsterdam: Excerpta Medica.

Frederking, W. 1953–1954. Über die Verwendung von Rauschdrogen (Meskalin und Lysergsäurediäthylamid) in der Psychotherapie. *Psyche* 7:342–64.

———. 1954. Meskalin in der psychotherapie. *Medizinischer Monatsspiegel* 3:5–7.

Gasser, P. 1995. Katamnestische Untersuchungen zur psycholytischen therapie. *Yearbook of Cross-Cultural Medicine and Psychotherapy* 1995:143–62.

Geert-Jörgensen, E., M. Hertz, K. Knudsen, and K. Kristensen. 1964. LSD-treatment: Experience gained within a three-year-period. *Acta Psychiatrica Scandinavica*, 373–82. Suppl. 180.

Gnirss, F. 1959. Untersuchungen mit Psilocybin, einem phantastikum aus dem amerikanischen Rauschpilz Psilocybe mexicana. *Schweizer Archiv für Neurologie und Psychiatrie* 84:346–48.

———. 1963. Therapie der neurosen mit phantastica. *Schweizer Archiv für Neurologie, Neurochirurgie und Psychiotrie* 92:234–36.

———. 1965. Neurosentherapie mit psycholytischen Stoffen. In *Psychiatrische Pharmakotherapie in Klinik und Praxis*, ed. F. Kielholz, 135–51. Bern, Stuttgart: Huber.

————. 1995. Personal communication.

Grof, S. 1967. The use of LSD 25 in personality diagnostics and psychotherapy of psychogenic disorders. In *The Use of LSD in Psychotherapy and Alcoholism*, ed. H. A. Abramson, 154–90. New York, Kansas City: Bobbs Merrill.

————. 1972–1973. LSD and the human encounter with death. *Voices: The Art and Science of Psychotherapy* 8:64–76.

————. 1975. *Realms of the Human Unconscious*. New York, N.Y.: Viking.

————.1983 *LSD-Psychotherapy*. Pomona, Calif.: Hunter House.

Grof, S., R. A. Soskin, W. A. Richards, and A. A. Kurland. 1973. DPT as an adjunct in psychotherapy of alcoholics. *International Pharmacopsychiatry* 8:104–15.

Hausner, M. 1968. Psyckolyticka psychotherapie. *Activitas Nervosa Superior* 10:50.

Hausner, M., and V. Dolezal. 1963. Prakticke zkusenosti s halucinogeny v psychoterapii. *Ceskoslovenska Psychiatrie* 54:328–35.

Hausner, M., and V. Dolezal. 1963. Group and individual therapy under LSD. *Acta Psychotherapeutica et Psychosomatica* 11:39–59.

Heimann, H. 1962. Zur Behandlung therapieresistenter neurosen mit modellpsychosen (Psilocybin). *Schweizer Archiv für Neurologie, Neurochirurgie und Psychiatrie* 89:214–20.

Hofmann, A. 1959. Abwandlungsprodukte des Psilocybin und Psilocin. *Helvetica Chimica Acta* 42:2073ff.

Hofmann, A., R. Heim, A. Brack, and H. Kobel. 1958. Psilocybin, ein psychotroper Wirkstoff aus dem mexikanischen Rauschpilz Psilocybe mexicana Heim. *Experientia* 14:107–9.

Hofmann, A., R. Heim, A. Brack, H. Kobel, A. Frey, H. Ott, T. Petrzilka, and F. Troxler. 1959. Psilocybin und Psilocin, zwei psychotrope Wirkstoffe aus mexikanischen Rauschpilzen. *Helvetica Chimica Acta* 42:1557–72.

Hollister, L. E. 1961. Clinical, biochemical and psychologic effects of Psilocybin. *Archives Internationales de Pharmacadynamie e de Therapie* 130:42–52.

Hollister, L. E., R. O. Degan, and S. D. Schultz. 1962. An experimental approach to facilitation of psychotherapy by psychotomimetic drugs. *Journal of Mental Science* 108:99–100.

Johnsen, G. 1964. Three years experience with the use of LSD as an aid in psychotherapy. *Acta Psychiatrica Skandinavica* 40:383–88. Suppl. 180.

―――. 1967. Indications for psycholytic treatment with different types of patients. In *The Use of LSD in Psychotherapy and Alcoholism*, ed. H. A. Abramson, 333–41. New York, Kansas City: Bobbs Merrill.

Keeler, M. H. 1965. Similarity of schizophrenia and the Psilocybin syndrome as determined by objective methods. *International Journal of Neuropsychiatry* 1:630–34.

Kristensen, K. K. 1963. Kliniske erfaringer med psilocybin. *Nordisk Psykiatrisk Tidsskrift* 17:177–82.

LaBarre, W. 1938. *The Peyote Cult.* New Haven.

Ladewig, D. 1994. Conclusions, with special regard to clinical aspects. In *50 Years of LSD. Current Status and Perspectives of Hallucinogens*, eds. A. Pletscher and D. Ladewig, 223–28. New York, London: Parthenon.

Leary, T. 1962. How to Change Behavior. In *Clinical Psychology*, ed. G. S. Nielsen, 50-68. Kopenhagen.

―――. 1964. The religious experience: Its production and interpretation. *Psychedelic Review* 1:324–46.

―――. 1969. The effects of consciousness-expanding drugs on prisoner rehabilitation. *Psychedelic Review* 10:29–44.

Leary, T., R. Alpert, and R. Metzner. 1964. *The Psychedelic Experience.* New York: University Books.

Leary, T., G. H. Litwin, and R. Metzner. 1963. Reactions to Psilocybin administered in a supportive environment. *Journal of Nervous and Mental Disease* 137:561–73.

Leary, T., and R. Metzner. 1967–1968. Use of psychedelic drugs in prisoner rehabilitation. *British Journal of Social Psychiatry* 2:27–51.

Leary, T., R. Metzner, M. Presnell, G. Weil, R. Schwitzgebel, and S. Kinne. 1965. A new behavior change program using Psilocybin. *Psychotherapy: Theory, Research and Practice* 2:61–72.

Leuner, H. 1959. Psychotherapie in modellpsychosen. In *Kritische Psychotherapie*, ed. E. Speer, 94–102. München: J. F. Lehmanns.

―――. 1960. Über psychopathologische schlüsselfunktionen in der modellpsychose. *Medicina Experimentalis* 2:227–32.

―――. 1961. Psychophysische korrelationen unter der einwirkung von psycholytika (LSD Psilocybin und ähnl.). *Medicina Experimentalis* 5:209–14.

———. l962a. *Die experimentelle Psychose*. Berlin, Göttingen, Heidelberg: Springer.

———. 1962b. Ergebnisse und probleme der psychotherapie mit Hilfe von LSD-25 und verwandten substanzen. *Psychiat. Neurol.* 143:379–91.

———. 1963. Die psycholytische therapie: KIinische psychotherapie mit Hilfe von LSD-25 und verwandten substanzen. *Zeitschrift für Psychotherapie und medizinische Psychologie* 13:57–64.

———. 1966. Psychotherapie mit Hilfe von halluzinogenen. *Arzneimittelforschung* 16:253–55.

———. 1967. Present status of psycholytic therapy and its possibilities. In *The Use of LSD in Psychotherapy and Alcoholism*, ed. H. A. Abramson, 101–16. New York, Kansas City: Bobbs Merrill.

———. 1968. Ist die Verwendung von LSD-25 für die experimentelle psychiatrie und in der psychotherapie heute noch vertretbar? *Nervenarzt* 39:356–60.

———. 1971. Halluzinogene in der psychotherapie. *Pharmakopsychiatrie—Neuro-Psychopharmakologie* 4:333–51.

———. 1981. *Halluzinogene*. Bern, Stuttgart, Wien: Huber.

———. 1987. Die psycholytische therapie: Durch halluzinogene unterstützte tiefenpsychologische psychotherapie. In *Ethnopsychotherapie*, eds. A. Dittrich, and C. Scharfetter, 151–60. Stuttgart: Enke.

———. 1994. Hallucinogens as an aid in pychotherapy: Basic principles and results. In *50 Years of LSD. Current Status and Perspectives of Hallucinogens*, eds. A. Pletscher, and D. Ladewig, 175–90. New York, London: Parthenon.

———. 1995. Personal communication.

Leuner, H., and G. Baer. 1965. Two new short-acting hallucinogens of the Psilocybin group. In *Neuro-Psychopharmacology Vol. 4*, eds. D. Bente, and P. B. Bradley, 471–73. Amsterdam, London, New York: Elsevier.

Leuner, H., and H. Holfeld. 1964. Psycholysis—Psychotherapy under the influence of hallucinogens. *Physicians Panorama* 2:13–16.

Ling, T. M., and J. Buckman. 1963. *Lysergic Acid (LSD-25) & Ritalin in the Treatment of Neuroses*. Sidcup, Kent: Lombarde Press.

Lipp, F. 1990. Mixed concepts and uses of entheogenic mushrooms. In *The Sacred Mushroom Seeker*, ed. T. Riedlinger, 151–60. Portland, Ore.: Discorides Press.

Malitz, S., H. Esecover, B. Wilkens, and P. H. Hoch. 1960. Some observations on Psilocybin, a new hallucinogen in volunteer subjects. *Comprehensive Psychiatry* 1:8–17.

Mascher, E. 1966. *Katamnestische Untersuchung von Ergebnissen der psycholytischen Therapie.* Göttingen: Medical dissertation.

Massoni, R. S., and F. Lebensohn. 1964. Las drogas alucinogenas: su importancia en psicoterapia asistencial. *Acta psiquiatrica y psicologica America latina* 10:128–32.

Metzner, R., and Editors of Psychedelic Review. 1963. The subjective aftereffects of psychedelic experiences: A summary of four recent questionnaire studies. *Psychedelic Review* 1:18–26.

Metzner, R., G. Litwin, and G. M. Weil. 1965. The relation of expectation and mood to Psilocybin reactions: A questionnaire study. *Psychedelic Review* 5:339.

Metzner, R. 1998. Reflections on the Concord Prison Project and the follow-up study. *Journal of Psychoactive Drugs* 30:427–28.

Nieto Gomez, D. 1962. Psicosis experimentales con Psilocibina. *Neurologia, Neurocirurgia, Psiquiatria* 4.

Pahnke, W. N. 1962. *Drugs and Mysticism: An Analysis of the Relationship between Psychedelic Drugs and the Mystical Consciousness.* Cambridge, Mass.: Philosophical dissertation.

Passie, T. 1985. Field observations in Mexiko.

———. 1987. Field observations in Mexiko.

———. 1995a. Ausrichtungen, methoden und ergebnisse früher meskalinforschungen im deutschsprachigen Raum. *Yearbook of the European College for the Study of Consciousness* 1993–1994:103–11.

———. 1995b. Die psycholyse in den skandinavischen Ländern. Ein historischer Überblick. *Yearbook of Cross-Cultural Medicine and Psychotherapy* 1995:183–220.

———. 1995c. Psilocybin in der modernen psychotherapie. *Curare* 18:131–52.

Passie, T., J. Seifert, U. Schneider, and H. M. Emrich. 2002. The pharmacology of Psilocybin. *Addiction Biology* 7:357–64.

Perez de Francisco, C. 1964. *Psicosis experimentales con psilocybina y LSD.* Mexico City: Medical dissertation.

Pletscher, A., and D. Ladewig, eds. 1994. *50 Years of LSD. Current Status and Perspectives of Hallucinogens.* New York, London: Parthenon.

Quetin, A. M. 1960. *La psilocybine en psychiatrie clinique et experimentale.* Paris: Medical dissertation.

Reda, G., G. Vella, I. Cancrini, and E. D'Agostino. 1964. Studio clinico e psicopatologico della psilocibina. *Rivista sperimentale di freniatria e medicina legale delle alientazioni mentali* 88:7–76.

Rinkel, M., A. DiMascio, A. Robey, and C. Atwell. 1961. Personality patterns and reaction to Psilocybin. In *Neuro-Psychopharmacology Vol. 2,* ed. P. B. Bradley, 273–79. Amsterdam: Elsevier.

Roquet, S., and P. Favreau. 1981. *Los alucinogenos de Ia concepcion indigena a una nueva psicoterapia.* México D.F.: Ediciones Prisma.

Roquet, S., P. Favreau, R. Ocana, and M. R. Velasco. 1975. *La existencial a través de psicodyslepticos: una nueva Psicoterapia.* Mexico City: Instituto de psicosintesis.

Rosenbohm, A. 1991. *Halluzinogene Drogen im Schamanismus.* Berlin: Reimer.

Rydzynski, Z., and W. Gruszczynski. 1978. Treatment of alcoholism with psychotomimetic drugs: A follow-up study. *Activitas Nervosa Superior* 20:81–82.

Salguiero, E. G. 1964. *A psicose experimental pela psilocibina: estudio clinico-labortorial em voluntarios humanos.* Lissabon: Inquerito.

Sandison, R. A. 1954. Psychological aspects of the LSD treatment of the neurosis. *Journal of Mental Science* 100:508–18.

———. 1959. The role of psychotropic drugs in individual therapy. *Bulletin of the World Health Organization* 21:495–503.

Sandison, R. A., and A. Spencer. 1954. The therapeutic value of Lysergic Acid Diethylamide in mental illness. *Journal of Mental Science* 100:491–507.

Sandison, R. A., A. Spencer, and J. Whitelaw. 1957. Further studies in the therapeutic value of Lysergic Acid Diethylamide in mental illness. *Journal of Mental Science* 103:332–42.

Savage, C. 1962. LSD, alcoholism and transcendence. *Journal of Nervous and Mental Disease* 135:429–35.

Savage, C., and S. Wolf. 1967. An outline of psychedelic therapy. In *Neuro-Psycho-Pharmacology,* ed. H. Brill, 405–10. Amsterdam: Excerpta Medica.

Schulz-Wittner, G. 1989. Mit psychoaktiven substanzen unterstützte psychotherapie bei negativ prognostizierten patienten: Neue katamnestische Ergebnisse. Göttingen: Medical dissertation.

Sercl, M., J. Kovarik, and O. Jaros. 1961. Klinische erfahrungen mit Psilocybin (CY-39 Sandoz). *Psychiat. Neurol.* 142:137–46.

Sherwood, J. N., M. Stolaroff, and W. W. Harman. 1962. The psychedelic experience—A new concept in psychotherapy. *Journal of Neuropsychiatry* 4:69–80.

Soskin, R. A. 1975. Dipropyltryptamine in psychotherapy. *Current Psychiatric Therapies* 15:147–56.

Soskin, R. A., S. Grof, and W. A. Richards. 1973. Low doses of Dipropyltryptamlne in psychotherapy. *Archives of General Psychiatry* 28:817–21.

Steinegger, E., and H. Heimann. 1966. Pharmakochemie und psychische Wirkung von drei mexikanischen zauberdrogen. *Mitteilungen der Naturforschenden Gesellschaft in Bern* 23:83–99.

Stevenin, L., and J. C. Benoit. 1962. L'utilisation des medicaments psychotropes en psychotherapie. *Encephale* 51:420–59.

Stoll, W. A. 1947. Lysergsäure-diätlhylamid, ein phantastikum aus der mutterkorngruppe. *Schweizer Archiv für Neurologie und Psychiatrie* 60:279–323.

Styk, J. 1994. Personal communication.

Swain, F. 1963. Four Psilocybin experiences. *Psychedelic Review* 2:219–43.

Vernet, I. 1960. Actions psychologique et therapeutique de la psilocybine. *Medecine et Hygiene* 18:420.

Villoldo, A. 1977. An introduction to the psychedelic psychotherapy of Salvador Roquet. *Journal of Humanistic Psychology* 17:45–58.

Wasson, R. G. 1958. Les premieres sources. In *Les champignons hallucinogenes du mexique*, R. Heim, and R. G. Wasson, 15–44. Paris: Museum d'histoire naturelle.

———. 1980. *The Wondrous Mushroom.* New York: McGraw Hill.

Yensen, R., and D. Dryer. 1995. Thirty years of psychedelic research. The Spring Grove Experiment and its sequels. *Yearbook of the European College for the Study of Consciousness* 1993–1994:73–102.

6

PRISONER BEHAVIOR
CHANGE AND
EXPERIMENTAL MYSTICISM:

TWO CLASSIC STUDIES FROM THE
HARVARD PSILOCYBIN PROJECT

DIANE CONN DARLING, RICK DOBLIN, AND RALPH METZNER

THE CONCORD PRISON STUDY

In the pre-prohibition days of the late 1950s and early 1960s, many innovative experiments were conducted using new potent hallucinogens. Such experiments were conducted in mental institutions, prisons, theological seminaries, private homes, and in the offices of practicing psychiatrists. The goals varied somewhat, but the intentions can be understood to be of an exploratory and healing nature. One of the best known of these early studies was the Concord Prison Project, conducted by Timothy Leary and associates under the auspices of Harvard University's center for Research in Personality.

Rick Doblin earned his Ph.D. in public policy from Harvard University's Kennedy School of Government. He is the founder and president of the Multidisciplinary Association for Psychedelic Studies (MAPS, www.maps.org), a nonprofit research and educational organization. MAPS's goal is to help develop legal contexts for the beneficial uses of psychedelics and marijuana.

One of the first studies of the Harvard group was to investigate the effects of psilocybin on "normals" in a nonclinical, nonexperimental but warm, supportive setting. Results were evaluated by a question-naire, which showed that "88% of their subjects . . . reported that they had learned something of value about themselves and the world, while 62% claimed the experience of psilocybin changed their lives for the better." (Leary et al. 1963).

Subsequently, Leary sought a controlled setting where measurable long-term results could demonstrate that psilocybin might be a powerful catalyst of behavioral change. He found it in Concord Prison, where, between February 1961 and January 1963, with the cooperation of the prison bureaucracy and staff and of thirty-two inmates, his team con-ducted in-house experiments using psilocybin in a unique setting of openness and mutual support. The behavioral criterion of insight and personality change was to be the recidivism rate (the rate of return to prison after release) of the prisoners who had participated in the project.

The concept of the program was to be radical. Leary's philosophy of research was to design it as a "collaborative group program; we avoid as much as possible the traditional doctor-patient, research-subject, or professional-client relationships." (Leary et al. 1965). Over a period of around eighteen months, small groups of inmates were selected and matched with controls. All were evaluated with a battery of standard psy-chological tests, which were then "fed back" to the project inmates, giv-ing them insight into their current psychological conditions. The Harvard team then explained in some detail the anticipated subjective effects of psilocybin and encouraged the men to relax and not fight the experience. They were also encouraged to decide upon their own specific personality change programs, such as, "I want to understand what drinking means to me." Then, in a relaxed, informal setting, they were dosed on up to three separate occasions with escalating amounts (20–70 mg) of pure Sandoz psilocybin.

In every session, one of the two team leaders and (after the pilot study) one inmate from an earlier group also dosed with smaller amounts (5–10 mg) of psilocybin to demonstrate solidarity with the subject inmates and to establish collaborative trust. The group was ide-ally, to quote Gerald Heard (1959): "concerned but not anxious, interested but not engrossed, diagnostic but not critical, aware of the seriousness and confidential value of what is being conveyed and all the more incapable of coldness or shock, aloofness or dismay . . . Any sense of fear or alienness means that the root danger and origin of all breakdown, i.e., separation is present."

After the return to baseline consciousness, subjects attended lengthy discussion meetings to work through their experiences and to integrate what they had learned into their everyday lives; then they were retested with the identical battery of tests, and the results again fed back to them. A second (and occasionally a third) all-day session followed with further discussion meetings.

The subjects who were granted parole during the span of the study were included in a special preparole group, where they were coached on employment opportunities and certain legal and other difficulties that they might face upon release from prison. A nonprofit organization, Freedom Inc., was created to coordinate postrelease efforts, but, as Leary noted, "This phase (post-parole) of our program was never fully developed. We now realize that it is necessary to set up a halfway house where members can meet regularly and discuss mutual problems along the Alcoholics Anonymous lines. For practical and material reasons, we were limited to irregular individual contacts with group members" (Leary et al. 1965).

The Harvard team made mighty efforts to stay in touch with the eleven inmates who were free in the Boston area. After failing to draw them to a meeting at Leary's offices at Harvard to plan a self-run halfway house, staffers resorted to meeting with the ex-cons in the evenings one-on-one in restaurants and bars. In one case, Leary even took one prisoner into his home and gave him a job at Harvard (the job was to find a job). The intention was to provide a network of friendly support aimed at keeping them out of trouble. Two case histories were reported, both concerning study members who apparently successfully reintegrated into normal working and living environments (Leary 1976).

The rationale of the program was based on Thomas Szasz's groundbreaking work on the game-quality of conduct. Leary explained it thus:

A game is any learned behavior sequenced with roles, rules, rituals, values, specialized languages and limited goals. Self-defeating games are maintained largely through inability to recognize the features and rules of the game one is involved in, and through inability to detach the self from its actions . . . Thus many of our procedures are designed to reduce helplessness. Relationships that imply or emphasize power differences are avoided, as much as possible. This is the rationale for the feedback of the test results and interpretations. Maximum responsibility for his own change process is given to each prisoner.

    . . . We have found that in a benign, supportive setting and with a favorable set, psilocybin can produce a state of dissociation or detachment from the roles and games of everyday interaction. This detachment, or temporary suspension of defenses, can provide insight and perspective about repetitive behavior or thought patterns and open up the way for the construction of alternatives. If the defenses are abandoned in a non-anxiety provoking situation, the experience also serves to establish a quite profound level of trust and communication between members of the groups (Leary et al. 1965).

In follow-up personality testing, a few changes of statistical significance were found. Minor improvements in scores of project participants on the California Psychological Inventory were noted, including Sociability, Sense of Well-Being, Socialization, Tolerance, and Intellectual Efficiency. Socialization-maturity and achievement scales also improved, all significantly more in the study group than in the controls, who were never exposed to the program. However, only seven of the thirty-two subjects were available for final testing, thus muddying the importance of the resulting scores. In addition, the practice of feeding back results to subjects probably tended to make the subjects test-wise, which could account for all variances. Further, there is a known tendency of short-timers to increase their conformity to staff and community norms just prior to release.

Eighteen months after the termination of the project, recidivism rates for subjects were reported as not different from the expected base rate for Concord Prison as a whole. Of all men released from Concord 56% had returned two and one half years later. Out of the thirty-two involved in the project, four were still in prison, one had escaped, and eleven remained free, a recidivism rate of 59%.

Here the research statistics got fuzzy and perhaps a little creative to demonstrate the hypothesis that psilocybin therapy was effective in reducing the crime rate. In their paper published in *Psychotherapy: Theory, Research and Practice* (Leary et al. 1965), the researchers broke the numbers down into types of return: due to parole violations and due to new crimes. They found that, compared to a 50/50 incidence in the prison population as a whole, only 7% of project participants were returned for new crimes, with 52% returned for parole violations. "One and one half years after termination of the program the rate of new crimes has been reduced from 28% to 7%, although if parole violations are counted the overall return rate has not changed. It is proposed that these results warrant further research into the potentials of the methods used, especially since no other method of reducing the crime rate exists." (Leary et al. 1965; Doblin 1998).

Rick Doblin published a follow-up and critique of the Concord experiment in *The Journal of Psychoactive Drugs* (Doblin 1998), which was later republished in the Winter 1999–2000 issue of *MAPS Bulletin*. In it, Doblin states that his intention was:

> to raise awareness in a new generation of students and researchers about what this author believed at the beginning of this follow-up was a successfully proven approach to behavior change. It was also hoped that this follow-up might help to catalyze additional research extending and expanding on Leary's pioneering study and its reportedly promising results (Doblin 1998).

He was able to locate records for twenty-one of the original thirty-two subjects and interviewed two of them as well as three of the researchers. The criminal histories he located recorded activity for the 2.5 years following release from the incarceration in which the inmates participated in the psilocybin project, as well as up to thirty-four years later when the follow-up study was conducted. The figures closely approximated those given by Leary et al., so Doblin assumed that the lost folders were likely a random subset of the entire cohort.

Though he found some minor irregularities in Leary's group's reporting of recidivism rates among several papers published over several years, he found two big problems. The first was that the reported researchers had compared recidivism rates of study inmates who had been released for an average of ten months, with the recidivism rate of all Concord prison inmates who had been released for an average of thirty months. As the probability of recidivism is a function of how long someone has been out, rising over time, the comparison was invalid. Using a graph indicating the recidivism rate as a function of time, Doblin determined that the control rate was 34.3%, compared to the experimental group's 32%, a 2.3% reduction (not the 23% reported), which is not significant and is the same as a finding of no treatment effect.

The other flaw Doblin detected was in the assertion that parole violations were of a lesser gravity than new crimes, thus that the program actually reduced the crime rate overall. Leary reported that only two prisoners were returned for new crimes and fourteen for parole violations of a minor technical nature, which were found possibly due to extra supervision the subjects received, as they were known to have taken part in this experiment. Doblin's research revealed that many of the subjects who were returned to prison on parole violations had actually violated their parole by committing new crimes for which they were subsequently convicted. In addition, some subjects who had simple parole violations not associated with a new crime were released and subsequently rearrested for new crimes all within the follow-up period of 2.5 years.

Through comparing the findings of the follow-up with Leary's reported results, it was possible, with some difficulty, to discern Leary's method of categorization between new crimes and parole violations. Leary's method counted only the reason for the first reincarceration postrelease, ignoring everything occurring after that. Thus, the distinction between parole violations and new crimes is largely meaningless, since the majority of what Leary considered "parole violations" were caused by incidents that later led to convictions for new crimes.

If "parole violation" is defined as "return to prison for anything short of an incident that led to a new conviction, such as not reporting to the parole officer, not keeping a job, associating with known criminals or suspicion of or arrest for a new crime but no new conviction" (Doblin 1998), the actual recidivism rate for new crime in the twenty-one psilocybin subjects at 2.5 years post-release was 71%, with fifteen of the twenty-one subjects having returned to prison. In the ensuing 31.5 years, the total recidivism rate was 76%, with only five subjects never having been reincarcerated. There is thus no treatment effect, in terms of reduced recidivism rate for new crimes, at the longest point in time for which base rate statistics for a control group are available.

In a communication on Doblin's discovery of statistical error, Metzner (1998) wrote: "We fell victims to the well-known 'halo effect,' by which researchers tend to see their data in as positive a light as possible." He suggested the mistakes made were "unconscious mistakes of overenthusiasm," rather than deliberate faking, "if only for the reason that our own results clearly show the inconsistencies."

As part of the follow-up, Doblin located three of the experimental subjects and interviewed two of them. He also brought these two to meet with Leary in 1996, several months before Leary's death.

> Both experimental subjects expressed their gratitude at being able to participate in the experiment. Both felt they had benefited personally from their psilocybin experiences and did not suffer any long-term negative problems linked to their psilocybin experience. Both had vivid memories of their psilocybin experiences. Neither had taken a psychedelic drug on their own after the experiment (Doblin 1998).

One of the subjects was a success story and hadn't returned to prison, while the other who had asserted: "I firmly believe that I would never have gone back to prison if I had had help [post release], if someone would have guided me, taken an interest. Who the hell wants to do time?"

For his part, Leary expressed great enjoyment in the meetings and recalled the elation he felt after an experimental session, having brought to the prisoners a degree of mental freedom. When asked what changes he would make in the experimental design if he were doing the protocol today, he again emphasized the need for a halfway house-based support system.

Doblin concludes:

> The failure of the Concord Prison Experiment to generate a reduction in recidivism rates should not be interpreted as proof of the lack of value of psychedelics as adjuncts to psychotherapy in criminals. Rather, the failure of the Concord Prison Experiment should finally put to rest the myth of psychedelic drugs as magic bullets, the ingestion of which will automatically confer wisdom and create lasting change after just one or even a few experiences. Personality change may be made more likely after a cathartic and insightful psychedelic experience, though only sustained hard work after the drug has worn off will serve to anchor and solidify any movement toward healing and behavior change. Psychedelic drug experiences are not sufficient in and of themselves to produce lasting change. Leary, who wrote about the importance of set and setting, knew this as well as anyone, and wrote, "The main conclusion of our two year pilot study is that institutional programs, however effective, count for little after the ex-convict reaches the street. The social pressures faced are so overwhelming as to make change very difficult." (Leary 1969) . . . Whether a new program of psilocybin-assisted group psychotherapy and post-release programs would significantly reduce recidivism rates is an empirical question that deserves to be addressed within the context of a new experiment (Doblin, 1998).

THE GOOD FRIDAY STUDY

In 1962, scientifically legitimate explorations with psychedelic drugs were a small but growing innovation in Europe and America. Associations were formed that held conferences on the topic; papers were published internationally reporting breathtaking results with particularly difficult kinds of psychiatric patients. During these heady days of experimental ferment, Walter Pahnke, a physician and minister who was studying for a Ph.D. in Religion and Society at Harvard with Timothy Leary as his principal academic advisor, conducted a study of psychedelic religious experience that became known as "the Good Friday Experiment." It was a well-designed controlled, double-blind experiment to investigate the relationship between the experiences recorded in the literature of spontaneous mysticism and those reportedly associated with the ingestion of psychedelic drugs.

The study was also designed as a test of the set-and-setting hypothesis, in that it used subjects (divinity students) who presumably had a religious orientation (set) and it was conducted in a chapel during a religious service (setting).

Knowing that there was much resistance among mainstream religious people to the growing idea that genuine mystical experiences could be had from a drop on the tongue or a little pill, Pahnke chose his measuring instrument carefully. Using classical and modern writings on mysticism, particularly W. T. Stace's *Mysticism and philosophy* (Stace 1960), Pahnke developed a questionnaire with a nine-category typology of the mystical state of consciousness, which continues to be a touchstone for inquiry into mystical states today. Briefly, these aspects of religious experience are:

1. Feeling of unity, internal and external. Internal unity is described as "the loss of usual sense impressions and loss of self without becoming unconscious." External unity is "a sense of underlying oneness . . . felt behind the empirical multiplicity."

2. Transcendence of Time and Space. The loss of the usual sense of time, personal and impersonal, as well as orientation to the three-dimensional world. Sometimes described as "eternity" or "infinity."

3. Deeply Felt Positive Mood. The most universal of these are joy, blessedness, and peace, experienced intensely, even overpoweringly.

4. Sense of Sacredness. "A non-rational, intuitive, hushed palpitant sense of awe and wonder."

5. Objectivity and Reality. "Insightful knowledge or illumination felt at an intuitive, non-rational level and gained by direct experience" with "certainty that such knowledge is truly real."

6. Paradoxicality. There is "a loss of all empirical content in an empty unity which is at the same time full and complete."
7. Alleged Ineffability. Where words fail, perhaps due to the paradoxical nature of the essential phenomena.
8. Transiency. The mystical state passes and normal waking reality is restored.
9. Persisting Positive Changes in Attitude and Behavior—toward self, others, life, and the mystical experience itself.

Pahnke then set up the experiment using standard personality testing, and psychological and medical exams to select ten pairs of white, male, psychedelically naïve, Protestant divinity students matched for past religious experience, religious background, and general psychological make-up. These subjects met together in groups and were coached by leaders experienced with psilocybin on how to deal with the experience: "go into the unexplored realms of experience during the actual experiment and not try to fight the effects of the drug even if the experience became very unusual or frightening" (Pahnke 1963).

On Good Friday 1962, these students plus ten group leaders (research assistants) met together in the basement chapel of Boston University's Marsh Chapel and all were given identical capsules. Half contained an active placebo (subjects and leaders were expecting an inactive placebo) containing nicotinic acid, and half contained psilocybin (30 mg for the subjects and, at the insistence of Leary and over the objections of Pahnke, 15 mg for the assistants). Half an hour later a standard service, actually being conducted in the larger sanctuary upstairs by Rev. Howard Thurman (who was Martin Luther King's mentor), was piped in to the lower chapel, which had the usual accoutrements of a Protestant chapel, such as stained glass windows, religious symbols, and pews.

The physical effects of the nicotinic acid (facial flushing and prickly sensations) set in very quickly, leading the controls to believe for a time that they were the ones receiving the psilocybin. Shortly after, when others began remarking on such details as the spectacular candlelight, it became apparent to all who was tripping. This loss of the double blind was anticipated and not considered significant, as the purpose of the experiment was to "determine whether volunteers who received psilocybin within a highly supportive, suggestive environment similar to that found in the ritual use of psychoactive substances by various native cultures would report more elements of a classical mystical experience . . . than volunteers who did not receive psilocybin" (Doblin 1991).

Immediately after the 2-1/2 hour service, individual reactions of both subjects and controls were taped, as was the group discussion that followed. In the following week, each subject wrote an account of his experience and completed a questionnaire designed to measure the factors listed earlier on a qualitative, numerical scale. Six months later they were interviewed again and completed a follow-up questionnaire.

The results showed that in all but one of the nine categories, subjects in the experimental group experienced significantly higher scores than the controls. The one exception was the experience of a "positive mood of love," which was reported by the controls also. The difference between the two groups persisted and even increased slightly in a six-month follow-up interview conducted by Pahnke.

In short, "The experience of the experimental subjects was certainly more like mystical experience than that of the controls who had the same expectation and suggestion from the preparation and setting. The most striking difference between the experimentals and the controls was the ingestion of thirty milligrams of psilocybin, which, it was concluded, was the facilitating agent responsible for the difference in phenomena experienced" (Pahnke 1966).

Over the ensuing years, until his death in 1971 from a diving accident, Pahnke maintained his conviction that the various psychedelic drugs held great potential for research into the mystical experience:

> The results of our experiment would indicate that psilocybin (and LSD and mescaline, by analogy) are important tools for the study of the mystical state of consciousness. Experiences previously possible for only a small minority of people, and difficult to study because of their unpredictability and rarity, are now reproducible under suitable conditions. The mystical experience has been called by many names suggestive of areas that are paranormal and not usually considered easily available for investigation (e.g.,

an experience of transcendence, ecstasy, conversion, or cosmic consciousness); but this is a realm of human experience that should not be rejected as outside the realm of serious scientific study, especially if it can be shown that a practical benefit can result. Our data would suggest that such an overwhelming experience, in which a person existentially encounters basic values such as the meaning of his life (past, present and future), deep and meaningful interpersonal relationships, and insight into the possibility of a personal behavior change, can possibly be therapeutic if approached and worked with in a sensitive and adequate way (Pahnke 1966).

Pahnke boldly suggested a biochemical commonality with such ascetic practices as breathing and postural exercises, sleep deprivation, fasting, flagellation with subsequent infection, sustained meditation, and sensory deprivation as possible triggers for mystical states. He was careful to emphasize that the drug itself was a facilitating agent, a necessary but not a sufficient condition, to be followed up with sincere work after the experience. He suggested that the drug-induced mystical experience could be regarded as "gratuitous grace," and indirectly acknowledged the heretical nature of his assertions.

A quarter century later, researcher Rick Doblin published the results of his long-term follow-up study of the Good Friday Experiment. He located nineteen of the original twenty subjects. With sixteen of them he conducted interviews and readministered the six-month follow-up questionnaire, which Pahnke had designed for the experiment so long ago.

Doblin found that for the volunteers he was able to test, "the scores of persisting positive and negative changes in attitude and behavior have changed remarkably little for either the controls or the experimentals despite the passage of between twenty-four and twenty-seven years between the two tests" (Doblin 1991). For the experimental group, scores in the mystical categories actually increased by several points, while for the controls, the changes were negligible.

In the interviews, subjects reported vivid memories of their Good Friday experience and characterized it as one if the high points of their spiritual life. Some compared it to subsequent mystical experiences and found the drug experience more intense and had a wider emotional range than their nondrug experiences. They felt the experience had significantly affected their lives in a positive way, enhancing their appreciations of life and nature and deepening their sense of joy and their commitment to their life's work. They felt their appreciation of unusual experiences and emotions was deepened, as well as their equanimity in crisis and their solidarity with beings unlike themselves (women, minorities). They reported that the feelings of timelessness they experienced reduced their fear of death and emboldened them to take risks in life and participate in political struggles:

"When you get a clear vision of what [death] is and have sort of been there . . . you would also know that marching in the Civil Rights Movement or against the Vietnam War in Washington [is less fearful] . . . because you've already been there. You know what it's about. When people approaching death have an out-of-body experience . . . [you] say, 'I know what you're talking about. I've been there. Been there and come back. And it's not terrifying and it doesn't hurt . . . '"

Another subject said:

"The more that I let go and sort of died, the more I felt this eternal life, saying to myself under my breath perhaps, "It has always been this way . . . O, isn't it wonderful, there's nothing to fear, this is what it means to die, or to taste of eternal life . . . " Just in that one session I . . . gained experience . . . I could never have gotten from a hundred hours of reading or a thousand hours of reading."

Some of the subjects in the long-term follow-up reported difficult experiences that were not noted in Pahnke's reports. One went into a state of paranoia about the darkness in the chapel and the bars on the windows. He went outside and was followed and brought back by a group leader. He attributed his problem to resistance, "reluctance just to flow." Beyond his emotional struggles, this subject reported strong feelings of authentic oneness "perhaps the same as a classical mystical experience . . . "

"GOOD FRIDAY EXPERIMENT"

Experimental and control groups at six-month and long-term follow-up, shown as percentages of maximum possible scores.

CATEGORY	EXPERIMENTALS		CONTROLS	
	SIX-MONTH	LONG-TERM	SIX-MONTH	LONG-TERM
1. Unity				
A. Internal	60	(77)	5	(5)
B. External	39	(51)	1	(6)
2. Transcendence				
of Time and Space	78	(73)	7	(9)
3. Deeply Felt Positive Mood	54	(56)	23	(21)
4. Sacredness	58	(68)	25	(29)
5. Objectivity and Reality	71	(82)	18	(24)
6. Paradoxicality	34	(48)	3	(4)
7. Alleged Ineffability	77	(71)	15	(3)
8. Transiency	76	(75)	9	(9)
Average for the Categories	60.8	(66.8)	11.8	(12.2)
9. Persisting Positive Changes				
in Attitude and Behavior	48	(50)	15	(15)
10. Persisting Negative Changes				
in Attitude and Behavior	6	(6)	2	(4)

At six-month follow-up, Exper. N=10, Control N=10
Long-term follow-up (in parenthesis), Exper. N=7, Control N=9
$p < .05$ for all category comparisons at both six-months and long-term

Another subject who also had difficult moments related his experience of indecision about which of his perceived brilliant color streams to follow out, precipitating a painful existential moment of death. However, afterwards he found he had unconsciously made an important career choice in which he felt great confidence and with which he followed through.

Doblin stated that the difficult experiences reported by the majority of psilocybin subjects he interviewed "were significantly underemphasized in Pahnke's thesis and in the subsequent reporting on the experiment." In fact, Pahnke never reported that one subject was injected with Thorazine as a tranquilizer during the experiment, a grave omission.

As it happens, the venerable Huston Smith was one of the leader-subjects in the Good Friday Experiment. In a 1996 interview with Tom Roberts he relates his experience (Smith 2002):

until the Good Friday Experiment, I had had no direct personal encounter with God of the sort that bhakti yogis, Pentecostals, and born-again Christians describe. The Good Friday Experiment changed that . . . the gestalt transformed a routine musical progression into the most powerful cosmic homecoming I have ever experienced . . . that God loves *me* and I *him,* in the concrete way that human beings love individuals, each most wanting from the other what the other most wants to give and with everything that might distract from that holy relationship excluded from view—that relation with God I had never before had.

Smith recalls that the scene inside the chapel was one of:

a mounting disorder . . . half of our number were in a condition where social decorum meant nothing and the other half were more interested in the spectacle unfolding than in the service proper. In any case, from out of this bizarre mix, one of our number emerged. He arose from his pew, walked up the aisle, and with uncertain steps mounted the chapel's modest pulpit. Thumbing through its Bible for a few moments, he proceeded to mumble a brief and coherent homily, blessed the congregation with the sign of the cross, and started back to the rear entrance of the chapel and through its door . . . When (the subject's) guide didn't respond to his leaving the chapel, I sprang to my feet and followed him out (Smith 2002).

What followed was a merry chase with this man on a mission, who strode into the campus of Boston University, where Pahnke and Smith shortly blocked the subject's progress. They walked the subject back to the chapel and Pahnke injected him with Thorazine. This subject's long-term feelings about the experiment were heavily negative and he adamantly refused to participate in Doblin's follow-up.

Doblin guesses: "Pahnke probably did not report his use of the tranquilizer because he was fearful of adding to the ammunition of the opponents of the research. Fears that the negative aspects of the experiment would be taken out of context and exaggerated may have been justified . . . His silence . . . may perhaps have been good politics; certainly it was bad science" (Doblin 1991).

In his discussion of the long-term follow-up, Doblin notes:

> the experiment's fascinating and provocative conclusions strongly support the hypothesis that psychedelic drugs can help facilitate mystical experiences when used by religiously inclined people in a religious setting . . . twenty-four to twenty-seven years later . . . all psilocybin subjects participating in the long-term follow-up, but none of the controls, still considered their original experience to have had genuinely mystical elements and to have made a uniquely valuable contribution to their spiritual lives. The positive changes described by the psilocybin subjects at six months . . . had persisted over time and in some cases had deepened . . . The long-term follow-up interviews cast considerable doubt on the assertion that mystical experiences catalyzed by drugs are in any way inferior to non-drug mystical experiences in both their immediate and long-term positive effects . . .

Coverage of the Good Friday Experiment in both the scholarly and popular media was broad and largely but not universally positive. Doblin speculates that Pahnke's underemphasis on the difficult psychological struggles of most of the psilocybin subjects may be in part responsible for the unpreparedness of the many subsequent formal and informal experimenters for this aspect of the experience.

> The widespread use of psychedelics, both in medical and nonmedical settings, which began in the 1960s is still currently taking place, apparently largely underground. Such use was partially founded upon an optimism regarding the inherent safety of the psychedelic experience which did not fully acknowledge the complexity and profundity of the psychological issues associated with

the psychedelic experiences. With some proponents of psychedelics exaggerating the benefits and minimizing the risks, a backlash against these substances was predictable. With the intriguing connection reported by several psilocybin subjects between mystical experiences and political action, the backlash in retrospect may have been inevitable.

In the balance, Doblin asserts that despite the above, additional studies utilizing a multidisciplinary team are justified and that "Renewed research can be expected to require patience, courage and wisdom from all concerned."

References

Doblin, R. 1991. Pahnke's "Good Friday Experiment": A long-term follow-up and methodological critique, *The Journal of Transpersonal Psychology* 23 (1).

———. 1998. Dr. Leary's Concord Prison Experiment: Experiment—A thirty-four year follow-up and methodological critique. *Journal of Psychoactive Drugs* 30 (4):419–26.

Leary, T. 1968. *High Priest*. Second Edition, 1995. Berkeley, Calif.: Ronin Press.

———. 1969. The effects of consciousness-expanding drugs on prisoner rehabilitation, *Psychedelic Review* 10:20–44.

Leary, T., G. Litwin, and R. Metzner. 1963. Reactions to psilocybin in a supportive environment. *Journal of Nervous and Mental Diseases* 137: 561–73.

Leary, T, R. Metzner, M. Presnell, G. Weil, R. Schwitzgebel, and S. Kinne. 1965. A new behavior change pattern using psilocybin. *Psychotherapy: Theory, Research and Practice* 2 (2):61–72.

Leary, T., and R. Metzner. 1968. Use of psychedelic drugs in prisoner rehabilitation. *British Journal of Social Psychiatry* 2:27–51.

Metzner, R. 1998. Reflections on the Concord Prison Project and the follow-up study, *Journal of Psychoactive Drugs* 30 (4):427–28.

Pahnke, W. 1963. Drugs and mysticism: An analysis of the relationship between psychedelic drugs and the mystical consciousness. Harvard University: Ph.D. dissertation.

———. 1966. Drugs and mysticism. *International Journal of Parapsychology* 8 (2):295–313.

Pahnke, W., and W. Richards. 1966. Implications of LSD and experimental mysticism, *J. Religion and Health* 5 (3):175–208.

Pahnke, W., and W. Richards. 1969. Implications of LSD and experimental mysticism. *Journal of Transpersonal Psychology* 1 (2):69–102.

Smith, H. 2002. The Good Friday Experiment. In *Hallucinogens; a reader,* ed. C. Grob, 64–71. New York, N.Y.: Tarcher Putnam.

Stace, W. T. 1960. *Mysticism and Philosophy.* London: MacMillan.

7

A Note on Current
Psilocybin Research
Projects

Rick Doblin, Ph.D.

THERAPEUTIC STUDIES

The first U.S. government-approved scientific investigation in thirty years of the therapeutic potential of psilocybin was concluded in the fall of 2003. At the University of Arizona at Tucson, Dr. Francisco Moreno, with the assistance of Dr. Chris Wiegand, administered psilocybin as a potential therapeutic treatment to ten subjects with treatment-resistant chronic obsessive-compulsive disorder (OCD). The Tucson study is funded by the Heffter Research Institute and MAPS. This study was initiated after the publication in the medical literature of several case histories in which patients with OCD self-administered psilocybin mushrooms in a nonmedical, recreational context. They reported that their OCD symptoms were reduced or eliminated for varying periods of time after their mushroom experience.

A second study of the potential therapeutic use of psilocybin was approved by the Food and Drug Administration (FDA) to begin in the fall of 2003. This study, headed by Dr. Charles Grob at Harbor-UCLA examines the use of psilocybin-assisted psychotherapy in treating anxiety and pain in terminal cancer patients. It was inspired by research in the late 1960s and early 1970s in which LSD-assisted psychotherapy was administered to cancer patients, after which significant reductions were reported in the amount of narcotic pain medications that the patients required. Dr. Grob's psilocybin research project is being funded by the Heffter Research Institute.

MAPS is sponsoring research into the use of psilocybin and LSD in the treatment of cluster headaches. Cluster headaches are a rare, severely painful form of headache that is related to but different from the more common migraine. John Halpern, M.D., and Andrew Sewell, M.D., McLean Hospital, Harvard Medical School, are initially analyzing and organizing responses to a questionnaire posted on www.clusterbusters.com, an organization run by and for people with cluster headaches. Medical records are also being gathered to supplement questionnaire reports. Preliminary data suggests that psilocybin and LSD do provide significant relief in some people for whom available alternative prescription medicines provide little or no relief. These reports and records will be used to design a randomized, dose-response study of psilocybin and LSD in people with episodic cluster headaches. The goal of the research is to explore the use of psilocybin and LSD both in interrupting an ongoing cluster headache cycle and as a prophylactic (cycle-interrupting) treatment for cluster headaches.

NONTHERAPEUTIC STUDIES

There are also on-going nontherapeutic psilocybin research projects taking place in other countries. One project studies the effects of psilocybin on binocular depth inversion, binocular rivalry, neuropsychology and synaesthesias. It is headed by Dr. Torsten Passie, M.D., at the Medical School of Hannover, Germany. The study involves the use of medium doses of psilocybin to examine the effects on neuropsychological measures (attention, reaction time, etc.), perceptual changes, and subjective effects.

Subjects participate in one session, which lasts most of the experimental day. To reduce the psychological discomfort of the subjects, the subjects are largely free of experimental procedures so that they may experience the psilocybin state in an open and relaxed manner. This study is being funded by the Medical School Hannover, Department of Clinical Psychiatry and Psychotherapy, and by MAPS.

Another study, funded by the Heffter Research Institute, is headed by Dr. Franz Vollenweider, University of Zurich. It involves a series of examinations of basic physiological parameters and information processing strategies. This team has completed a five-dose, dose response psilocybin study in about seventy individuals. Dr. Vollenweider is also in the development phase of a study of the potential psilocybin-assisted psychotherapy in the treatment of subjects with eating disorders.

For more information on these projects, see:
http://www.maps.org/research

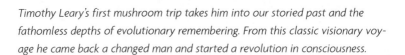

8

The Initiation of the "High Priest"

Timothy Leary

Timothy Leary's first mushroom trip takes him into our storied past and the fathomless depths of evolutionary remembering. From this classic visionary voyage he came back a changed man and started a revolution in consciousness.

I was first drugged out of my mind in Cuernavaca, August 1960. I ate seven of the Sacred Mushrooms of Mexico and discovered that beauty, revelation, sensuality, the cellular history of the past, God, the Devil—all lie inside my body, outside my mind.

In the days of Montezuma this town called "horn-of-the-cow" was the center of soothsayers, wise-men, and magicians. Cuernavaca is the southern anchor point of a line running from the fabled volcanic peaks Popo and Iztaccihuatl over to the volcano of Toluca. On the high slopes of the volcanoes, east and west of the capital grow the Sacred Mushrooms of Mexico, divinatory fungi, *teonanácatl*, flesh of the gods.

In the summer of 1960, Cuernavaca was the site of considerable activity by American psychologists—soothsayers, medicine men, would-be magicians—from the North—vacationing on grants and working in the lush valley of Morelos in sight of the snowy peaks of the legendary volcano. A (certain) villa served as summer headquarters for four American psychologists: Timothy Leary and Richard Alpert of Harvard, Frank Barron of California, and Richard Dettering of San Francisco.

The happenings of that summer in quiet Cuernavaca were to set up reverberations that have echoed now for years. Many of the scientists who were working and vacationing there that season have had their lives dramatically changed, and none of them will ever completely escape from the mysterious power, the challenge, the paradox of what started to unfold. The setting, the surrounding, is a key factor in the outcome of any visionary voyage, whether you use mushrooms or marijuana or LSD or Ary beads, and in this regard the Cuernavaca mushroom-eaters were fortunate.

The Spanish-style villa . . . was a rambling white stucco house with scarlet trim, surrounded by gray stone walls. Down below was a sloping lawn ringed by flowers. Next to the upper terrace was the swimming pool, lake blue, and the lawn fell away downslope to a lower green terraced lawn. The villa had been built by Mexican Moslems and remodeled by Mexican Viennese. It was colorful, open, and lush.

Summer days . . . swimming trunks before breakfast . . . ontological discussions . . . the cold grapefruit eaten by hot poolside . . . clear hot sun burning tanned skin . . . the startle value of iced drinks . . . the shouts of Jack Leary and Pepe, the Mexican boy, chasing ducks on the lower lawn . . . thunder and earth . . . the sudden cooling splash of the evening rain . . . the sky over the volcanoes . . . candles at dinner.

A frequent visitor was Gerhart Braun, anthropologist-historian-linguist from the University of Mexico. With him would come Joan, his girlfriend, and Betty, who wrote poetry and cracked jokes.

Gerhart had been studying the Aztec culture and translating old texts written in Nahuatl, the language used by Aztecs before the conquest. He had discovered repeated references to the use of Sacred Mushrooms by Aztec soothsayers on ceremonial occasions to predict the future, to feel better, to solve mental problems. His curiosity aroused, Gerhart had asked around about the mushrooms and discovered they grew on the volcanic slopes near Mexico City . . .

So we drove up to the village of San Pedro near the volcano of Toluca and walked around the marketplace asking about the Sacred Mushrooms. There was much thoughtful shaking of the heads by the shopkeepers—and conversations in low Spanish in the back rooms. Old Juana was the one to see. She would come to the market. Wait right here under the arch. She'll come soon.

We stood there for an hour while the sandaled, market-day crowds padded by. An old woman, back bent, gray stringy hair, black shawl, eyes down, creaking stiffly: Senora Juana. She brushed by us, not responding to our hail. On the outskirts of town Gerhart caught up with Juana. She stopped and they began to talk. We stood back and waited and watched.

Gerhart returned to us, smiling. Okay. It's all set. She'll get the mushrooms next Wednesday and I'll meet her in the marketplace next Thursday.

The following Thursday Gerhart phoned, excited. He had met Juana in the market. He had asked her if she was sure they were safe. She popped two of them in her mouth before his eyes. The mushrooms were resting now on the shelf of his refrigerator. See you Saturday.

The day of visions dawned sunny and clear. Gerhart and his group arrived and I met them on the lawn. We stood in a welcoming circle, (eight of us: myself, Gerhart, Joan, Ruth and Dick Dettering, Mandy, my girlfriend, Whiskers, and poet-Betty). Gerhart lectured us on the trance-giving mushrooms, pushed out of history's notice until the last decade when they had been discovered by Weitlinger and Shultes and the American mycologists, Valentina and Gordon Wasson. By now they had been eaten by a few scientists, a few poets, a few intellectuals looking for mystical experiences. They produced wondrous trances.

There were two kinds, females and males. The lady mushrooms had the familiar umbrella shape, but black, ominous, bitter-looking. The males' anatomy was so phallic there was no reason to ask why they were called males.

We moved out to the pool. The mushrooms were in two large bowls, male and female separate, on the table under the huge beach umbrella. Gerhart was lecturing now about dosage. Six males and six females. The effect should begin after an hour. Then he stuffed a big, black, moldy-damp mushroom in his mouth, made a face and, chewed. Gerhart was voyager number one.

I picked one up. It stank of forest damp and crumbling logs and New England basement. They tasted worse than they looked. Bitter, stringy, filthy. I took a slug of Carta Blanca and jammed the rest in my mouth and washed them down.

Everyone was listening to his own stomach, expecting to be poisoned. Quite a picture, six of us sitting around the sunlit terrace in our bathing suits, waiting, waiting, asking each other how many did you take? Males or females? Do you feel anything?

Two people did not partake: Ruth Dettering was eager to eat, but she was pregnant. She had been a nurse and I was glad she was going to be out of trance. I talked to her about how to call for an ambulance and stomach pumps. Whiskers was a friend of a friend, a sensitive logician, hesitant, pedantic, dressed in bathing trunks over flowered undershorts, and green garters and black socks and leather shoes and a silken robe. He had been appointed scientist and was taking elaborate notes of Gerhart's reactions.

Suddenly
   I began
       to feel
Strange.
Going under dental gas. Good-bye.
Mildly nauseous. Detached. Moving away
                       away
                             away
From the group in bathing suits
On a terrace
   under the bright
       Mexican sky.
When I tell this the others scoff
Hah, hah. Him. Power of suggestion.
Skepticism? Of my mind? Of me? Of mind? Of my?
Oh, now no. No matter.
Dettering says he feels it too.

Oh my friend. Do you feel tingling in the face?
Yes.
Dental gas?
Yes.
Slight dizziness?
Yes. Exactly.
Whiskers making notes. Rapid whiz pencil.
Lips obscene gash brown stained beard.
Flowered underpants peeping out from bathing trunks,
green socks,
black shoes
thin shoulders
Bending over note pad
Viennese analyst.
Comic. Laugh. Laugh. Laugh. Laugh. Can't stop.
Laugh. Laugh.
All look at me.
Astonishment
More laugh laugh laugh laugh
Whiskers looks up, red tongue flicks from shrubbery.
Lick lips.
Stomach laugh. So funny that I . . .
Laughing, pointing . . .
The rabbi! Psychoanalytic rabbinical rabbit!
Convulsed in laughahafter.

> *pomposity of scholars*
> *impudence of the mind*
> *smug naïveté of words.*

If Whiskers could only see!
Stagger in hahahouse. Roaring. Into bedroom.
Fahahalling on bed
Doubled in laughahafter.
Detterings follow, watch curiously, maybe scared.
Funnier.
Then
Dettering begins to lafhahahaf.

Yes, he laughs too.
You see, Dickohoho? The impudent mind?
Comedy? Yes.
Only Ruth standing there grinning quizzically.
Starting back to terrace
My walk has changed
Rubber legs
Room is full of water
Under water
Floating
Floating in air-sea
Room
Terrace
People
All
Under
Water
BUT NO WORDS CAN DESCRIBE

Out on terrace
Trance has hit the others.
Gerhart
Sprawling on chair, staring up at umbrella
Eyes popping, big as melons
Gone
Gone
Gone
Babbling.

No, see Whisker pencil flying
Hear Gerhart voice
    an orange spot, I should say twenty
    centimeters in diameter, now changing
    to purple, now being approached at an
    angle of forty-five degrees by an
    alternating band of yellow and red . . .

Scientists at work
Funny, funny too.
Long, lanky Gerhart in straw sombrero
Gleaming, staring, eyes fixed in space
Tufted goatee bobbing up and down as he tapes
out visions.

Dettering swims up.
Point to Gerhart
We lafhafhafhaf
Swim to poet-Betty
On the beach by flowers.
Face turns up
Gone, gone, gone.
I took nine.
Nine, she sighs.
Betty makes hissing noise.
Eyes tender. All woman inviting.

Ruth Dettering standing by the door.
Swim to her through water, suddenly
Ominous.
Have you ever swum
On moonless night
In southern sea
Where sharks may be?
And felt that dread
Of unknown
Black peril?
Swimming in ocean of energy
With no mind to guide.
Look, Ruth. I can tell you that this
thing is going to hit me real hard.
Harder than anything that has ever
happened to me. And to the others, too.
Ruth listens hard, nodding her good

nurse head. You may have six psychotic nuts
on your hands. I think you should send
the kids downtown to the movies, and
the maid too, get her out of here, and lock
the gates and for god's sake stay close
and keep your eyes on things.

How do you feel having all this
Going on around you?
Ruth grins.
So envious I could
Scream.
Sitting on chair
Feeling cold doom
Sky dark, air still
Soundless like
Ocean
Bottom
World stops spinning
Somewhere
The big celestial motor
Which keeps universe moving
Is turned off and the whole business
Terrace, house, lawn, city, world
  coasting
      coasting
          dropping
              through space
                  without
                      sound
Mandy floats from beach chair
Swims by, I watch her go
Inside door loosens hair
Falls down over shoulders
Looks out in bikini wet tresses falling
Mermaid eyes see far away.

Old Dettering floats over
sea-toad face
bloated
purple-green warts
froggy
We stand looking down over
allgreen grass blade leaf petals in
focus sharp clear shining
changing waves color
like
floodlight slides
at summer dance hall
kaleidoscope.

Mandy and I lie side by side on beach chair
her knee hits mine they merge
no difference between skins
last abstraction of self and self's body gone
hairs on leg (my leg?) tripled move in sharp
perspective
like little fleas in Tivoli sideshow in Copenhagen
no word spoken
five us sit on terrace
still staring space
catatonic silent withdrawn
Ruth I talk
She psychiatric nurse
I good patient.
She talks earnestly about . . . reality

                              You must try LSD
                              and mescaline and
                              see if they are
                              different from
                              mushrooms

Listen tolerantly.
Pity her.
Poor creature.

Thinks such affairs important.
Mind games. Head trips.

Whiskers walks in kitchen completely dressed, he is going to town.
He is so serious about the comic game in which he is trapped. Whiskers
seems so can't bear funny.

On patio
Scientist Gerhart giggly, sitting peacefully.
Lost contemplation.
Joan by side
But
She is fighting spell
Fluttering,
Talking
Refusing to relax.

Holds bowl of mushrooms in hand
Hostess pushing cookies at church tea.
Have another, one more makes all the difference.
I eat a second.
Have another, one more makes all the difference.
I eat a third.

Swim along veranda to bedroom
Shades drawn. Dark.
Betty feels isolated. All woman un-tilled earth. I am
sorry tender.
Her black hair
drawn back big pony tail.
Cherokee princess great beauty.
Hummingbird words swoop from mouth.
How do you feel?
I sit trying to answer. Can't talk.
Can only look jeweled patterns,
swirling tapestry work in closed eyes.

What is she asking me? Oh, yes, how do I feel?
Far far gone.
She sits silently behind bead-work face. Do you
have anything on your mind? Do you want to talk?
She wants close. Intimacy. But,
I drift off to cavern of sea light.

Gerhart and Joan come in.
Fall on another bed.

In Mandy's arms
Her body warm foam rubber
Marshmallow flesh
My body gone
Fallen into her
Two leafy water plants
Twined together, undulating warm bermuda sea
deep
Entangled so that no one
Not even plants themselves can tell
Which leaf
Which stem
Belongs to which.
Gone again, gone into
Palace by Nile
Temple near Hong Kong
Babylonian boudoir, Bedouin pleasure tent
Gem-flash jewel
Woven color silk gown movement
Mosaics flaming color Muzo emerald Burma rubies
ceylon sapphire
Mosaics lighted from within glowing, moving,
changing.
Hundred reptiles, Jewel encrusted. Hammered
Moorish patterned
Snakeskin.

Snake mosaic, reptiles piled in
Giant, mile-square chest
Slide, slither, tumble down central
                                drain
                                One
                                By
                                One
                                By
                                One
Such happy beauty
I lift up head to laugh
From around come answering chuckles.
Who? There are others here?
Eye open
Gerhart and Joan on next bed laughing
Next to me mermaid, laughing.
Put hand on hip where
Skin pokes through bikini lacing
Hand up soft back until fingers
Sink in quicksand of flesh through skin through ribs
Close eyes
Moving belts like
Inlaid Moorish patterns

Plummeting back through time
                        snake time,
                        fish time
Down through giant jungle palm time,
            green lacy ferny leaf time
Watching first life oozing,
                writhing
                twisting up.
Watching first sea thing crawl to shore
    Lie with her. Sand-rasp under cheek,
            Then float sea-thing, down
                    Deep green sea dark

I am first living
Thing I
Am.

Laughter in dark room IT IS INTERESTING TO CONTEMPLATE
A TANGLED BANK CLOTHED WITH MANY PLANTS OF MANY
KINDS. *Gerhart sitting up in dark shouting* WITH BIRDS SINGING
ON THE BUSHES WITH VARIOUS INSECTS FLITTING ABOUT.
Oh God don't let this end AND WITH WORMS CRAWLING
THROUGH THE DAMP EARTH *Gerhart goatee bobbing* AND TO
REFLECT THAT THESE ELABORATELY CONSTRUCTED
FORMS SO DIFFERENT FROM EACH OTHER *Gerhart gone in*
ecstasy AND DEPENDENT ON EACH OTHER IN SO COMPLEX
A MANNER *I know his ecstasy* HAVE ALL BEEN PRODUCED BY
LAWS ACTING AROUND US *We are high. High Priests.*

THESE LAWS TAKEN IN *ancient evolution trail* THUS FROM
THE WAR OF NATURE, FROM FAMINE AND DEATH *down to*
fishy bottom Float with plankton THE MOST EXALTED OBJECT
WHICH WE ARE CAPABLE OF CONCEIVING NAMELY *down*
the littoral Tumbling past coral reef THE PRODUCTION OF THE
HIGHER ANIMALS DIRECTLY FOLLOWS AND *barnacled sea*
cliff Fathoms down through tangled jungle THERE IS GRANDEUR
IN THIS VIEW OF LIFE *Once we were all double-celled creatures*
Remember that WHILE THIS PLANET HAS GONE ON CYCLING
ON ACCORDING TO THE FIXED LAWS OF GRAVITY *Once we*
all drifted down soft red-walled caverns FROM SO SIMPLE A
BEGINNING ENDLESS FORMS MOST BEAUTIFUL AND MOST
WONDERFUL *Our neurons remember* HAVE BEEN AND ARE
BEING EVOLVED *Do you remember*

Then begins Blake's long red voyage EVERY TIME LESS THAN A
PULSATION OF THE ARTERY *down the blood stream is* EQUAL IN
ITS PERIOD AND VALUE TO SIX THOUSAND YEARS *floating,*
bouncing along the labyrinthian tunnels FOR IN THIS MOMENT THE
POET'S WORK IS DONE *artery, arteriole* AND ALL THE GREAT
EVENTS OF TIME START FORTH *through every capillary* AND ARE

CONCEIVED IN SUCH A PERIOD *through pink honey-comb tissue world* WITHIN A MOMENT: A PULSATION OF ARTERY *along soft watermelon channels* EVERY SPACE LARGER THAN A RED GLOB-ULE OF MAN'S BLOOD *part clotted scarlet swamps coagulate* IS VISIONARY, AND IS CREATED BY THE HAMMER OF LOS *tumbling through caverned heart hall, ventricular* AND EVERY SPACE SMALLER THAN A GLOBULE *sliding down the smooth aortic chute* OF MAN'S BLOOD OPENS *slow bumping* INTO NARROW TUN-NELED PLEXUS INTO ETERNITY, OF WHICH THE VEG-ETABLE EARTH *feel heart's muscle motor prodding us*

Chuckles from across room
All fall in soft laugh
Some scene
Four sprawl in darkened room
Opium den of purest dreams
> *Oh you worldling looking in think*
> *you evil no you wrong evil in your*
> *mental coin your evil makes me*
> *compassion laugh*
> *here is no evil*
> *but*
Diamond virtue
Pure blue blueness
Beyond desire
Only
Needle moment
Buddha unity

> *That's*
> *why we laugh do you understand*
> *thinking about that paradox*
> *of mental evil and*
> *the mind-less clean diamond that's*
> *why we laugh*
Words and thinking

Are not as important as we
Said and thought
And so we four drugged ontologists
Lift up heads and laugh
Mandy stone carved semitic mask above water
don't sleep don't sleep
Miss the beauty if you sleep
No one sleeps

Head fall back on bed. Floating, tumble weed, wind driven. CERTAIN
SEEDS, FALLING ON WATER BECOME DUCKWEED. *Dropping
again down shaft of time.* WHEN THEY REACH THE JUNCTION
OF THE LAND AND THE WATER THEY BECOME LICHEN. *See
tiger jungle cats, sinewy. Good-bye.* REACHING RICH SOIL, THEY
BECOME WU-TSU, THE ROOT OF WHICH BECOMES GRUBS,
WHILE THE LEAVES COME FROM BUTTERFLIES, OR HSU. *See
reptiles jewelry. Good-bye.* SO GOD CREATED THE GREAT SEA
MONSTERS AND EVERY LIVING CREATURE THAT MOVES,
WITH WHICH THE WATERS SWARM. *Now I see the straggly shore
creatures. Good-bye, dear friends.* THE YANG CHI GRAFTED TO
AN OLD BAMBOO WHICH HAS FOR A LONG TIME PUT
FORTH NO SHOOTS, PRODUCES THE CH'ING-NING. *I am
drifting down past flowering sea life. Good-bye.* AND GOD MADE
THE BEASTS OF THE EARTH ACCORDING TO THEIR KINDS
AND THE CATTLE ACCORDING TO ITS KIND. *Drifting down
through the history of my body which is all body down to the red, wet,
warm beginnings.* AND GOD SAW EVERYTHING HE MADE, AND
BEHOLD IT WAS VERY GOOD. *I am down to the center.*
    To the single point of origin. Hello.
    lay pulsing softly center
    of all life and time
    I the giant eye . . .
    Giant eye I
    Giant eye
    Eye
    I

Lying ecstatic eyes closed on a Triassic-Jurassic sedentary rock formation, one hand on Mandy's vertebrae hearing interstellar voices from the Mexican patio, light years away. Voice calls. Where are you? Here! I am lying unicelled looking up up up through the spiral unfolding of two billion years seeing it all ahead of me, ovum, segmentation, differentiation of organs, plant, fish, mammal, monkey, baby, grammar school, college, Harvard, Mexico, Cuernavaca. They want me way up there. Is it worth the whole journey? To start the two billion-year cycle once again? No. Why bother? Let's move over to the Precambrian sludge, no too wet, abysses, overlying waters, narrow littoral rocks, let's try that cenozoic snaky jungle. Ah, yes.

IT IS NOW EIGHT O'CLOCK STOP MUSHROOM EATING BEGUN AT FIVE O'CLOCK STOP EFFECT STARTING TO WEAR OFF STOP WANT TO STAY HERE BUT CAN'T STOP RETURNING SOON STOP HAVING MOMENTS OF NON-TRANCE CONSCIOUSNESS STOP STOP STOP BUT THE ENRAPTURING VISIONS RETURN AND CLUTCH OF MIND LOOSENS STOP IMPACT OF NOW-WORLD HITS RETINA AND DON'T STOP.

Mandy and I peer out of cage at earthlings
Acapulco friends who have just arrived
Humor of situation pushes over brink to laughter.

Friends listen to Dicko orate
Shoots nervous glances in our direction
Wildly funny
    then I realize responsibility
    and role as host
    and walk out to porch and have
    friendly conversation with new arrivals
    explaining what is
    happening and telling them to go to
    kitchen for drink and we will be
eating supper in an hour or so they are
relieved and we conclude our
    perfectly normal conversation

Quiet waters roll and Dettering
Old rumpled crocodile paddles up
    Dettering reports that the rest of the
    crowd had landed back on shore and
    were gathered around the kitchen
    table
    Whiskers had returned and Gerhart
    was dictating notes to him.
I INTEND REMAINING OUT HERE LONG AS POSSIBLE STOP
HAVING WONDERFUL TIME STOP WISH EVERYONE WERE
HERE
    on livingroom couch
    head in flesh pool of Mandy's lap
    Plastic forms spinning in eyelid.

    Ruth standing above us
    ¿Qué tal?
    Join us in the kitchen, everyone talking
    No, Ruth.
    Good-bye Ruth.
    ¿Adónde vas?
    To slinky sea bottom.
    Ruth leans down and shakes my shoulder.
    Take me with you. Tell me what you see.
    No. No. Dear nurse Ruth.
    I can't.
    Ask marlin to take you with him on slippery,
    divy
        skimming jumping for joy across and
            under the sun-specked ocean
    Ask your blood to sing the song of voyage
            down to wine-red cavern of your
            heart.
    Can they speak your language? No?
    Neither me. My voice trails off as I head

down

again

Head falls through
Butter belly and
Melon womb to
Sofa cushions
     Mandy is getting up to check
     on guests
At the far end of the pool Mandy and I sit
on beach chairs. She climbs on lap. We throw
heads back and watch gray clouds skudding along
black sky.
Magic mushrooms
Sculpting clouds
Into Roman emperors
     Greek gods
     Football scrimmages
Cavalry charges
We sit for full half-hour
No words
Soft laughter at secret we share
Then
The gray masses change back to clouds for
longer and longer periods and all
at once my legs feel cramped and the chill of
night air and
the trance is over.

The time was 9:07 and the journey into the other half of the cerebral cortex had lasted four hours and seven minutes from the time of eating.

And that was the trip.

It was the classic visionary voyage and I came back a changed man. You are never the same after you've had that one flash glimpse down the cellular time tunnel. You are never the same after you've had the veil drawn.

In the seven years since eating seven mushrooms in a garden in Mexico I have devoted all of my time and energy to the exploration and description of these strange deep realms.

9

Initial Experiences from the Harvard Psilocybin Project

Ralph Metzner

I had my first psychedelic experience with synthetic psilocybin in 1961. Professor Leary had decided to initiate a prisoner rehabilitation project, and I had applied to be a graduate student research assistant. Growing out of Leary's own experience and his philosophical-humanistic values, he had decided that those giving the psychedelic to the convicts should have experienced it themselves. This was fine with me since I was eager to explore this wondrous experience I had heard so much about.

It was a chilly Sunday afternoon when I arrived at Tim's house. Two other graduate students, Gunther Weil and Lyn K., were involved in the session, as well as Gunther's wife Karin, and the prison psychiatrist, Madison Presnell, and his wife. After we had made ourselves comfortable in the living room, Tim gave everyone six little pink tablets, each containing 2 mg of psilocybin. He took probably a smaller dose. It had already become the preferred policy to not stress the role of guide or teacher, but rather to work on the assumption that we were fellow explorers. Nevertheless, in sessions in which he participated, Tim generally set the tone of the experience.

My first reaction was lassitude. I lay down on the floor and stretched out, feeling very relaxed and yet very alert. Tim had said there would be a period like a decompression or slight disorientation. My body seemed for a while to be in a strange sort of limbo. All of a sudden, I found myself in a completely new and magical world. The little green strands of the shag rug were writhing and undulating like a mass of worms, yet in a most delightful way. The lights reflecting off the glass coffee table top sparkled with a kind of moist luminescence. The furniture, the walls, the floor were all pulsing and undulating in slow waves, as if the whole room was breathing. I felt I was inside a living structure, like a vast cell. The rate of the waving motion seemed to be coordinated with my breathing.

This extraordinary sensory fluidity was not at all disturbing; in fact, it was extremely pleasurable. There was clear rational awareness that this was a room with solid walls and a floor, etc. The ordinary world was not erased—it was expanded, enlivened, and made infinitely more interesting. For example, I became totally engrossed in contemplating the fascinating edges of things, the curiously beautiful patterns of light and energy weaving around and radiating out from them. The telephone was a veritable marvel of diamond-studded, gem-encrusted, crystalline sculpture—yet also moving, breathing, and changing as if it were alive.

Simultaneously with this unbelievable sensory feasting, Gunther and I were engaged in a kind of verbal interplay, a mock-serious philosophic exchange that had us both convulsed with laughter. Words and concepts exploded in my brain with multilevel ripples of meanings that set off cascades of feeling and physical sensations. Deep philosophic questions arose and dissipated in a stream of paradoxes and absurd riddles punctuated by convulsive giggles.

When I closed my eyes, fantastically beautiful and intricate geometric depth patterns were interweaving behind my eyelids, washing, colliding, and streaming by at great speed. Occasionally, there would be images of precious stones or different parts of bodies, but nothing stood still long enough to congeal into anything definite. It felt as if my eyes were giving off a white-hot radiance; my mouth and the sense organs in my face and the rest of the body were glowing, flashing, oozing with liquid light; my nerve fibers crackling with white lightning; my blood stream felt like a seething stream of lava. My skin was embracing me, enwrapping me, in an alternately wet and dry, hot and cool almost unendurably pleasurable embrace . . .

A moment of panic occurred that illustrated the fantastic amplifying power of the psychedelic. When I looked at the faces of the others, they were bright and strong and clear. I thought, "This is how archangels look." They were somehow naked, shed of a fog of dissimulations, anxieties and hypocrisies. Everyone was true to his or her own self and not ashamed. I looked at them without shyness and with frank admiration. At one time all the faces were suffused with a soft greenish light.

I looked at Karin across the room and told her she was beautiful, and I loved her. She just looked back without saying anything. Then she got up and started to leave the room (probably to go to the bathroom). I began to panic. I implored her not to leave, that dreadful things would happen if she did. Lyn, who was sitting next to me, said it would be all right, but I got more and more upset and terrified, pleading with Karin not to leave. Karin said she would be back, but I said, "No, no, don't leave!" She asked, "What will happen if I leave?" I replied, in a tone of desperation, "Something terrible will happen . . . the music will stop."

When she got up and walked through the door, somehow I identified that action with all the feelings of abandonment and loss I had ever experienced. It was a moment of acute anguish. But when she was gone, I felt fine, amazed, and relieved. I said to Lyn, "She left, and it was all right." And Lyn said, "Yes, it was all right."

Then, holding Lyn close, I suddenly felt myself shrinking in size . . . I was very rapidly regressing into childhood consciousness. I actually felt for brief moments what I had felt as an infant, even to the feel of a baby bottle in my mouth. Then, just as rapidly, I was shuttled back to my adult awareness.

At a certain point I noticed that the intensity of the experiences began to diminish, like a slow gliding down. My body felt very warm and relaxed. I understood how my normal perception of the world was constricted and limited by many prohibitions I had somehow accepted. For example, I went outside and on the porch was a box. I looked inside and saw that it was garbage and immediately turned away. Then I realized I didn't have to turn away, that it was okay to look at it, that I had a choice and was not bound by a set of rules regarding what could or could not be experienced and perceived.

This was to me perhaps the most significant revelation of this experience: that I was basically in charge of what I could perceive and think about, that I was not bound by external forces but rather made choices that determined the extent and quality of my awareness. To exercise my newfound freedom, I made some snowballs and threw them at the screened window of the room in which the group was sitting. I felt greatly exhilarated. Tim must have sensed my expansive mood because, with a grin on his face, he picked up some pillows and tossed them gently at the window from the inside toward me. The brief interchange had an edge of freshness and spontaneous clarity that made me feel superbly happy.

That first experience with psilocybin had an immeasurable effect on my life. It was radically and totally different, yet during the course of the experience I felt closer to my true self than I had ever been, more aware of my innermost feelings and thoughts. I had also been fully and intensely aware of people and things around me and did not lose the reality perceptions that govern our ordinary world. Rather, ordinary perception was enriched and enlivened beyond comparison. It was clearly false that these drugs were "hallucinogenic" in the sense of hallucinating something that isn't there.

I could see how much sensory phenomena could be attributed to a temporary suspension of the perceptual constancies, those mechanisms that keep the visible shapes and sizes of things constant, even though the optical image is obviously changing. An illustration of that happened during this session when I was lying on my side on the ground and Gunther rolled a ball toward me. As the ball approached me, it grew enormously in size, as the retinal image would. Also, I could trace the constant slight rhythmic oscillations I noticed to the moving of my eyes, which, under the drug, became magnified. All the mechanisms that filter, screen, and regulate perception seemed to have been suspended. As Huxley put it, the mind's "reducing valve" had been inactivated.

The week after that initial session, we began the prison project. My second exposure to the drug took place behind prison walls. We wanted to avoid giving the convicts the feeling that they were to be guinea pigs in the drug experiments of a mad professor, so we decided that some members of the project would always take the drug with them. My first trip in the prison environment, among convicts, was a visit to hell. My anxiety was magnified to terror, loneliness to profound abandonment, and discomfort to agonizing despair, all accompanied by horror visions of devouring machine-monsters. Then, while feeling trapped in the depths of isolation:

From a very long way off I heard a tiny voice saying quietly, "I get this feeling of being alone in the universe, just the self." It was a human voice and there were others! Cautiously, incredulously, I opened my eyes. A scene of incredible peace and serenity presented itself. Gunther and two of the men were sitting quietly, talking, bathed in a stream of afternoon sunlight coming through the window. One of the convicts was lying on the bed peaceful and relaxed, smoking and reading a paper. Two others were sitting silently, playing chess. A wave of relief washed over me. The prison walls were down; the whole world was wide open. Objects again had that extraordinary depth-dimension, as if there were soft crystalline formations in the space between them and me. People had mellow greenish faces and shining eyes. Someone said, "There is one of everything." In some strange way this oneness of everything is the essence, the essence of feelings: one joy, one sadness, one terror, one pleasure.

Suddenly, there was chaos as the prison psychiatrist burst in. "Everybody back to prison routine, change of guards, out of this room!" There was a mad scramble as everyone put together their belongings, straightened their clothes, and tried to force peacefully dissolved identities back into the mold required in prison life. As we walked out through the prison yard, I could feel the guards watching us. "Control, easy now," I said to myself. As the heavy doors clanged shut behind us with loud rattling of keys, the grim strangeness of it all sobered our thoughts.

The revelations of this experience were perhaps even more far-reaching than those of the first session. I began to see how the suggestibility factor operated: feelings of fear or guilt or blame could be triggered by chance remarks, and these negative emotions could drastically alter the course of the experience. Conversely, a warm word or a reassuring touch of the hand could provide instant comfort to someone racked by inner pain.

We entered into a contract with each of the convicts who volunteered for the study. We told them what little we knew about the drug, about our own experiences, and stated the goal was to facilitate insight that would enable them to make a noncriminal adjustment to life outside once they were paroled. The agreement also called for psychiatric interviews and psychological tests before and after the sessions and written reports on each experience.

The results of this work with about thirty convicts were published. They showed that there were profound, measurable personality changes in the men and an apparent, though ambiguous, reduction in the rate of recidivism. Subjectively, the men almost always regarded the sessions as beneficial, even those that were painful. Contrary to dire warnings of many professionals, there was never a moment of violence. Actually, in our research we found that the most violence-prone subjects were psychiatrists and theologians, who had massive repression systems that could be exposed by the drug experience.

As a result of my work in the prison, I grew to like and respect some of the men very much. Al was a man of somber mien and the enormous heavy muscles of a weight lifter. In one session, all in the group were touched as we saw him enter totally, incongruously, into the consciousness of a little boy, expressing wide-eyed, innocent wonder and delight at the photographs in a *Family of Man* book, or the feel of water running over his hands and the look of intense inner searching that came over his face when he saw his arm turn into an eagle's talon.

Donald was in his fifties, serving a twenty-year sentence for armed robbery. In one of his sessions, he had visions of lines and patterns that he traced with careful, probing eyes as he saw in them the patterns of his life. "Does it have any meaning?" he asked, and after a long silence, answered his own question, slowly and haltingly, but deliberately: "Is ego our god? Do we do things so as to have a good image of ourselves in our own eyes?"

We talked for a long time. Those of the group that were on longer sentences or were not to be released organized a study group after the project was terminated. They continued to meet on a regular basis for years after, working on self-help, self-understanding, becoming guides and helpers for younger convicts. Such was the power of those few initial revelations.

A high-dose experimental session with psilocybin that we ran in 1963 exemplified some of these complex dynamics (and risks), as well as illustrating Tim Leary's laid-back, humorous, and yet caring style of supporting our explorations. Tim gave us a lot of leeway in setting up the sessions. Several of us, with two years of experience, had decided to explore the effects of a higher dosage of psilocybin, to see if it would compare to LSD, which we had also started to use by that time. Some took 40 mg, I took 60 mg, and George Litwin, with his pioneering spirit, had decided to take 80 mg. These dosages, though higher than any we usually took, were still well below toxic levels. However, it was in this session that I came closest to suicide than I ever did in the years of working with psychedelics.

When the drug began to work, George was shaking violently. As I looked at him, his face looked strangely distorted and seemed to be coming apart in layers, like one of M. C. Escher's weird paintings. When he spoke, his voice sounded nonhuman, as if his mouth was filled with metallic mud. He was talking about finding the button that made his heart stop or go.

As I looked around the room I saw great bands of moving streams of energy particles traversing the space, passing through and between myself and the other people. We all seemed to be part of these moving, ever-changing bands of energy. They were familiar to me from mushroom sessions, when I had seen them as luminous vibrating filigree networks. But this time the intensity frightened me. As my fear level increased, the energy bands congealed and stopped moving; they took on a grayish hue, like prison bars. All at once I felt immobilized and trapped, like a fly in a gigantic metallic spider's web. I couldn't even talk and explain what was happening to me; my voice felt paralyzed.

Everyone, including George (who was no longer shaking), seemed to be frozen into immobility by these metallic web-cages. I felt my mind was paralyzed too. I couldn't think or understand what was happening. I couldn't tell whether what I was experiencing was real or a drug-induced hallucination, an experience psychiatry refers to as "derealization."

I did, however, decide I should try to call Tim for help, on the telephone. Gunther Weil, who seemed to sense my dilemma, accompanied me to help with the dialing. The telephone set was wiggling and jiggling like a demented jellyfish. Somehow, we managed to reach Tim on the line. Since I felt so totally unreal, I wanted his help to establish some kind of "reality." I said, "Tell me something real, Tim, what's happening over there?"

Tim immediately got the message and started to tell me, "Well, Jack's sitting at the table eating a hamburger. Susie's watching television with her hair in curlers. Michael's drinking a beer . . . " I started to feel a little better. These were messages from "reality." Nevertheless, I told him we needed help and would he come over.

While waiting for Tim to arrive, I was holding on to my sanity with the thought that when he got here, he would free us all from this monstrous spider's web we were caught in, which also had the effect of making us speechless. At least, it felt like I couldn't hear, say, or understand anything. I felt completely dehumanized, not even like a biological organism, more like a mechanical puppet or device.

I was so relieved when Tim came through the door. I could see him moving freely through the sticky web of gray steel bands. But then, after a few minutes, as I watched in horror, he too became trapped in them: his movements slowed down, became mechanical, robotlike, his voice thickened and slurred, and I plunged into despair as I realized he, too, was helplessly caught. Near the apartment building was a train track, on which a high-speed train rumbled by with thunderous noise every now and again. Such was the depth of my despair that I remember wishing that the train would crash through the building and I would be killed, thereby releasing me from this hellish torment of feeling "dead."

This was before we learned how to take someone through a really deep psychotic experience, how to reach them in consciousness, set up communication, and bring them back. Tim and the others simply laid me out on a bed and hoped for the best.

After some hours of objective time and a hellish eternity in subjective time, I noticed the intensity of the experience beginning to diminish somewhat. I remembered I had taken a drug and knew the effect was beginning to wear off. I felt like a living human being again, though thoroughly shaken by what I had gone through. We needed to learn how to bring a person back from psychotic hell-states, as well as preparing for ecstatic heaven-states.

I learned to understand the experience of constricting energy bands years later, when I read Stanislav Grof's account of experiences in the Basic Perinatal Matrix II, in which the fetus experiences the mother's powerful uterine contractions, but there is as yet no cervical opening, hence no possibility of moving through and out of this position. Grof relates this perinatal stage to subsequent psychedelic experiences of feeling trapped, bound, crushed, "no exit," eternal stuckness, and the like.

As we proceeded with our explorations, still under the aegis of the Harvard University Psilocybin Research Project, we were increasingly moving into the consideration of religious and mystical concepts and images. Such ideas were foreign to our humanist psychological orientation but were thrust upon us by the nature of the experiences. Sometimes when Tim was talking to groups about these kinds of experiences, he seemed inspired by an almost messianic fervor that made a powerful impact on his listeners. At the same time the issue of leadership, with its associated complex of idealization and disappointment, was beginning to rear its ugly head.

One strange and moving session on a cold November night in 1961 was particularly memorable for its focus on these issues. Six of us assembled in Dick Alpert's apartment: Dick, Tim, Michael Kahn, George Litwin and his wife Corky, and myself. Gunther Weil had said he would join us later, as would Maynard Ferguson, the musician, and his wife, Flo. Everyone was in excellent spirits. We had never all taken psychedelics together and were looking forward to it.

On the way to the session, Mike and I had been talking about the idea of the sin against the Holy Ghost, the one unpardonable sin. We had discussed it as a kind of universal projective test in the Middle Ages, revealing what you considered your greatest failing. Theologically, it was the attribution to the devil that really came from the Holy Ghost, thus cutting oneself off from the source of grace and redemption.

During the session, Mike returned to this topic and related our earlier thoughts. George, who had a marvelous sense for practical detail, was wondering about borderline sins. He asked Tim, as the only Catholic present. "What did the Church do with those rare cases which the existing rules didn't cover? How did it handle totally new events or occurrences? For example, take a peasant who comes to the priest and says, 'I took these pills last night, and I met Christ, and we shook hands and spent a wonderful evening together, but somehow everybody goes around telling me I'm bad.' How would the Church handle that? What would the priest say?"

When we had all finished being convulsed with laughter, I saw that George had stopped smiling and was looking at Tim, saying, "I'm serious."

I felt a wave of sympathy for George and looked at Tim, who said nothing. I looked at him very intently and repeated, "What would the priest say to George's question, Tim?"

Tim became very confused. He did not seem to hear and was fiddling with his hearing aid. We repeated the question. Then he looked at me in silence for a very long time. I became aware of how important the question had become to me. It was the question about this night, about our work, about our whole life, which had come to revolve so much around these drugs—was it good or bad? It had become a very basic question about existence and personal worth, the question to which each one must find his own answer. This was what I felt Tim to be saying by not answering the question: everyone must come to terms with his or her own condition. When I realized that this was what he meant, I felt tears streaming down my face, but not tears of sadness.

After a while, Tim began to tell a story about a Catholic man he used to know, who always referred to a boy with certain sexual habits as "the monster." I felt this was the priest's answer to George's original question about how to define sin; at the base of the Catholic concept of sin lies a strong disgust toward sexuality.

As I was trying to tell Mike how I felt about these two answers, the human one, and the Catholic one, I saw that Tim had "said" all these things unintentionally. He protested that he did not even hear half of what was going on, and that he felt like a figment of George Litwin's imagination. He said he was in a terrible bind and didn't know how to get out of it. He said he had always regarded us as equals and felt betrayed that he was suddenly being called upon to answer religious questions.

"What have you all been doing all these months?"

Mike, speaking very quickly, said some intense things about Zen masters and Buddha and Jesus, and that Tim had to suffer so that we could learn. All leaders have to go through the same process of awakening to the fact that they are being regarded as leaders, not as equals, as they would like to be.

Gunther said the time might come when he would decide to leave Tim because he disagreed with him and didn't want this pure thing corrupted. He saw Tim being sucked into an evil game because he was so naive.

The room had become almost totally dark. We all sat quietly for a long time, then Gunther said, "You know, Tim, only a Jew and a Catholic could have this sort of discussion."

Tim asked, "What is there of me to leave?" He had always regarded us as equal work-partners, as a group working together for common goals.

Gunther replied, "Yes, I see that now, I recognize the different roles we play. But there was a time when I exalted you, looked up to you, worshipped you. Now you have come down to a human level."

There was a terrible groan of protest from George Litwin.

"Wait a minute, wait ... I am neither Jew nor Catholic, so I can speak here with some impartiality. There was a time before when the Jews exalted a man and made him divine and then nailed him up when they discovered he was human after all. Whether it's a fact or not is irrelevant; it is a *tradition*, and one that we should cease to live by. It's the Jewish tradition that some people are closer to God than others. But there is another one, the one of the Declaration of Independence, where men gather together to draw up a petition in equality."

George was magnificent. He was fighting for a new start, away from the ancient modes of exalting people and then tearing them down, toward a vision of true equality between men and common goals and shared responsibility. Most of us heaved a profound sigh of relief. Maynard and Flo cheered.

The bubble had been broken. Tim got up and went to the kitchen and left the door open. A bright shaft of light streamed into the room. The depressing fog of incipient religious bigotry was dispersed. The tendency to over-idealize a potential leader had been clearly revealed and uprooted, at least for that group and that time.

This account is extracted from a longer essay entitled, "From Harvard to Zihuatanejo," published in Robert Forte, ed., *Timothy Leary: Outside Looking In* (Rochester, Vt.: Inner Traditions, 1990).

EXPERIENTIAL TEACHINGS OF THE MUSHROOM SPIRITS

The Mushroom Beings Would Help Us Return to Our True Nature

Leila Castle

Mushroom journeys spanning twenty years of a woman artist's life provided healing and visionary inspiration. They empower her connection to an ancient lineage of priestesses and have led her to a peaceful, beauty-filled life in a natural setting.

OAXACA, MEXICO 1975

The noisy bus clamored with chickens and babies crying as it labored up the mountainous dirt road. A young Mexican girl swayed in the aisle, playfully singing that Dion Warwick song, "Do You Know the Way to San Jose?" Traveling with friends in Mexico, we had decided to look for the sacred mushrooms in the mountains of Oaxaca. I imagined I was some kind of wild, tantric gypsy who had given up everything to the present path of adventure. I had experienced psychedelics before, but never mushrooms. Little did I know that I would be entering into an ancient pathway and that these plant spirits would be my teachers for many years to come.

As we stumbled off the bus in the thick darkness of San Jose del Pacifico at midnight, rifle-slung soldiers searched us and robbed us of a knife. Then we followed our friends through the forest to a hut that we shared with several Mexican families that night. I slept wrapped in blankets peacefully on the earthen floor, calmed by the innocent sound of the children's soft breath as they dreamed.

The next morning, as I wandered by myself down a dusty road, a little boy approached me, saying "*Hongos? Hongos?*" I followed him into the conifer-scented forest, feeling like I was in a fairytale. He led me to his home where his young mother, a beautifully radiant Indian woman stood in her doorway, resting a basket of freshly-picked glistening blue mushrooms on her pregnant belly. She invited me to stay.

By sunset we were perched on the edge of the forest ridge overlooking the Pacific Ocean far below, completely entranced by the mushroom beings. They sang sweetly for hours and showed me that the forest was alive and dancing with spirits. I watched, astonished, as clouds in the western sky began to form a gigantic, perfectly shaped mushroom cloud that looked like a nuclear explosion. They communicated to me that humans at this time on the planet had a choice: we could either follow the path of warfare and destruction that this mushroom cloud symbolized, or its antidote: the mushroom beings, who would help us return to our true nature and the ancient wisdom of the Earth and the interconnection of all life within Gaia.

I stayed in Oaxaca for six months, learning from the mushrooms and returning to the mountains many times. They continue to teach me their original message and to weave their spell through my life.

PALENQUE, MEXICO, VIRGO FULL MOON 1976

It was not long before I was back in Mexico, this time with a friend. We were camping in a hammock in the rainforest beside the Mayan temple ruins of Palenque in the southern state of Chiapas. On the full moon, we woke before dawn and walked to the nearby mushroom fields. To this day, this experience remains perhaps the most exquisite vision of pure earthly beauty and enchantment that I have ever had the blessing to witness. Everywhere cows lay peacefully in the fields, their graceful horns in silhouette on the sky like the Egyptian goddesses Isis/Hathor. Over the western mountains, a luminous milk-white Virgo full moon was setting, while to the east, in the still, starry-streaming, rainbow colors of impending dawn, the planet Venus, dazzling jewel-like, was joined by Comet West, with its great plumed tail flaring beside her. We gathered our mushrooms from the lush, emerald fields while these celestial spirits shone around us.

We spent the day among the temple ruins in deep communion with the mushroom beings. As the mushrooms and I joined together, I began to hear their childlike voices and see them coming toward me. They were made from rainbow light and carried brightly colored parasols that would turn into mandalas. As they approached, they came up into my inner vision as if looking into the window of my mind. They thought this was extremely funny, saying they were "tourists," and I realized that we were in fact touring each other's realms through the mushroom window of perception.

The temple gardens were exceptionally fragrant with orange blossoms warmed by the heat of the day and I felt completely intoxicated with bliss. I spent a long while doing cloud meditations, watching the clouds form and dissolve many different images, creatures, and beings in a constant stream. Butterflies and dragonflies flitted about gently everywhere as I melted into Mayan dreamworld visions, prayers, meditation, and laughter. Many years later I would learn this state is described as the "flowery dream." I had a very strong experience of opening to the spirit of my first child at this time, and indeed, he was conceived within a few months and born the next year between these two moons. I thank the goddess Ixchel for her blessings of beauty, creativity, and children in my life.

DESERT HOT SPRINGS, CALIFORNIA 1990

We set our intention together and gradually began coming on. At first I felt nervous and a little shaky, but then I began to feel the mushrooms spreading through me. I was very aware of body sensations, heartbeat, then it started to smooth as I began to surrender. I heard the mushroom beings' friendly voices after so long, greeting me, welcoming me, calling me "Little Sister." It felt wonderful, like coming home.

Entered their world. They took me to a rainforest where everything was magnificently alive and vibrant. Tree roots spiraled like snakes in the rich fecund Earth. The roots became snakes, *everything* became snakes, as I heard her say, "I am Mama Quilla," who is a South American moon goddess. I saw the radiant full moon illuminating a tree where a beautiful white plumed bird roosted in the upper branches and snakes coiled like roots at the base of the trunk. This was her manifestation. Then I became her; I *was* her. I felt myself embody this form, energy, and vision. Colorful, vividly patterned snakes, like pythons, were coiling within me. My body was completely made from this serpent energy that was winding, undulating, spiraling, slithering in an ecstatic dance within each cell. I just sat there in wonder. It felt very empowering to be dissolved into this form.

Then the mushrooms began to speak again. They were giggling and said: "Unless you get by the snakes, we won't tell you anymore." I knew they were joking with me about the snakes being guardians of the mysteries. I felt completely united with all of nature, the Goddess, the land, all of life. I understood that the mushroom beings are guardians of the Earth and that through our communion with them we learn to protect the well-being of the land. They showed me awesome realms of pure beauty. Everything seemed so simple in the quiet stillness of the luminous indigo desert night. This incredible dance of life is always going on in the most exquisite perfection and ecstasy, yet we ignore it, separate ourselves, lose our connection and our relationship with other life forms, thus creating all the problems our collective world now faces.

I realized a profound union with a global lineage of serpent priestesses, the *pythia,* oracular protectresses of the Earth. I saw how I was part of an ancient lineage through time and place and that my work has always been to perform this sacred ritual union with the mushroom spirits.

I was then given personal guidance about my children and the future. It was like visiting with the Grandmothers, I felt so much at home, welcomed and empowered by them to bring this sacred knowledge back into the world. The snakes were my adornments, my jewelry, symbols of this oracular power of the Earth to speak through her priestesses.

Tears streamed down my cheeks from the intensity of the beauty. I saw visions of tear-streaked masks of goddesses from Neolithic Old Europe. I felt the sacred moisture of the Goddess, her beauty and love. I anointed my crystals, my partner, and myself with my tears. A huge rainstorm came the next day. I felt very grateful to receive this experience from the mushrooms.

Knowing little about Mama Quilla, I later discovered she is the partner of the Incan sun god, Inti. As a pair, sun and moon, they are the primary Incan deities. Her priestesses were rainmakers.

PT. REYES, CALIFORNIA, IMBOLC 1991

We light candles and make a fire together in my big stone hearth, then sit and eat our mushrooms. We lounge quietly by the fire, sipping chamomile tea until the mushroom spirits become strong in us. I am wearing my white ritual dress and feel like the Goddess, full of love. Everything appears soft and blissful, love-soaked, as if made of nectar. I lay down and close my eyes. My body transforms into rainbow light and I feel its energy moving through me. There is nothing else. It is healing, purifying everything. I feel it moving through me, healing wounds through time, healing everywhere. I am spraying rainbow lights and hear the mushrooms tell me to be love, that there is nothing but love and to twine my heart with my partner's heart. I look at him and I have never seen him so beautiful. I see our hearts weave together like two serpents dancing. They coil upward like a caduceus forming one column. The mushroom spirits have taken my heart and given me a new one made from a substance that looks like clear crystal, but it is rainbow light emanating from a lotus mandala. We make offerings to the fire and pray for the Middle East. We make love for hours by the fire in this exquisite love nectar.

PALENQUE 1995

While in Palenque, Chiapas, Mexico to observe and celebrate the planet Pluto's entrance into the sign of Sagittarius, I realized I was there for the same Cancer full moon in January during which the experience with Mama Quilla and the serpent energy had occurred. As I made offerings of perfume to the Goddess sitting at the entrance of the Jaguar Temple, I noticed a great tree before me. It looked just like the tree with the coiling roots I had seen in the mushroom journey at Desert Hot Springs. There was a mysterious linking that collapsed time and space, completely independent of my conscious awareness.

None of this was planned. It was the language of the mushroom beings.

I journeyed that day nineteen years after I had witnessed the spectacular display of Comet West with Venus in the predawn sky. The mushroom beings were gentle and healing. I was not well and they told me I needed rest and to be very gentle with myself. As I sat within a temple portal gazing out into the surrounding ruins, the entire rainforest came alive in a kind of hyper-real clarity, very magical. Everything was there as it appeared normally, yet it was as if it were one body, *seamless,* including me. I became aware of an enormous spider goddess spirit whose web was the rainforest itself. I believe this was a form of the Mayan moon goddess Ixchel as weaver. I lay back inside the temple on a blanket and closed my eyes to dream. Fireflies began to appear, weaving patterns of light through my whole body until I was filled with their shimmering golden light, made of it. They said they would help me to get well. I bathed in this radiance for a long while and experienced a complete union with the rainforest and the spirit of the place.

Later, while resting in my hotel room, I realized I was quite ill. Fortunately, a friend came by to check on me who had an emergency homeopathic treatment kit and surmised that what I needed was Cantharis, or Spanish fly! It helped tremendously and immediately alleviated my symptoms.

In 1975, I was a twenty-two-year-old artist and dancer following a faery trail. Wandering and in need of healing, I journeyed to Oaxaca, where mushrooms opened realms that continue to guide and teach me: the experience of nondual consciousness, dharma, the preciousness of all life, deities, ancestors, sacredness of place, land and body, otherworlds. This path has led me in giving birth, mothering, working with children, teaching, traveling to sacred sites worldwide pioneering geomantic research, ritual and pilgrimage, organizing and producing educational and arts events, teaching, writing and publishing on the sacred feminine and sacred place, all with the intention to transform consciousness and actions that are tragically destroying the fabric of our lives and world.

Rich with loved ones scattered near and far, my life is simple. I live in the country along the California coast with the garden, apple trees, wild beaches, and deer. My children are grown, strong, and living their own lives, though we remain close. I have worked with botanical fragrance for over twenty-five years and created an original collection of natural botanical perfumes. Changing mediums I paint, write, and weave the arts, magic, prayers, and daily life.

Leila Castle is the editor of the book, *Earthwalking Sky Dancers* (Berkeley, Calif.: Frog, Ltd., 1996).

The Land of Eternal Waiting— Report of a Mushroom Experience with Maria Sabina

Frederick Swain

With the guidance of the curandera Maria Sabina, a forty-year-old American Vedantist monk is transported to a timeless realm and given a Mazatec identity.

Primitive religious rituals have always fascinated me and I have sought them out in my travels whenever possible. A few years ago I heard of the discovery of a new hallucinogenic mushroom in Mexico by the mycologist, R. Gordon Wasson. The religious rituals woven around the mushroom captured my imagination. I decided to investigate at the first opportunity.

In 1961, I went to Mexico to hunt for this mushroom. I had little knowledge of its nature. I knew that this species grows in the mountains of southern Mexico, and that there is a *curandera* (or shaman) in the village of Huautla de Jimenez, who performs religious mushroom rituals. I went to Mexico City with the hope of obtaining more detailed information before continuing on to the mountains, but I could not find anyone who had even heard of the mushroom. So I started out alone by bus to the village in the Sierra Mazatec range in the state of Oaxaca.

After a long day's ride we arrived at the town at Tehuacan, where a broken down public carrier, loaded with vegetables and chickens as well as people, took us to the village of Teotitlan in the foothills. In

Teotitlan there was no one who spoke English, and I speak no Spanish. I located a room at an inn and the following morning I began the frustrating ordeal of arranging transportation into the mountains. Finally, the postmaster agreed to drive me in his jeep. The next morning we rode off in a cloud of dust with two other Mexicans and extra cans of gas in the back.

The paths were narrow and forever winding upward, around, and over mountains, with hairpin turns and thousand foot drops over the side of the road. No one had penetrated the mountains for twenty-five days because twenty landslides had blocked the route due to the rains. We worked hard, digging through the smaller landslides with shovels or waiting for crews of local Indians to dig through for us. The larger slides we skirted by building logs and stones over the cliff, then gingerly inching the jeep around with only inches to spare. On the map, the route to Huautla de Jimenez looked less than fifty miles, but due to the winding roads, it was over a hundred. We arrived late at night, caked with mud and dead tired.

The following day I walked through the village, which was near the highest peak in the Sierra Mazatec. It seemed like the top of the world, the side of the mountain, with valleys below and the mountain peak above. As far as the eye could see there was nothing but mountains with the cloud-covered sky as a backdrop. The air was clean and cool from the rain and altitude. I loved it.

The Mazatecs guessed that I had come for the mushroom. Why else would a *gringo* come to Huautla? It struck them as humorous and whenever they saw me they would shape their hands in the form of a mushroom and pretend they were eating it. Then they would laugh and slap their knees and throw their arms hilariously around each other. I was the joke of the town. Other enterprising Mazatecs did their best to separate me from my money, but I held my own. Most of the Mazatecs didn't speak Spanish, only Mazateca, which is not related to any other language. However, I found a little girl who spoke broken English that she had learned in school.

With her help I learned the name of the *curandera* who performs the mushroom rituals: Santa Maria Sabina. She lived at the top of a peak overlooking the village. I decided to find my own way to her and started walking up the mountain, following the trails, asking directions, calling out the curandera's name. Women would run inside and shut the door, while men would stare and sometimes point the way. Finally, after a heart-pounding climb, I reached a point near the top where some Mazatecs came out to greet me. They announced that here was the home of Santa Maria Sabina.

Her hut was one room with a dirt floor, thatched roof, and mud walls. The household consisted of Santa Maria, her three sons, three women, and numerous children, all living in the same room. There was a wood fire in the center with no chimney. The smoke escaped through the walls, which had many holes and gaps where mud had fallen away. The damp, chilly wind came up the side of the mountain, over the ridge, and through the walls of the hut.

I approached the family with warmhearted friendliness. At first they were suspicious, but other Americans had been there before and gradually they became quite friendly.

I drew from my pocket a picture of the mushroom, which the Mazatecs call *teonanácatl*, meaning "God's flesh." Santa Maria's eyes brightened when she spoke of the mushroom. After watching me closely for a few minutes, she indicated she would have a mushroom ritual that night for my benefit. Since nothing more could be said, I went outside and lay under a tree to rest and wait for the night, as white fog rolled up from below and surrounded me.

When night came I reentered the hut and sat close to the fire while the household ate their dinner, which they offered to share. When we finished, straw mats were unrolled and the children were put to bed. The women went to bed also, leaving only Santa Maria, her three sons, and me.

In one corner an altar had been set up with two long candles and a glass vigil in the center, surrounded by bouquets of flowers. A straw mat was spread before the altar and Santa Maria sat on it cross-legged, motioning for me to sit beside her. The three men sat behind us. The candles were lit and she pulled a large bowl of fresh mushrooms from under the altar.

The heads of the mushrooms were brown and about an inch in diameter. The stems were long and white. She carefully examined each one, then deposited six in each of three cups, which she gave to the men behind us. She then gave me a cup with ten mushrooms. She took ten for herself. The mushrooms still had dirt on them and had been handled a great deal. I tried to ask that they be washed, but no one understood me. What could I do? I ate them, dirt and all.

No sooner had we eaten them than the three men began vomiting and spitting. I was surprised to learn this is what one is supposed to do, and there was a large pan placed by each of us for this purpose. They indicated that I, too, should throw up, but I felt no nausea, so I declined. This surprised them and they discussed the matter among themselves. I noticed Santa Maria did not throw up, either.

I asked for more mushrooms, feeling that if I should not have more, Santa Maria would not give them to me. She looked me in the eye a moment, then put eight more mushrooms in my cup. I had eaten five when one of the men excitedly tapped me on the shoulder asking how many I had eaten. I showed him fifteen on my fingers and he slapped the side of his head and the three began saying, "No! No! No!" No one other than Santa Maria ever eats fifteen of this particular mushroom. They were really afraid for me, but Santa Maria remained undisturbed and said nothing. This was comforting. She sat quietly facing the altar and began chanting something like canticles, with rich, vibrant, tender tones.

Within half an hour I saw vivid, flashing colors. Then a clammy chill came over me and I began shaking. My joints began to stiffen a little, but within fifteen minutes these toxic effects subsided and I felt wonderful. All the fatigue of the day left me and I felt strong and light of body. My back straightened and I began to meditate on the colors.

Her chanting was fascinating, a rising and falling crescendo. The notes had a crisp freshness that carried authority. Intricate art motifs appeared in vivid colors, with a predominance of light blue, but also greens and reds in various shades. The motifs unfolded in a long panoramic view. They formed a spiral and I traveled down the spiral. My sense of sound was heightened and I heard distant music.

Of course, I cannot be certain, but it seemed to me that all five of us were having the same experience. Our consciousness changed many times during that night. It seemed we all changed together, which I attribute to the control Santa Maria exerted over us. The states of consciousness seemed to vary with the rhythm of her chants.

The motifs subsided and our surroundings transformed into a light, warm glow that engulfed us. Dancing celestial eagle gods appeared. Their lines and colors were so sharply focused that they seemed much more real than anything I normally see with my eyes. The dancers were accompanied by sensitive, ethereal music with a background of drums. The timing was fast but soft and the eagle gods were exceedingly graceful, fully absorbed in their dancing. They became ecstatic and we became absorbed with them. It was wonderful.

But where was the hut, the altar, the damp ground, and the sleeping people? The candles had been extinguished, so I took a match from my pocket and lit it. Everything seemed to be in order. As I put my mind on the hut, it came into focus, but the vision of the dancers also remained. Somehow the two worlds intermingled. If I concentrated on the hut, it was predominate. But if I concentrated on the vision, the hut receded. I had control of my will and intellect. I was able to point my mind in any direction, though I felt I was in turn influenced by the emotional content of the visions, much as emotions influence the mind in normal circumstances.

I turned my match to Santa Maria. What a surprise! She seemed transfigured. Her eyes shone with a glow that seemed to light up her head. She looked thirty years younger. There was not a wrinkle on her face. Her skin was light, clear, almost translucent. Here, she was master of the world of the mushroom. She was regal, absorbed in ecstasy. During the day she was a humble, poor Mazatec, but at night she was queen in her strange, mythological realm. I blew out my match and returned to the vision with enthusiasm.

The dancing soon came to an end, the music stopped, and the eagle gods vanished. A new scene quickly took shape, in which all five of us sat a few yards apart from each other in a semicircle at the center of a vast, endless desert. We were merely sitting in silence, each absorbed in his own thoughts.

I grappled with the nature of reality. I felt I was on the verge of a discovery, a new realization that I couldn't quite put my finger on. It was an eerie feeling. Time stood still. Gradually the feeling came that we had been sitting there for an extremely long time. It seemed that we had always been sitting there. Then a name came to me, as though I had always known it: *The Land of Eternal Waiting*. We were waiting there, eternally, though what we were waiting for, I didn't know. But we were definitely waiting.

The memory of my past life began to dim. When had I lived my life on Earth? Many years ago, if I had lived there at all. I began to worry. Would this never end? I certainly didn't want to remain here forever. I was losing my identity. I tried to arouse my memory by recalling the names of my father and close friends. At first the names were dim, as if out of some distant past, but with a little effort they returned quite clearly. Still, I felt I had lost contact with life on Earth. I was really worried that I had died from mushroom poisoning without realizing it, long ago. Perhaps I really *was* in the Land of Eternal Waiting.

Silence had become a part of me. It seemed years since I had spoken, but I forced myself to speak. To my surprise, the Mazatecs responded in English. I swear it. There was some kind of telepathic communication between us. I was later told it sounded to them like I was speaking Mazateca.

They said, *Yes, we really are in the Land of Eternal Waiting. This is reality, your true abode. Your life on Earth never happened, it was only a dream. You have been sitting with us all along, dreaming a very long time. Now you are awakening from your dream, coming back to reality. We belong here together. This alone is real.*

It seemed strangely true, more real than anything I had ever experienced. I was awakening from a dream, a veil had been lifted. The past was shattered. Wow!

We talked a long time on the subtle nature of reality, which they explained with patience and kindness. Usually the Mazatec are a simple, childlike people, absorbed in their struggle to survive. But here in the night with the mushroom, they were highly articulate and presented their views with wisdom and insight. Finally, we returned to silence.

But something still disturbed me: if I were dead to the world, I might as well make the best of it. If I had really died many years ago, my family and friends were probably also dead by now. Though I was in rapport with these people and I really seemed to belong with them, I was damned if I would continue sitting here throughout eternity. Is that all there is to do? This might be reality, but it was senseless, purposeless. I felt like a fool. I began to get mad, really hot.

I turned to them and shouted, *You're all crazy and so am I. We're all mad, stark raving mad. We can't sit here like this forever! We're absolutely crazy!* They politely nodded their heads in agreement. *Yes! We're all crazy. However, this is reality nonetheless. There is reality even in madness.*

They had an irrefutable answer for everything. I was finding out too much of the truth. They tried to soothe me, but I would not be soothed.

I announced I was leaving, though I didn't know where to go. Only the endless desert lay before me. I stood to walk away, but my legs were like rubber. I was so wobbly I couldn't take a step. This made me even more furious. I felt I was being tricked.

Under the influence of the mushroom, one's power of concentration is far more pronounced than normally. You become deeply absorbed in whatever you may be thinking. There is no external distraction. Whatever you do is emotionally intense.

My situation called for drastic action. I really had to get away. I threw my head back and willed myself out of that place. It was as though a charge inside me ignited. I exploded upward like a rocket, instantaneously, straight up through the sky. The others followed me, sucked up by the vacuum of my ascent.

I emerged in a delicate ethereal upper region of space standing calm, collected, and free. I was immediately master of myself and my surroundings. I realized that everything is a state of mind. I am free and master of myself. I am whatever I believe myself to be, if my belief is strong enough. My mind was released from its struggle and I felt the strength of a giant, like a god. Yes, this was *It,* the real moment of truth.

The Mazatecs sat cross legged beside each other while I remained standing, deeply absorbed in my realizations. They looked at me and chanted, "*Santos, Santos, Santos,*" in unison.

This distracted me from my thoughts and I said, *What? What is that? Santos? Who is Santos? Am I Santos?*

They answered, *Yes, you are Santos. Now you are coming to know your true self.*

They waited a moment for this to sink in. Well, I really began to feel like Santos, whoever he is. I became identified with a mental image of Santos that took shape in my mind, accompanied by a feeling of ecstasy. I seemed to move automatically, not guided by my will, but by my emotions. My emotions overflowed. I felt a diving rhythm in the core of my heart. I rose on one foot, light as a feather, and turned slowly on my toes. I had perfect physical control and began to do the eagle dance. I danced with my arms and torso more than my feet. Then I began to chant in Mazateca and moved and swayed to the rhythm of my chanting. It all came as naturally as breathing the air.

The dance did not take place only in my mind. I really did do the eagle dance with my physical body. At one point I became vaguely aware I was dancing in the mud hut. I could sense and even see many people crowding into the hut. Other Mazatecs in the area were apparently pushing in to watch me. I could see them if I wished, or I could be lost from them in my dance of ecstasy. Their presence didn't disturb me as it normally would. I was absorbed in my dancing and my identity as Santos, oblivious to all else.

I don't know how long I danced. Somewhere my chanting changed into a song in Mazateca. Normally my voice is quite ordinary, but in that state of consciousness, tones came from my throat that are unimaginable to me, long sweet, beautiful exotic tones flowed out with strength and power, without effort. The following day I was told my voice carried through the valley below and was heard all over Huautla de Jimenez. Everyone in the surrounding area heard me. Those in the immediate vicinity came crowding into the hut to watch. It must have been quite a performance. As I write this account, I drift off and relive the whole thing.

When my wonderful lovely songs came to an end, I began to lose my feeling of godhood. I changed completely. I became a child. I lay on the floor like a child crying for its mother. Not its earthly mother, but some kind of divine, godly mother.

After lying on the floor for some time, I began to return to my normal state of consciousness. The effects of the mushroom wore off rather quickly. The visions ceased. My surroundings lost the vivid colors. Everything looked disgustingly normal. The transition took about twenty minutes. The only thing that remained was the emotional impact of the experience.

I stood up rather sheepishly and lit a cigarette. It was four o'clock in the morning. I had been under the influence of the mushroom for seven hours, about two hours longer than the Mazatecs, due to the larger quantity I had eaten. Perhaps my experience was more intense than theirs, for the same reason. I was not the least tired. Physically, I felt in excellent condition. I could not detect any ill effect or any form of hangover from the mushroom.

At daybreak, Santa Maria initiated me as a Mazatec. She rubbed a green, earthy substance into my arms, chanted, and proclaimed me her son. But we could no longer communicate with one another by words, only sign language.

When I descended into the village that day, I found the attitude of the people toward me very different from the day before. No one made fun of me. Everyone came to me and I tried to talk. They would talk among themselves, point at me, put their arms around me. Even prices came down. Cigarettes were cheaper, beer and food were all less than the day before. Yes, indeed, these were my people.

After a few days I had to leave Huautla, though I wanted to stay on. I was running out of money and the food and lack of good water was beginning to tell on my health. I wasn't much use to their worka-day world. All I was good for was eating mushrooms, so I left them, with reluctance.

I don't recommend the mushroom to anyone. Even though they are physically harmless, each person responds differently, according to temperament and psychological makeup. For those who seek the hidden depths of the unconscious mind, the possibilities of explo-ration are unlimited. The variations are endless. One can enter mythological realms and mental worlds undreamed of. If one gives spiritual meaning to these experiences, as the Indians do, the results are far more significant.

Sometimes, even now, I think perhaps Santa Maria was right when we were sitting in the Land of Eternal Waiting. Maybe I am still sitting there, dreaming. Perhaps I have only resumed my dream of living in this world. Perhaps my being here is only the product of my imagination. How can I really know? Can we ever be really sure of anything? But if all is a dream, I must say the dream I like best is the one where I shoot up through the sky and become Santos. Man, that's really living!

The late Frederick Swain was, at the time of writing, an American Vedantist monk and student of Gyatri Devi. He also collaborated on the Harvard Psilocybin Project. This report is excerpted from *Psychedelic Review*, no. 1, 1963. Reprinted with permission.

A Mazatec Indian Curandero's Healing Practice Using Psychoactive Mushrooms

Bret Blosser

An anthropologist reflects on his experience participating in three mushroom healing ceremonies with the Mazatecs of Tenango and on the future of entheogen-based healing among Mexico's indigenous people.

Tenango is a region of rugged, steep limestone hills and valleys in the Mexican state of Oaxaca. The vegetation is mostly evergreen tropical forest, coffee, or *milpa* agriculture. The Mazatecs of Tenango are in contact with mainstream Mexico through coffee commerce and a good road with bus connections to Puebla and Mexico City.

The *curandero* (healer), whom I refer to here as R, is about fifty years old, monolingual in Mazateca, soft-spoken, and solid. He is a respected member of the local community. R and his sons C (about twenty-eight) and P (about twenty-three) are primarily corn, beans, and coffee farmers. C is also the local medic, who refers patients who need more advanced attention to the hospital or to his father, depending on the nature of the disease. Both sons have lived outside of the Sierra and are considered cosmopolitan Mazatecs. They are married, have young children, and live adjacent to R and his wife, L. Both sons seem dedicated to learning mushroom healing. Their wives are also involved.

These people befriended me in 1985, when I was hiking alone in the high Tenango backcountry looking for vertical caves. The Sierra Mazateca contains world-class vertical cave systems. R then agreed to introduce me to his methods of healing involving psychoactive plants. He uses several: *piziete:* San Pedro cactus; a tall, pink or white blossoming tobacco grown near the house; *Hojas de la Pastora (Salvia divinorum)* grown away from trails in remote coffee plantations; and three species of wild mushrooms. R conducted two ceremonies during which I consumed the raw leaves of *S. divinorum.* The leaves quickly moved me somewhere beyond my body, companionship, and the ordinary dimensions. R's sons emphasized that the mushrooms were slower and better for learning.

In 1988, I visited during the rainy season, when mushrooms are available. I stayed for ten days and participated in three ceremonies. Two were specifically for me and one was for a patient. The format of these ceremonies varied somewhat. The two performed for me centered on introducing me to the format and technique of mushroom healing. I also learned about using San Pedro and about singing/praying.

FIRST MUSHROOM HEALING CEREMONY

At about 8 p.m., C says, "Listen, he has started." I hurry over to R's house with my flashlight and copal incense. I open the door carefully. The room is brightly lit by a bare bulb. R sits by an altar table, chanting. P indicates a chair facing the altar by a long table against the far wall. The chant ends.

I look around and smile at the patient and family. The patient, Lazaro, is on a chair further back. His wife and child are on a *petate,* a woven mat. L sits on the bed by R, who is next to Lazaro. P's wife, A, is in the back on a petate with the two kids. They talk and we wait until about 9 p.m.

R gives me a double handful of *pajaritos.* "There are some little *derrumbes* in there, too," says P. R gives everyone an amount, quite a bit to the patient. Later A tells me she ate twenty and her two kids (about four and five years old) each had two, their first.

R has a small handful of derrumbes, including some pretty big ones. They are gray-capped with whitish-gray stems stained a black-blue. I set the handful he gave me on the table and begin munching, chewing well. R and others make "yee-ouch!" sounds and swing their heads, remarking on the acrid taste.

We sit and wait again. There is a tiny crucifix on the wall and a candle stub on the crossbeam behind it. There are no flowers, but San

Pedro is on the altar. Copal smokes on coals in a potshard on the floor. The lights have been turned off and a faint light shows above a wall and under the door.

R begins with, "*In el Nombre, en el Padre, en el Hijo, en el Spiritu Santo,*" and some lines about the trinity and so on. Then he chant-sings. Everyone starts chanting, singing, talking at their own paces, some in musical relation to R. L, in particular is complementing his lines with echoing higher notes and phrases, particularly on a closing refrain.

R brings the singing-talking to a halt. His flashlight goes on. Speaking through P, R has me orient my chair as the others are, to the altar "where the sun will rise." R talks for awhile with L and others, then begins another set. We all join in. I am feeling cold and wishing I'd brought my jacket.

Then comes a cramp or ache in my shoulders, arms, and legs. It is blocked, lost energy, and I realize that I must face this, not try to transcend or avoid it. I try cramping down harder in each area, which gives me a wonderful relaxation-release with some psychic optics results. Nice. It feels correct to take it on. I try moving the afflicted areas one by one, singing with my arms billowing as wings. I try massage, especially of quadriceps and belly. (My belly has become the object of attention of the whole extended family during the last couple of days, due to my constipation, which now, of course, has taken on its somatic-psychic dimensions. Rather humbling. I go to study shamanism and end up getting treated for clogged guts.) Aside from the frustration and discomfort of this physical preoccupation, it does feel like I am facing an aspect of myself that is a problem and potential opening. At one point in the session I feel content, coming to terms. Sometimes I get release into vision and energy.

After a set or two, R asks if I want San Pedro. Yes. He gets up in the dark and walks toward me. I hold out my hands and receive some San Pedro. The changing of wads and the spitting on the dirt floor give me something to do to get me through some weird stretches.

R belts out strong songs, which become more intricate and interwoven as the night progresses. Everyone else is chanting and singing. Sometimes R signals an end to a set, or sometimes Lazaro's chatter increases in volume and we halt to give him the floor. He jabbers urgently and eventually R interjects a comment or two, then starts up another set.

Twice, toward the end, he has me sing-pray in Spanish. I sort of falter, though I have plenty of inspiration when I am singing anonymously in English. I do not want to take time away from the patient, so I keep it short. The next morning I was told that energetic, continuous song-prayer is the mark of doing well. When songs are short, cut off, it indicates the work of *brujos* (dark sorcerers) to shut off your visions.

Between late sets, R seems to be counseling Lazaro. P explains that he was telling him that a curandero whom he had been treated by earlier was actually making him sick!

Finally, around 3 or 4 a.m., the lights go on and we sit around talking, relaxed and happy. Late in the morning we all have chicken *caldo* prepared by the patient's wife. P tells me that this is Lazaro's second session and he will return for more sessions until he is well.

SECOND MUSHROOM HEALING CEREMONY

We begin at 8 p.m. in R's room. P sets petates with blankets on the floor in back and plays with his little son. His daughter curls up on the bed. The kids laugh and smile a lot and we all admire them.

At about 9 p.m., R sets a chair in front of the altar table where four piles of pajaritos sit. He dedicates them chanting, "En el Nombre, etc." We sit and they talk for awhile longer. R hands me a double handful, perhaps a bit less this time. We all begin munching. R finds them gritty and begins dipping them in water. We have a great laugh about our teeth getting black as we chew the mushrooms.

We sit more quietly. It rains. I collect my intentions, feeling my way into it. All day I have been visualizing a flower in my afflicted areas. My imagination has been lucid due to after effects from last night's session. To avoid my multifarious changing impulses, I decide to set a few intentions as I go along and stick with them. I opt for a strategy of clear, sustained attention to the sound and happenings in 3-D space, rather than going for the dream visions that come easily, but sort of carry me away. So, my intention is self-possession and sobriety. This turns out well; I am self-possessed the whole time, objective about the mushroom state. I try not to be bothered by any aspect. I minimize thought and attend to clarity and sustained attention.

R turns the lights out. After awhile, P asks if I *"tienes."* Yes.

R begins the introductory chant, "En el Nombre . . . " saints' names, and more. R takes San Pedro on a banana leaf back to his seat. After awhile, he begins to sing the same song that starts each session. It has a churchy, hymnlike sound. Another song goes by and then L and P begin their own chant-prayer-songs.

I rev up. I find that singing in English goes well. Mostly I use simple phrases with variations and play with tone, pitch, speed, isolating a word or two of the phrases, like, "Let the energy go, let it jump, let it twist, let it flow." I try to tie my rhythm and pace into R's, complementing his singing. "Let my feet flower, let my legs flower . . . " Sometimes I sing choir style high notes from the chest, strong and loud. Sometimes I push forward energetically, urgently.

Rain showers pulse through, pounding harder and harder on the tin roof. We all sing-pray loudly up into that intensity. Sometimes I just talk into the mushroom night: "Don't leave me here, don't let me be stupid, take me on, take me over . . . " R leads on with a driving, pulsing, intricate style, but it seems he has less force and variation of style than last night.

When he stops, we all do. Perhaps there is a cue in Mazatec or perhaps they listen for his ending. In the *pausas* he talks quietly with the others. He calls out to ask how A is. She does not talk or sing in the song sets but expresses more softly. P lets out intense bursts of fast, earnest, forceful words but never sings. L mostly echoes on the refrain but sometimes embellishes and sings a phrase or so of her own in her beautiful voice. We do several sets.

I never break into vision or into the intense "drenched in a psychic rain" feeling of the previous night, but I feel strong and clear. I am asked a couple of times how I feel and reply, "Strong and clear," or some such. I wonder if my sober approach has cut the vision. I note that I did not intend to be high. Now I sing, "I intend to be very, very high."

R gets up and lights a candle. He talks seriously between sets. He perceives the attack of bad people, which has the effect of putting a stop to vision and one feels one cannot sing more. These bad people are envious. They believe that I am bringing a lot of money to the family or that I am getting gold out of caves for them. C says they consciously send *mal aire* (bad air, also referred to as *viento,* wind).

I feel like the session could end now. I have not got much inspiration. It is about 12:30. R sings more sets and I get inspired and do some good singing and work. P tells me it is time for me to say or sing what I ask, in Spanish. I sing for a strong life, a path, health for me and friends, and to learn to cure. A clumsy song. Eventually P asks if I am down *(bajar)*. Yes. It is 1:30.

R and P talk for a long time, apparently expressing frustration over P's efforts or career. It seems sessions serve the purpose of requesting direct aid from God for life situations, for asking for general well-being, and for discussing life situations.

REFLECTIONS

The candle is important. It must be pure beeswax, not the kind sold by vendors in the market. R makes them from beeswax from a local woman. The candle is lit for a bit at the start, then put out with a flower, not by blowing, when the effects begin. It is lit during the ceremony if there is a problem. It gives strength. The next morning I was to *limpiar* (clean) myself by wiping the candle through the space just off my body. This felt good.

There is a strong prohibition against sex after the session. Four days is the period most often mentioned, but C said five is better and a week is better still. I was told that if I do a ceremony back home, I must be sure that my companions follow the same prohibition, or it will come back on me. Before the first mushroom session, I was asked if I had broken this prohibition after the previous ceremony, a Hojas de la Pastora ceremony more than a year before. If I had, R would have given me a small amount of mushrooms because I could go crazy.

There is also a prohibition against offering anyone anything to eat or drink during the four days, *cuidar los dias,* to guard the days.

The mushrooms are generally picked for these ceremonies by widows or very trusted people. They must not have any sexual contact from the time they first spot the mushrooms, which might be just sprouting and not yet ready, until they deliver them.

C and P explained R's role: "He is like a guide leading us up a mountain. He gets to a certain point and waits for us there. We have to reach him, then he leads on to the next point." I did experience his songs as bursts of energy that boosted me on.

About the curandero's visions: "It is like a television. At first it is dark or white. Then you see something. What is that? A person appears. Christo. The person explains it to you (the problem and the cure)."

"The Gods are like judges. God is the ultimate, but there is a defender. The curandero speaks to the authorities on behalf of the patient. He has very good contact with them. He is like a government lawyer. He knows all the articles and laws very well because he has to touch on so many points."

Healing ceremonies that involved the use of mushrooms, morning glory seeds, *Salvia divinorum,* or peyote were a basic part of Mesoamerican health systems before the Spanish invasion. Plant-based healing methods were generally tolerated by colonists and colonial authorities, but entheogens (certain psychoactive plants or other substances) were identified as means for invocation and communication with the devil, and as evidence of pacts with the devil.

The church mounted a sustained and thorough campaign to eradicate entheogen-based healing, divination, and religion. They succeeded in eliminating entheogens from local religious practices everywhere except for among a few peyote-using northern groups. The use of entheogens in healing and divination in Mesoamerica has survived only in the highlands of the states of Oaxaca and adjacent Puebla among Mazatecs, Zapotecs, Cuicatecs, Chinantecs, Mixes, and Otomis. This cultural continuity reflects centuries of deliberate and considered resistance to repression by the colonial church and legal system, which was firmly established even in those rugged sierras. Today, at least in the Mazatec area with which I am familiar, patients and their families have recourse to both western and ancestral Mazatec ways of healing.

Unfortunately, there are forces in modern Mexico that threaten the continued viability of entheogen-based healing among Mexico's indigenous people. These healing methods are not directly attacked as illegal, although most of the entheogens themselves are illegal in Mexico.

However, as a result the career-path of the traditional healer is no longer attractive to young people. Formerly, plant healing was one of the few bodies of specialized knowledge that a young indigenous person might study, master, and use to pursue a profession that was both prestigious and economically rewarding. Healers were formerly held in such high esteem in the Sierra Mazateca that, within living memory, all top political leaders were also mushroom shamans. Traditional healers are still accorded great respect, play key roles in their communities, and benefit economically from their practices. Though some young people do undergo training and enter the profession, fewer are doing so because other career paths offer equal or greater prestige and greater economic reward.

In the anthropological literature, it is often reported that healing expertise is transmitted from grandparents to grandchildren. This makes particular sense in the case of mushroom-based healing. The healer's extended family gathers for the ceremonies of the mushroom season. The transformations of the mushroom reach the child prenatally when its mother attends a ceremony. The mushrooms also sweep through a child too young to partake, but old enough to attend. Around the age of five a child may be given a mushroom to eat. Then it is allowed to dream in its mother's arms as songs go on through the night. To kids who grow up attending these ceremonies, mushroom spaces are a familiar part of their neighborhood. The children in healers' families thus begin their training before they are born and continue training as they participate in family life. Ideally, some of a healer's children and grandchildren undergo training with their grandparent in healing ceremonies and other special ceremonies.

Mazatecs from families other than the cuandero's are very positive about mushrooms but will only experience them a few times during their lives, mainly when they have recourse to a mushroom ceremony because of a health crisis.

Bret Blosser is a graduate student in anthropology at Tulane University studying with Huichol Indians in Jalisco, Mexico. He teaches a field program in Native American studies and environmental issues in the American Southwest for the Sierra Institute of the University of California, Santa Cruz.

I Was Awed by the Mysterious Precision and Generosity of the Mushroom Spirits

Raoul Adamson

A psychologist in his fifties experiences psychological insights, manic overexuberance, magic energy chants, materialization phenomena, and painful precognition with humble gratitude.

On the way to the cabin in the woods by the river, we stopped at the house of the grower. He gave us handfuls of moist, fleshy fungi, colored in delicate strands of ivory, silver-gray, and violet. They had the texture and sensuous feel of flesh. Taking them into my mouth tasted like doing oral sex on engorged genitalia. "Flesh of the gods," indeed, and goddesses too! But they are also *los niños*, the "little princes" that Maria Sabina sings of in her *veladas*, her all-night healing ceremonies.

The first thing I noticed was the closed-eye visions of multihued geometric lattices and filigree webs, sparkling and shimmering; but this time they had a fluid quality as well, as if some divine nectar was dripping sensuously into my brain and body from these pulsing lattices. I noticed the patterns quickly turned ugly and tacky if I had the least glimmer of distrust or suspiciousness.

I got a sense that the "little people" of the mushrooms were meeting the spirits or egos of my inner organs. Each organ, like each plant, had an indwelling spirit with a self-conscious identity; indeed, the inner organs seem to be much like plants, with their pouches, vascular stalks, and fibrous branchings. Some of them were not in a good mood, feeling out of sorts. The little mushroom folks were making them feel better by tickling them from inside and making them laugh. Happy laughter, like that of a child, gurgled up from my insides.

There was a presence in the room that my partner and I both sensed, of a majestic elven-king, but he was elusive, not directly visible, as if playing hide and seek with us. The walls of the room were pulsating, seemingly breathing, as if we were inside a gigantic organic cell. The walls became quivering, porous membranes. Looking into the fireplace, the burning logs turned into a vision of a vast underground city, with myriad lights and glowing fires among buildings and moving shapes. As I kept looking, on the other side of the fire there was an opening into the vastness of cosmic space, studded with stars.

From a center within myself, lines of choice radiated out in all directions. The forward radiations were lines stretching into the future, and the backward lines the memories that connect us to the past. We were in the still center of what William James called "the theatre of simultaneous possibilities."

I was given insights into certain behavior patterns I learned in childhood. One was my tendency to be helpful to people, so that they will love me. The mushroom spirits suggested it would be better and more forthright to just ask for the affection I want, like my dog, who rolls over with great obviousness when she wants her belly rubbed. I was also shown how my anger, unexpressed because of my fear of its violence, ties the expressive side of my nature into knots of hidden resentment and somatic distress. Several painful childhood experiences that led to that kind of entanglement flashed by in quick succession.

We felt blessed, in full recognition of the sacredness of all life and all lives, ours included. The mushroom spirits were supremely generous in the way they showered us with insights and delights of the senses. Their quality of serene wisdom, combined with delightful giggly humor, permeated our consciousness.

Another time, on another journey with the mushrooms in the same setting, the geometric structures became visible to me with my eyes open, filling the space around me. I was walking outside on a trail through the forest and kept lifting my feet high to step over them. We were walking through a forest of crystals.

Later, while lying down, I felt my face changing. A mask was being removed from my head, neck, and shoulders, like a lizard shedding skin. I oscillated between a reptilian crawling posture and mammalian crouching one. I thought my conceptual human mind had been suspended, parked like a car in the garage, so that my innate body wisdom could make the changes needed for healing.

Stimulated by music of East Indian drumming and chanting, I started to make strange explosive, trilling and rolling sounds that unzipped walls of resistance in my psyche. Echoes of aboriginal and prehistoric chants and dance movements flashed through my awareness. Barbarian consciousness, I realized, is one in which healing can take place from within, naturally, because there is no overlay of civilization, with its rules and conventions. I felt I was turned inside out, with my inner organs externalized, exposed to view, as if hung out to be washed and dried in the fresh air, and charged with sunlight.

My partner, a psychotherapist, was asking me pointed questions. They engaged my mind and attention, but I was unable to think about them in the usual way. Instead, I was verbalizing a stream of consciousness, with words in different accents and voices and nonlinguistic sounds mixed in. The theater of possibilities had become a madcap farce, with various characters alternating speaking through me in rapid succession. I felt as if an alien power was using my vocal apparatus to talk.

The imagery became more laced with aggression and violence, though I didn't feel any anger or hostility. It was as if someone had pushed the "read-out" button on my computer and various patterns of aggressive behavior in the collective consciousness came pouring out of me: images of warfare, civil strife, anti-Semitism, racial violence, ethnic hatred, Spaniards against Indians, rednecks, bigots, torture, mayhem. Occasionally the stream of vicious verbiage was punctuated by maniacal laughter.

I managed to insult my partner several times, casting slurs on her ethnicity, but she was mercifully unmoved, mindful of the nonpersonal nature of my eruptions, which continued for a couple of hours. Once, when I got too obnoxious, she reminded me that a large-bodied friend was right next-door; I backed off right away. I felt like an ape-man gone berserk, a mushroom maniac. Then, suddenly, I transformed into an aged Indian beggar woman, sitting in the dust by the side of a road, terminally weary, poor, and hungry. The mania was over.

I believe this mushroom mania was triggered by a too-high dose, which was also accompanied by a mild stimulant. This led to the explosive expression of feelings and rampant projection of images, rather than processing them with mindfulness and conscious attention, as is possible with more moderate amounts.

A third mushroom session occurred a few weeks later, again in the setting of the house in the forest by the river. My journey companions were again my partner and a close woman friend who is Basque. We set up our energy shields, each with different qualities and colors, in the four directions.

In late summer afternoon sun the crown of my head felt fiery hot. Standing by the door looking outside, the sunlight was filtering through tree tops, flashing and sparkling where it touched a fern leaf, a romping dog, friends next door; even the chrome and edges of the car glowed with vibrant intensity.

Inside, I was on my hands and knees when I noticed that my hands and forearms had turned into lizard paws. I used them to beat rhythms on the floor. Lizards had been appearing more and more in my experiences lately. I'd come to appreciate their quality of attention: how they sit motionless staring at you with one large unblinking eye, then flit like lightning and disappear, or crawl with sinuous, slow deliberation under a rock. The feeling of crawling like a lizard was very pleasurable to me. I sensed healing vibrations spreading out from my spine. I remembered, from my time of working with autistic and retarded children, that there is a process of facilitating sensory-motor integration that consists of "cross-pattern crawling."

Pursuing a healing intention, I initiated a conversation about my chronic constipation. Various unpleasant childhood experiences were easily seen to have created an aura of discomfort around the prosaic act of defecation. Humor and laughter emerged quickly as the obvious antidote to excretory distress. I remembered how delighted I was when I heard my six-year-old son sing while sitting on the toilet—it had never occurred to me to sing under such circumstances. The woman said she made up funny chants for shitting when she was a child. Sitting back in her chair she talked about how important full-belly laughter is for healthy elimination. I sensed a whole group of her Basque elders and family members standing behind her, as if prompting her. Then she said, "Beware the man, who when he laughs, his belly does not jiggle: he has a constipation problem."

I said, "What is this, a Basque proverb that you've just channeled?" I felt like my conceptual mind had checked out again, and I couldn't quite understand what was being said. So I asked her to repeat the proverb.

When she did, there was a bolt of energy from her voice that shot right to my lower abdomen, the *hara center*, causing me to laugh with a jiggling belly. Then her laughter and my partner's added to mine seemed to be sending a jetlike stream of energy from my belly up my vertical axis. I had been sitting on the couch and suddenly found myself lying face-down on the floor six or seven feet away; although I have no memory of flying through the air. When I recovered from this, I said, "So this was the sound that hurled the man across the room, caused his kundalini to rise up to his crown chakra, and maybe cured his constipation problem!"

I couldn't think; my mind had been parked somewhere. I started to make sounds of a computer breaking down, followed by chants, rhythmic beatings of my hands on my body, and various animal sounds. While these sounds were coming out of my mouth, my face and hands were going through expressive gestures that seemed like part of some masked demon dance, with bulging eyes, flaring nostrils, and gnashing teeth. I thought we were in the midst of some kind of ceremonial dance theater from Tibet or Bali.

A year after the above experiences, I undertook another mushroom journey with my Basque friend. Our intention was to explore certain alchemical themes.

While I was watching the familiar geometric lattices taking shape in front of my eyes, I felt slightly frustrated that I was not quite there yet. I got a vision of an organic furnace, dark in the center, with fire glowing around the outside edges. Then I remembered the alchemists' secret equation: the alchemical vessel or furnace, in which the work of transformation takes place, is the practitioner's own body. So I decided to bring the image of the partially burning furnace into my body. I identified with it, embodied it. The process worked. I felt more energy being generated within me, until I was fully charged, cooking.

I thought about Jung's statement that the alchemists projected their unconscious contents into matter. I realized that this is only partially right. I saw that they *consciously, purposively*, projected chosen archetypal images into matter, including the matter of their own physical body. The alchemical artist, through an act of imaginal perception, structures archetypal symbols, such as the alchemical furnace, or retort, into matter.

We had a small brick of piñon incense, which we lit and placed inside a holder shaped like a kiva. At first, the little chunk was black except for two burning corners from which the fragrant smoke was curling up. We both realized it was a little elf, a furnace elf, with a dark chunky body and two enormous fiery, smoking eyes. This furnace elf was gleefully, fiercely burning itself up, releasing fragrance in doing so. It became a frog-faced fire-gnome. Then we saw an old man wearing a bear pelt. Next it became a bear-shaman fire-gnome elder.

As we were drifting off to sleep, the Basque woman described an image of a blue spiraling line of light coalescing into a blue kernel. An inner voice told her, "Find the blue stone on the crystal glass by the large feather." In my living room, which she was not at all familiar with, there was a large macaw feather on top of a bookcase. Near the feather was a book on sacred geometry called *The Power of Limits: Proportional Harmonies in Nature, Art and Architecture*. It had a figure of a spiral with the golden section on the cover. On top of the book lay a magnifying glass. Book and glass had been there for months; we had not talked about it. I got up and looked at the glass by the feather. On the circular lens, which was on top of the golden section spiral, exactly in the center of the glass, lay a single kernel of blue corn.

Neither my friend nor I had placed the corn kernel there, nor ever seen it before, nor was there any other blue corn anywhere in my house. It was a demonstration of materialization. I looked at the clock and it was exactly 3:00 a.m. We were both in awe at the precise, elegant, nonchalant generosity of the magic mushroom spirits.

The last mushroom journey I am going to relate here illustrates the power of intention in shaping altered state experiences. Four years after the experiences described above, I was driving down the Oregon coast with my wife and stepson, on the last leg of our honeymoon. My wife had become pregnant, as we had hoped. We had visited the spectacularly beautiful mountains and islands of British Columbia, including camping in the Queen Charlotte Islands. We found a campsite by a stream, under some trees, a short walk from the ocean. It was the last night of our trip and I decided to take some mushrooms. The boy was asleep and my wife would attend. I wanted to see if I could tune in with the spirit of the child now forming in her womb. I took three grams of dried mushrooms after nightfall. I was supremely happy and couldn't have imagined or wished for a more positive and benign set and setting.

Nevertheless, to my surprise and chagrin, the experience had a negative tone to it. I felt restless and anxious, with a vague sense of oppression. Amazed, I noted the contrast between the serene, lovely setting, under the stars, and the frustrated, ill-at-ease inner feelings I was having. I examined my intentions, my set, to see if there was any attitude or unexamined negativity somewhere that could account for this strange and uncomfortable turn of events. I found nothing that made sense. I began to think, "This was a mistake, I made a mistake, this is not working out, I should not have done this journey." I ruefully resigned myself to feeling bad.

After about two hours of restless distress, the situation changed and I began to feel warm inside, accepting and trusting in the process, even as I failed to understand the message I was apparently being given. I walked in the moonlight and felt my entire body had become one large sense organ registering sense-stimuli and energy-fields in all directions. I walked to the ocean and wanted to surrender to its immense power.

However, a perception of increasing cold captured my attention, and I walked back to the tent. My instinct for self-preservation overrode any mystical or psychedelic self-sacrificial temptations.

It was four months later, during an experience with ayahuasca, that the meaning of the strange mushroom journey finally became clear to me. My wife had a miscarriage a week or so after our return from the trip. The ayahuasca spirits showed me that my experience under the mushroom, where I had intended to tune in to the child being conceived, was exactly how one would imagine the experience of an embryo that was going to miscarry: feeling oppressed, restless, uncomfortable, ill-at-ease, and that a mistake had been made. These were apparently not how I felt personally, but they were the feelings of an endangered embryo. This exactly reflected my intention.

I was again awed by the mysterious precision and generosity of the mushroom spirits. They had given me exactly what I asked for, an experience of the child that was coming in. I didn't know how to interpret it because the possibility of a miscarriage never occurred to me. I realized then that many of our dreams and visions might be prophetic or precognitive, but go unrecognized as such. The more mundane and ordinary precognitions go unrecognized because we haven't recorded them: the fateful and disastrous ones, because we don't want to see something dangerous or terrible.

I Was Being Told to Paint with the Blood of the Heart

Kate S.

An artist now in her fifties found the mushroom showed her a vision of an ongoing struggle between human and alien beings from another dimension. The presence of a wise friend rescued her. Later, she received guidance for her artwork.

This experience happened in a circle of fourteen people, guided by a shaman. Each participant was asked to choose an intention going into the session, such as a question or an area of concern, in hopes that the participant might gather information. I had two questions: the first had to do with understanding my restlessness, and the second had to do with whether I should take on a project of illustrating a deck of Tarot cards.

I ate 3 to 4 grams of mushrooms around 5:00 in the evening. In a short period of time I had gone very deeply into my experience. Although the shaman was guiding us through various exercises that we had reviewed earlier that day, I was so deeply engaged that I was only partially able to hear his words.

I was catapulted quite beyond the room into a realm where reptilian people were in a battle with human beings of our planet. They were from a different dimension of reality and through some opening or tear between our two worlds, they were able to make their way into ours. They were trying to take over our minds and bodies and were extremely focused on domination over our species. I felt I was experiencing some distant time in the beginning of our human presence on this planet.

I was being shown the history and inner workings of these reptilian beings and the long-standing war that raged between our species. Most of them were a sort of lizard-man combination. They stood as a person would stand, on legs, so that they were as tall as me or even taller. Their skin was bumpy and scaled, greenish, pinkish, bluish. They had long dark-pinkish tongues and seemed to communicate telepathically through deep intense glances of their eyes.

I was shown that the reptilian people were aware that humans commonly lost their focus and were asleep to the influences that surrounded them. This lack of centering cause a sort of hole in the human through which the reptilian people's influence could find its way in. Then the human being would consciously or unconsciously begin to act with the coldness of the reptilian attitude. It was a very tough situation.

The reptilian people seemed evil, in that their emotions were heartless, with no sense of compassion. All that moved them was their need to attain their goal and an insatiable appetite for power. As the experience unfolded, I was aware that they had been at this project of trying to control human people for many thousands of years. They understood all of our modern technology and communication methods. They understood our psychology. They had found a way to disguise themselves as humans and bind humans to them through false friendships and relationships, even to win humans over to actually becoming lizard people.

As I lay on my mat, I wondered if any of the people in the room had been taken over by the lizard people. I realized how fearful I was feeling and I did not want to get into projecting my fear onto the others. I was very aware that I was under the influence of a mind-altering substance and I reminded myself that the experience was bound to last only a few more hours.

I tried to shift myself out of this fear, but to no avail. I was working hard to keep calm because the whole of myself, even my body, was terrified. What I had seen had shifted my understanding of my world. I got up to use the bathroom, thinking that by moving my body perhaps my experience would shift also. But when I made my way back to my mat, I found I was still gripped in fear.

Finally, I remembered that I could call on a spirit helper for protection and advice. This turned out to be quite an interesting experience. I called for Jesus, to whom I had not related much since I was a child. He seemed to have the sort of benevolence, love, and power that would protect me from the reptilians. I also called for the spirit of a horse I once had, thinking that its force and energy would help me. Neither Jesus nor the horse appeared.

I then thought about contacting my father, who had died two years before. As I did this, I remembered an experience from my childhood that I had not thought of for ages. My father had badly frightened my mother by coiling up a dead rattlesnake and putting it into our freezer where she would find it. Upon remembering this, I wondered if perhaps he was somehow connected to the reptilian people. If he wasn't, he certainly was a trickster and could not be trusted. This was the first time during the evening that anything personal entered into my experience.

Then, all of a sudden, S appeared to me. This was surprising because I was under the impression that spirits who come to help are the spirits of the dead. But I had been doing experiential personal work with S for quite awhile and had a very deep trust in his presence. I was also aware of his own history of journeying into nonordinary states. I wondered if I had somehow contacted his dreaming body, as Castenada would call it. Seeing S helped me immensely. He told me that I was safe and advised me to take an interest in what I was seeing. He said that I had passed through the door into another world and that the information I was gathering was important in understanding our position on this planet. So, with his help I was able to relax, calm down, and let go of the fear.

Having people or places just appear occurs frequently in my inner work. They seem quite important, so usually I make efforts to allow them and not control them. However, the reptilian beings were still making me too uncomfortable with fear, so I did opt to remove myself from their world.

Soon after, the shaman leading our circle asked everyone to sit up and we began our first round of song. Each member of the circle would in turn allow sound to come from him or her, which would reflect their experience. To me, my voice sounded like that of an old American Indian. I found it very soothing.

I was very thankful for the singing and I did not see the lizard people again after this break. When I again lay down on my mat, my second question, about illustrating Tarot cards, was addressed.

I saw myself lying on the floor. There was a cylindrical hole in my chest over my heart. In the hole was a can, which was filled with the blood of my heart. Resting in the can was a paintbrush. I knew I was being told to paint with the blood of the heart.

I did not get a specific answer to my other question about restlessness, or at least not one that I understood, but I was exceedingly calm the next day. Perhaps my extra energy was scared out of me during the experience!

I felt rather timid about sharing my experience of the lizard people with the group because it seemed so strange. I was shown something that is hard to understand and also hard to explain, but I knew that it was connected to the primitive reptilian brain that we all have. Sometimes now when I see a cruel situation or hear someone spouting disconnected, loveless words, I think perhaps they're coming from the reptilian influence.

I had gone much deeper than most of those around me. My sensitivity to entheogenic substances is very high and a little goes a long way. I now keep my doses light in guided journeys so that I can participate by staying in relation to the circle and guide.

The shaman walked into our circle the next morning wearing a black shirt with two green lizards circled on it. I laughed. I realized that he had been wearing it the night before.

Some years later, I do not think I would experience the same kind of fear in the reptilian people's world if I should ever encounter it again. Now I always begin with contacting my personal helper spirits and animal guides prior to undergoing entheogenic experiences, so I know that I am always safe no matter what I see.

I have often pondered the above experience. Perhaps I peeked into what the ancients called "the world of the salamander" (the element of fire). I notice that my restlessness becomes the strongest when I forget to connect with the things around me on a deep level. Keeping things impersonal was a characteristic of the reptile beings.

As for the Tarot cards, I have been steadily working on them and with them for a number of years now. It has been a wonderful journey.

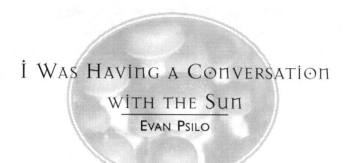

I Was Having a Conversation with the Sun

With the Sun

Evan Psilo

In the late summer, this psy-trance DJ and human rights activist makes an inner journey far, far from his home in New York City to vast alien realities. Then he returns to his body and explores with wonder its "systems of cyclic and fractal organic intelligence."

At about 1 a.m., I ate 8 grams of dried mushrooms, alone in my apartment. I lay on the bed to relax and meditate. In about 20 minutes, the fungal medicine began to seep its gnosis into my muscular system. I started to stretch and feel lethargic, but still a little nervous. Suddenly the rush came on, but my body was still tense with what I felt was an accumulation of emotional issues. I turned on my stomach with my knees bent to my chest, a position I'd seen in certain prayer forms, and I began bowing and rocking while mumbling and breathing heavily, my hands clasped in prayer. I engaged in thoughts, questions, and paradoxes that had been on my mind recently.

I was crying and praying feverishly when a tremendous tidal wave of energy came cascading in from all directions. Then there was a thunderous explosion of lightning in my head and I had a vision of massive iridescent storm clouds rolling and tumbling toward Earth from outer space. It was cosmic in scale, like a nebula. Awed, I asked, "What is this?" The response was, *This is the storm that is coming—you know!* I gave a huge scream like I was coming out from under ten thousand pounds of pressure.

Then commenced the visions. I was on my back and a wave of silent eternity began to cover me like the shade of a cloud. Behind the silence was a distinct presence of movement. I saw I was lying on the floor of a forest. My body began to dissolve into the soil, merging with the Earth. Ten thousand maggots began to eat my flesh, but the feeling was one of unimaginable ecstasy. As my flesh was returning to the cycles of life, I felt a new sensation of my spirit also returning to some forgotten home.

I sank down into the Earth and became a river, which flowed into an ocean. I was continuously experiencing more space to be conscious in and more life to be conscious with. I started wandering through various visions.

An old friendly Rastafarian couple appeared and looked down upon me in a kindly, parental fashion. Then an old man came to stand beside me. He seemed thousands of years old. He offered me his hand and as we walked he showed me many beautiful things, which made me feel very humble. I asked him about the singularity, or *eschaton*, and what that was all about. He said nonchalantly, *Oh, that!* He slowed down as if to say, *Get ready for this!* I felt a rumbling and saw, appearing over the horizon, a big luminous sphere like a great churning furnace of creation. It had networks of moving lights on it, like the sun, and I couldn't look at it very long. I knew creation wasn't finished.

Then I was a miniscule spaceship traveling at high speed through vast alien realities. The awareness in my body released itself into a geometric freedom of which it was composed. The defining attributes of crystalline, biological, technological, and mathematical principles merged into constantly changing objects and devices, each with a life of its own. All these were flying by and whizzing around along an endless galactic highway, passing through futuristic cities and technologically expanded realities. In the cities were pyramids made of luminous circuitry. There were majestically decorated aliens moving about, utilizing their technological interfaces with expert grace.

I thought I should check in on my body back on Earth. As I lifted the hair that was covering my face I found that somehow I managed to get myself into a very awkward position in the opposite corner of the dark room from where I was originally lying down. I rubbed my forehead and saw hundreds of eyes layered together like cells. In the space in front of me I could see gorgeous, morphing mandalas made of eyes and multidimensional jewels. I tried to focus on the surroundings in the apartment and saw eyes on everything. All matter and substance was alive and overflowing with personality.

I went to the roof of the apartment building to enjoy the air and stars. Looking up, the stars seemed to be transmitting messages between them. I could see little lasers of information crisscrossing on spiraling bits of light. One star zoomed right up to my face, like a computer-processed image of a white sphere, then disappeared. Images came from space of gearlike numeric systems, alien mathematical hieroglyphs, and cosmic calendars. I understood the goal of the Mayans and the purpose and challenge in creativity and science. I looked at the moon and it was surrounded by a mandalic vortex of colored light. This delicate geometric grid served specific functions based on the angles of the intersecting lines. I had never seen anything like that in nature before.

As I sat on the roof I explored this new enhanced state of perception and creative flow. One vision was of a particular individual, who could be considered a shaman, resting under a tree with mushrooms growing all over his body. I thought about LSD, which I once used regularly. Through a display of comical images, the changing hallucinations made fun of "the mild twentieth century chemical that makes psychedelic snobs," comparing it to the vast eons that the mushroom makes accessible.

Then I was introduced to some beings that seemed to be from a future where, through their emotionally honest relationships and their technology, they would travel back into time, into history to explore various realities from different perspectives. They would search events and relationships and patterns in different times, such as chanted mantras or collective scenes, to find rare portholes of cosmic information or particular patterns valuable for developing future programming.

I navigated through various archetypal realms of the collective human subconscious as it manifested as complete realities. Reality felt as if it were made of flowing tactile emotions. When I got up to stand, I was surprised by an enormous weight on my shoulders, like I was lifting the entire city as I stood. Finding my balance, the weight became comfortably a part of my body.

I went back down to my bedroom. As I lay down again I felt the shifting weight in my muscles and bones. My body started to burn a little and I couldn't help but squirm and move like a gigantic creature. As I found my breath, I also discovered the endless wonders of biology taking place in a million different places inside my body, which I could freely explore. I was flowing through my blood circulation and with various electrical impulses that traveled along nodes and intersected pathways and grids, causing wonderful uncoilings and spastic releasing of tensions in my body that I understood had been building up for years. I was filled with wonder at the incredible systems of cyclic and fractal organic intelligence and the myriad cellular forms vibrating with purpose. It was amazing to comprehend the massive organism in which I live.

I started to make sounds I had never heard before. Every shift in resonance and tone led to strange significance and new, textured sounds. The sound was not a separate thing but an open channel of the biological, temporal, emotional, the light, color, and form.

My cat scratched the door and I let her in. With eyes wide open she hopped through mythical and fantastical appearances. She perched on my shoulder and purred. With her permission, I fell into her being. The purring was no simple fleshy vibration; it was a resonating echo in a cavernous abyss, home to a timeless ecstatic life. Her purring was as loud and strong as a generator that keeps the planet's heart beating. When I became separated from her by reacting with awe, she kicked my tranced butt out of her sensitive universe.

I suddenly felt like I was wasting time and the peak was beginning to subside, so I went back up to the roof. The sun was rising and the sky was ineffably beautiful. The air and colors and details of everything were alive, filled with light and beauty. I looked at the tops of some buildings and they literally smiled with their architecture, moldings, and windows. They stretched upwards and outwards on top, as buildings do in cartoons.

I lay down to enjoy the clouds and the sun. The clouds seemed enthusiastic to show what they could do. I could interact with them and guide which way the winds would take them, making spirals and shapes in the clouds that were real and not a perceptual distortion. I squinted my eyes to the sun, which poured forth rich, brilliant energy and warmth. I was having a conversation with the sun, receiving intelligent information and wisdom from our star. I saw curved flares being slowly emitted from its surface. I felt how different dimensions coexist beyond our conventional understanding of space and time. I contemplated dark matter as space spirit. I had numerous revelations dealing with different stunts and wonders of the infinite and the balance between simplicity and complexity, repetition and change. I also felt very connected to the collective happenings, of outside activity, so I decided to go to the Park.

I walked a couple blocks to Central Park. The trees and plants and stones were radiant with thriving life. I could see the growth happening before my eyes. I even tried to communicate with the Gaian spirit, but it felt new and strange to both of us to try to communicate on a personal level. The cooperative communication and general awareness exhibited in the ecological matrix of life was stunning enough as it was.

I sat down by one of my favorite waterfalls. As I relaxed to the sound of falling water and slowed my breath, I straightened my back and, like a xylophone, seven ascending tones clinked up my spine, "tink tink tink tink tink tink tink!" The freedom in that core moment of alignment was peaceful and astounding.

A woman was sitting behind me and when I looked at her she seemed to blossom like flower petals blooming in time-lapse. She embodied various mysterious goddess archetypes. I let myself gaze at her briefly, but I sensed fragility in the air, so I decided to move on. Looking back again at her she removed her hands from her thighs and released what I can only describe as babies: birdlike newborn entities of the space spirit that I previously mentioned that flew into the air. Whether they were malevolent spirits previously possessing her or new autonomous consciousness born of her, I couldn't tell, but she seemed elated after this occurrence.

The marvelous way in which we are all communally involved and closely connected became apparent to me. I felt the potential for great healing and delicate forms of loving communication, but also the potential for evil magic, selfish manipulation, or spirit possession born of fear. Waves of children laughing and the busy chaos of daytime in Manhattan filled the air. I went back home to contemplate and rest from this exciting trip.

The next day my vision was incredibly acute, sharper than I remember it ever being. I also found out that the previous day the sun's solar flare activity was higher than it had been in a hundred years.

The physical healing I experienced from that trip was amazing. Serious muscle tensions had been completely released. I was more in tune with my body as a result of the mushroom medicine. Psychological fears and habits that I had carried with me for years were healed. The visions I had experienced were enough to keep my imagination and intellect busy for years.

The mushroom experience is sacred because it is real, a part of the wonderful workings of organic and ecological intelligence. Mushrooms are healing medicine and a most remarkable tool for religious or spiritual understanding. Sensitivity, empathy, humor, and intuition are enhanced. So-called psychic experiences and precognition can be normal senses in these states. The tryptamine hallucinogen experience is timeless and cosmic; the essential consciousness of life and love and all that they entail become apparent and important in these experiences.

Any powerful tool begs a mature and humble approach. The experience offered by mushrooms may seem archaic, but it must be studied if we wish to develop the sciences of *psyche* and *soma*. This and other cherished methods of developing awareness must be protected and defended, in the name of science, religion, and the creative imagination.

SHADOW, BE MY FRIEND

GANESHA

This forty-one-year-old actor and healer communes with spirits of plants, water, stars, and lizards. He meets the great god Pan and gains insight into the union of Nature and Spirit.

I was invited to participate in a medicine circle to be held in a natural setting of the Sierra Madre Mountains of California. The medicine was to be the sacred mushrooms, the "Little Princes." All of the shamanic circle work I had done up to this point had been indoors with a rather formal structure. This event would be looser, with freedom to leave the circle during the journey to commune with Nature. There would be three rounds during the evening, times to come together around the fire and share our experiences.

The group leader thought of himself as a guide, both in the physical world, taking us to a special location, and as a guide to the inner wealth of Nature to be found there. It would be a gathering of medicine men and women contributing equally to shaping the event in the moment.

I had formulated certain intentions to take to the circle. I wanted to move more into my higher self, but I did not want to use spirituality to evade looking at my Shadow. I also wanted to determine if my sexual life brought my best self forward. Further, a relationship had just ended for me, and I wanted to ask the medicine to affirm my life path. I wanted to review my behavior over the past year of this relationship

235

with equanimity and clarity, so that I could learn any inherent lessons. Never one to scrimp on intentions, I would also ask for vision around my healing work, to be able to love more, stay open to others, and be more generous in my giving.

On the Friday afternoon in early August, eleven of us gathered at the trailhead. The trek into the wilderness took about two hours, during which time civilization melted away. Finally, a fairly steep descent down a rocky trail brought us into a womblike space bordered by trees, a high rock wall, and rushing water of a large creek. It was an ideal location in terms of its privacy and access to the creek, large rocks, and stretches of vegetation.

After our hot and sweaty hike in, everyone stripped to refresh themselves in the clear cool stream and nearby mountain pools. I added to my intentions the desire to commune with the nature spirits.

After an evening circle of stating our intentions, we slept. The next morning, we all fasted in preparation for the evening session. We spent the day swimming, hiking, and exploring the surrounding area. As the afternoon wore on, we gathered wood for a fire and then moved into more restful activities, such as napping, yoga, journaling, and healing massage.

The guide would be taking medicine along with us, while his wife would be abstaining as our sitter. She would ground our connection to the physical world and tend the fire in the fire pit against the massive vertical rock wall.

We all laid our pads and sleeping bags in a semicircle around the fire. At dusk, we each ingested about three grams of dried psilocybin mushrooms.

When I first started coming on to the medicine, I wondered if perhaps I had taken too much, as I felt it very strongly. I got cold and fearful, even paranoid, and my legs were shaking. I knew that the depth and strength of the session often corresponded to this coming-on period. It would be a profound session.

To ride out this uncomfortable part of the journey, I burrowed into my sleeping bag and stayed nestled for perhaps forty-five minutes. I saw colored lights and geometric forms and became aware of tension in my body. I used my meditation training to release. I knew this to be clearing and centering for the visions that would come.

When my discomfort subsided, I poked my head out and oriented myself. I rose and moved away from the circle to an area I had spotted before the session. There I knelt on a soft sandy bed, bordered by tall lush plants. Next to me, the creek narrowed into a strong flow of water that descended to a gentle waterfall. The plants were luminescent, glowing with an inner light that spilled out into the ether around them. I sensed the presence of faeries in this natural garden. I could hear them speak in sweet singsong tones.

Two plants to my right were vividly communicating with me. I asked them if I could stay and play, and they welcomed me without hesitation. As I relaxed into my new situation, I became aware of many presences. In a tree that hung over the pond dwelt a grandfather spirit, very old and wise. In the running water, I sensed water elementals and knew them to be undines. A white presence was hovering over a nearby pond. This I took to be the deva of this area.

I opened to simply observe the existence of these beings and to receive whatever communication they offered. They were transmitting qualities rather than thoughts: a blissfulness and ease from the faeries, a contagious there-ness from the undines, a quiet dignity from the tree spirit, and buoyancy from the pond deva.

I began to hear animal noises, wild cries, coming from the high rocks. I made out the form of our guide hanging from a rock. The sounds were coming from him. He came over to me, and I greeted him. I could feel the energy in the embrace go all the way to our core, and I knew in that instant how profound healing work could be. The experience was so powerful that I had to sit down.

He returned to the rocks, and I returned to my place by the pond. I became aware of a bright, pulsating star overhead. It sent down a corridor of light to me, and I could see a webbed network of light going out from the star into the rest of the sky. The star seemed to come closer to me and transmit its energy directly.

Eventually the star withdrew and my vision dissolved, so that I perceived no more than a star in the night sky. I turned back to the faeries, but they too had withdrawn. Feeling alone, I lay sobbing over my condition, the human condition, of aloneness. I cried for myself, separated from my family of origin, recently estranged from my lady and her little boy, whom I had come to love as my own. I cried for all the people who are alone. My thought was, "Every loved one goes away. All the loved ones go away."

Soon after, the journeyers were summoned back to the circle for the first round. The energy of the night shifted to a feeling of joy and revelry. Drums, rattles, and other musical instruments were brought out. Up to this point, I had been subjective and subdued, but now I was swept up in the spirit of celebration and tribal community. I felt power rising up within me. I could feel it in everyone. I felt we were a group of shamans coming together to share our wisdom and our lore. I perceived qualities in myself of a healer. I listened intently to others as they spoke or expressed in other ways, holding them with my energy and supporting them with love and attention.

I had a sharp-sounding rattle that I had received from a Huichol shaman. During this first round, I felt it as an ally and an extension of my power. It was alive, keeping rhythm with the drum, punctuating the remarks of people as they talked. It seemed to be the rattle of a snake, activating and awakening reptilian energy in the Earth and kundalini energy in others and myself. When it came time for me to express in the round, I sang. I went on to pay homage to the Earth, then to the Heavens and back down again, uniting Above and Below within the human heart. My own heart felt open and present to give and receive love.

I perceived one woman as a Lizard Lady, embodying the energy of Lizard and expressing it. I encouraged her with my rattle. She came over to crouch directly in front of me and we had a face-to-face confrontation. We were two lizards having a showdown, but it had an electric sexuality and playfulness. As we locked eyes, I saw her face as convex, with everything else becoming a faint background. She emitted a guttural growl and I responded in kind. Then she seemed to flip backwards and retreat to her spot. I lay back and chuckled.

I saw our guide lurking in the shadows to my left. He began to play on his harmonica a lilting old-world tune. His countenance was dark and mysterious, as though he were the Pied Piper transporting us to another time and place. He maintained eye contact with me and through the music, I felt I could see into his deepest nature, that I knew his secret urges and desires and that they were mine, too. Still playing the harmonica, he picked up a log and began to dance with it on his shoulder, emulating the burdens and cares of life, but lightening the load with humor and charm.

A chant started, calling on the Shadow to come forward into our awareness. The Shadow was everything that is ignored, denied, and suppressed in our natures, that then has power over us and can even sabotage our lives. Focusing our awareness on it allows us to observe and accept it. Integrated, it becomes part of our larger conscious self and personal power. To face the Shadow is to have it as an ally.

As we chanted our invocation, the space around and through us changed to deep dark underworld images and the serpentine power of the kundalini. The rocks took on hues of orange and purple and a reptilian consciousness that caused them to shift and undulate. I spoke aloud: "Shadow, be my friend."

When Lizard Lady took the talking staff, I saw a palace chamber surrounding her as she spoke. The rocky trail leading down to our enclave became a stone staircase in England around the time of King Arthur. I saw our guide as a king, and the woman as a Druid priestess speaking before him in his chamber, bringing him a message of the sovereignty of Nature. It seemed to be a critical time when Nature was being denied and demonized by certain Christian forces.

One other circle participant was next to Lizard Lady and seemed to have the role of a counselor to the king. He sought to bend the King's ear and deny the sanctity of Nature.

As this vision continued, I saw a spirit appear at the top of the stairs. It was humanlike in its presence, but in its form was a glowing orb of white light. It seemed to bridge the gap between the past of the vision and current time. It moved down the staircase and hovered midway for the duration of the vision. It remained a nonintrusive presence that emanated a calm, potent truth of Beingness, observing and accepting the conflict that played out below.

I carry a sacred pipe in the Native American tradition, using tobacco as a medium of prayer. We lit the tobacco and passed the pipe around the circle. Prayers were verbalized and sent to Great Spirit on the wings of sacred smoke. Blessings were conveyed to loved ones. The passing of the prayer smoke was a unifying device, bonding the brothers and sisters present together in sacred space.

After the tobacco ceremony was concluded, the guide sat next to me and began to play a recorder. As he played, he gazed into my eyes as though to communicate something to me. My perception shifted and I could see him as the animal god Pan, the very spirit of Nature. He *became* Pan, with horns and hooves and animal sensuality. With extraordinary presence and allure, he transmitted an experience of the totality of the kingdom of Nature. I felt an excitement and a connection to the soul of Nature.

In the third round, I addressed the pain of ending my relationship. I had experienced terminations of relationships before, and I knew that in time I would get over the loss of this woman and that there would be others. What troubled me most was the loss of the child. I felt great sadness that he would feel abandoned by me. It brought up the pain of having an absent father myself for a good deal of my childhood. I had no answers. I knew only that I needed to proceed with equanimity. I knew I would honor my relationship with the boy and remain present in his life.

As I reflect upon the lessons of this journey and how my life has been influenced by it, I see that the central theme has been to honor Nature and its in-dwelling divinity. My connection to Nature and its beings, both physical and nonphysical, grows deeper daily. Through this journey and others, the Earth-based sexuality I envisioned has become a part of my own nature. Although I may still hear inner voices of sexual shame and guilt, I no longer give them credence, because I know of something larger. I continue to delve beneath the surface for that which is hidden in my motives and behaviors, in order to realize a more perfect whole. The experiences I had during this journey have contributed to a healing method that incorporates the energies of Spirit, Earth, and the life-force, all united by the inclusive principle of love, the most effective healing tool of all. And, finally, the tribal sense of community that I felt that night is something I am always seeking, and sometimes finding.

WHERE ANCIENT SPIRITS DWELL AND THE AIR HUMS WITH MAGIC AND MYSTERY

CAT L.

A woman writer in her forties takes mushrooms among the rocks and ruins of the Southwest and tunes into the spirits of the Ancient Ones who loved the land.

My partner C and I planned to take mushrooms together outdoors in a power spot. We prepared 5 dried grams of *P. cubensis* in advance by chopping it finely in a blender. Once we arrived at our destination, the dried material was added to a pot of boiling water along with instant miso broth to create a palatable mushroom soup.

The setting was the desert ruins of a vanished southwestern American Indian tribe, in a secluded wash between two cliffs. We set up a makeshift altar on a flat rock, where we placed a turquoise frog fetish, a candle, a rawhide rattle, a clay ocarina in the shape of a turtle, a carved stone pipe packed with sacramental smoking material, and a string of colored beads. We heard the distant rumble of thunder across the canyon; the air was electric and moist and the temperature a very pleasant 85 degrees. Masses of white cumulus clouds were assembling at the horizon while the sun shone brightly high above. A light wind carried the scent of sage and desert soil and the promise of an approaching storm.

Sure enough, a gentle intermittent sprinkle began to fall. I lit a bit of dried sage and asked the spirits to join us and give us their help and protection. We each took a ceremonial puff from our pipe. Somehow these actions served to ground and comfort us, for we knew we were about to embark on a powerful, potentially awesome journey, fraught with uncertainty and mystery. We each expressed our intent for the trip: mine was to experience what it was like to be one of the Anasazi people, the extinct inhabitants of this land, and also to be shown a way to help heal my mother's arthritic pain. C expressed a similar intention focused on healing and consciousness expansion. Both of us wished to learn whatever we could from the beautiful natural surroundings we had been drawn to for this journey.

The soup was pleasant-tasting enough, and we sat back and waited to feel the effects. A beautiful panorama spread out below us: a slight slope dotted with low brush, rocks, and sage, a large, beneficent-seeming cottonwood tree at the bottom of the wash and sheer canyon walls across from us. These multicolored layers of stone, formed eons ago, spoke eloquently of the natural forces that had shaped this land. I was keenly aware of the presence of the four elements: the electrically charged gusts of wind that heralded the approaching storm, the lightly pattering first drops of rain, the occasional flashes of lightning, our tiny candle flame, and the sandy earth and variegated rock formations all around us.

Soon, I began to feel heat rising in my blood, a pressure in the right hemisphere of my skull, a slight nausea, and rushes of energy in my body. When I closed my eyes, strange images appeared: bejeweled masks that moved and morphed, mosaic-like faces that approached and dissolved into new forms and colors as I watched. Liquid ambers, blood reds, flaming oranges and yellows, cerulean blues like molten lava bubbled and flowed across my eyelids. I opened my eyes. The world appeared normal, except that the large cottonwood tree in the wash below was undulating back and forth as if made of some gelatinous green liquid. The canyon walls were moving too, the layers shifting and rippling as if an invisible force were moving through them. I closed my eyes and again the strangely beautiful alien masks danced before me.

Feeling increasingly restless and nauseous, I began to move about, crawling on my hands and knees like some primitive animal, climbing up on a nearby rock and wrapping my arms around it. Unable to settle down, I crawled and crouched, digging into the soil with my fingers. A low growl rose in my throat, and I roared as the contents of my stomach erupted onto the ground. Relieved, I crawled back to my tarp and lay down, while the weird energy continued to course through my body. What is this magic, I wondered, that can so alter my perception and consciousness?

I listened to the buzzing of insects in the preternatural quiet that seemed suddenly to have descended on the place. An intense humming filled my head, an insect's buzz magnified a hundred times. The bejeweled visions were gone and now there was only a crisp darkness behind my eyes. The mysterious hum elicited the palpable sense of a presence nearby, a presence that wished to remain hidden but was clearly as aware of me, as I was of it. In retrospect, I call this phase of the journey "the Portal," perhaps the portal to the land of the dead or what Terence McKenna called "an ecology of souls." I wondered if I was to pass beyond the Portal that day.

Presently, I was drawn to the edge of our little rock-sheltered area, so I moved to the more exposed shelf at the outer boundary of the outcropping and lay on my back with my arms spread out and my knees bent. I began to writhe about, enjoying the sensation of the warm sun on my body. I undulated my hips in pleasure, feeling somehow that the sun was entering me erotically.

After some time, I became aware of a whistling noise behind me and turned to find my bemushroomed partner standing naked on the rock above me, calling me back from my tryst with the sun. Feeling energized and positively charged, I joined him and flung off my clothes as well. We embraced and lay down on the tarp, and enjoyed cuddling together and sharing observations about the weirdness and subtle difficulty of the trip. It seemed that this period of difficulty or strangeness was a necessary part of the experience that prepared the way for the heightened awareness and intensity of the journey that followed. We were definitely feeling sensual, but coordinating our bodies sufficiently to make love was out of the question, so we lay in a dreamlike silence together for a while, until a mourning dove's distinctive cry aroused us. We decided that it was time to gather ourselves and move on.

Summoning our attention to the task of repacking our belongings and leaving no sign of our presence at the site, we set out down the hillside toward the trail. The land seemed more alive than ever. Colors and scents were heightened by the moisture and by the changing light of the storm-dancing sky. A refreshing breeze blew across the desert. I felt safe in my bright orange poncho and exhilarated to be up and walking about. At that moment a small rabbit appeared at the side of the trail. It became aware of us at the same time and froze in its tracks and twitched its nose. I froze too, fascinated by this lovely creature just a few feet away. Her pelt was a soft creamy blonde color with rust highlights and she seemed to be imbued with a magical glow. Go ask Alice, indeed!

We headed on up the trail toward the ruins of a small dwelling consisting of four or five rooms. I stood next to one of the ruined walls, placed my palms on the surface and immediately found myself flooded with an intense emotion of wonder and sadness. I felt the presence of the ancient people who had lived here, knew them to be people just like me, who loved the land so deeply that they created dwellings patterned after the rich and beautiful canyon walls that surrounded them. It was as if they were engaged in a deep respectful dialog with the Earth as they designed their architecture in its image. The dwellings here echoed the variegated patterns of the landscape, wholly at one with nature and sheltering their human inhabitants with simple ease. My heart was touched by the ancestral spirits, which seemed to hover in the air around us and percolate up from the ground below. I wept joyously at the beauty and mystery of this deeply-felt presence. Here, it seemed, I did pass through the Portal to the realm of the Ancestors.

As the sun was setting, we decided it was time to start back. Our feeling of awe and appreciation for the continually unfolding beauty of the natural landscape remained strong and our energy was high and positive. The clouds were thickening and spectacular intermittent flashes of lightning pierced the sky. As we drove out of the area, our amazement and wonder at the divine beauty of the landscape deepened. The skies rumbled and flashed with thunder and lightning. The group of horses we had passed on the way in was there to see us safely on our way, and we paused briefly to whistle and click our good-byes to them. A long drive down dark rainy highways brought us back to our hotel late that night, where a warm shower and cozy bed awaited us. We thanked the spirits for their gifts and fell into a welcome and dream-blessed sleep.

For the next several days I experienced a distinct afterglow, a heightened appreciation for food, sex, and the simple pleasures of human interaction. I told my mother how much I had enjoyed the ruins, and how the trip had shown me why her father (my grandfather) had loved what he called "the Indian country" so much. I felt a strong emotional connection with her and with my grandfather when I shared this with her. Perhaps in some mysterious way, I had called in my grandfather's spirit to facilitate my own heightened awareness of his birthplace. It is a land where ancient spirits dwell in the rocks and ruins, and the air hums with magic and mystery when one is attuned to their frequency with the help of the fungal ally.

My Heart Was the Doorway to Greater Vision and Awareness

Abraham L.

In these accounts of mushroom experiences, a therapist in his forties identifies with and learns from his clients' heroin addiction as well as the regressed confusion of the insane and the suffering of his Jewish ancestors.

I was forty-one years old when, in a solitary, ritual setting I ingested the mushrooms with the intention of reviewing my life, personal relationships, and my work at a methadone clinic. After some initial body and emotional processing, I moved into experiencing an ecstatic appreciation of life and the flow of energy that was moving through me. Every moment was a beautiful birthing, rich with experience and information at all levels.

Remembering my intention to look at my work, I thought about heroin addiction. I wondered how heroin addicts actually feel, drawn so powerfully to the experience of their drug that they make great sacrifices for it. I opened to a kind of empathy for them, and for the injustice done them by the persecution and criminalization of their pursuit of a particular state of consciousness through a particular substance. After all, I was engaging in a similar pursuit through the ingestion of the mushrooms. I wondered if we were doing the same thing. I started looking at my bias, that what I did was okay, while what they did was sick. I began to see heroin addicts as possibly even more devoted to their quest for some experience of oneness than I am. Would I give up

everything, even face ridicule and social isolation, for what I am seeking? In some ways they seemed like devoted spiritual seekers who have
become martyrs.

At that point I noticed that I was doing a lot of thinking. My
thoughts seemed very interesting and exciting and the insight about
judging heroin addicts seemed useful, yet I lacked a sense of my full
body. When I moved more into my body, I recognized that the way to
explore this issue was to ask to experience what heroin is like, since I
had never tried it. I asked to have this experience in a prayerful way and
opened myself.

After a short while, I was no longer thinking of this issue, but I
noticed that I was feeling kind of flat. No pain, and kind of pleasant,
but without the ecstatic "birthing of the universe" feeling that I had
experienced earlier. I wondered if the journey had ended, but I definitely
felt I was still in an altered state, just without any sense of wonder or
aliveness. I then remembered my request and realized that I was experiencing the pain-less but joy-less experience of opiates.

As soon as I made this realization, I noticed that something was half in
and half out of my chest. I had no real reaction to it, no fear, and no incli-
nation or motivation to do anything about it. However, something in me
was rising to question whether this was a healthy thing to allow. As I
started to say, "Wait a minute!" the many-tentacled thing took on more life
and tried to get deeper inside me. I knew I wanted it out, but I didn't know
how and couldn't make it reverse itself. I felt powerless and impotent.

I opened inwardly for help. The next thing that entered my mind
was the Beatles refrain, "All you need is love." At first this seemed
silly—then I got it. An energy, a pink light that I can only describe as
Higher Love, started to flow through me. The more aware of it I
became, the more I opened to it, the more powerfully it flowed. The
creature began to back out of my body. At each step of its withdrawal
I felt more myself, connected to my spiritual energy, as though I had
been in a trance and had awakened.

The creature moved to a distance several feet from me. I felt
strength and commitment in relationship to it. When I sat up and
focused intently, it turned into a beautiful woman, very sexy and seduc-
tive. I felt aroused and drawn in, but when I became aware of being

manipulated, the being became very fierce and scary. It made other shape-shifting efforts to put me off balance.

I called on all the strength and wisdom of my spirit allies to support me. My vision expanded to a global view of this creature connected to a world-wide network that had tentacles into the addictive behaviors of all humans—not only those involved with drugs, but with all manner of greed, violence, and war. I faced the Beast, evil, the Devil, saying simply, "Keep your distance." I saw heroin addicts as just some of the instruments through which this entity sucked up power.

I asked for guidance and was told that I could not destroy it. Instead, I was to learn from it and keep very conscious of its nature and activity. As it was a part of the evolutionary journey of all humanity, I needed to learn to be with it in an appropriate relationship, to come to terms with it. It seemed to have a purpose in a planetary sense. Also, I understood that I was not alone. The energy that had come in to rescue me earlier was part of a network of light-worker beings of which I was one. This was an initiatory experience that I clearly remember.

As I returned to ordinary consciousness and my work, I have continued to be aware of this encounter. I more deeply respect and understand the Twelve Steps of AA, which are helpful teaching to so many self-defined addicts. I remember my own feelings of powerlessness as an isolated personality in the face of this force that intended to take me over. I remember the Higher Power, the great love, which, when I turn to it, frees me from the grips of the demon. I feel great compassion, understanding, and empathy for the addicts of the world, so easily seduced by forces ready to sap life-energy. And finally, I have made a commitment to align with that network of Beings who are engaging the dark forces and channeling the energy that liberates us.

Many years later, I was reconciling my relationship with my older brother, who was a homeless schizophrenic man. As I sought to connect with him, I remembered the above experience and found comfort in the teachings of the mushroom. Early researchers of psychedelics believed these substances could help therapists understand the experience of the mentally ill. I've verified the truth of this for myself, and pray that such research can someday again be conducted.

This time I was forty-five years old and in a group in a ritual setting. As I began to feel the effect of the mushrooms, a wonderful feeling of relaxation came over me. I was seeing beautiful patterns synchronized with the music. Some of the patterns appeared like Jewish letters and symbols streaming across in blues, golds, and silvers, colors I associated with Jewishness. This seemed to validate my recent explorations of my roots and my intentions to celebrate the Sabbath and Rosh Hashanah.

Then I became concerned with noises I was hearing from other group members. I became confused about whether I should be helping them. This confusion seemed familiar, in that I often feel uncertain about whether to reach out to others or stay in my own process. In this instance, the confusion seemed like an unsolvable puzzle and I saw myself as incapable of making any decisions or choices. I soon found myself in a chaotic place, unaware of where I was or of my surroundings.

The music was passing through me, saying, "There is no time," in long beautiful refrains. I noticed that I was singing these words, although there was no intention on my part to be singing. It was happening through me and I was observing. I again became aware of my surroundings and the presence of the group. I became more conscious of my part in forming the sound as I entered into a cocreative process. The sound felt like the vibration of Life, that was creating me, then coming through me with my added inflection. I noticed that I could move my mouth slightly and send the message in a particular direction or throughout the room. My thoughts could shift the message itself, so that it (I) would sing, "We are beyond time; time is no more."

I was alternating between periods of peace and periods of confusion. Sometimes I had no understanding of where I was, only that I was in a place that I could not comprehend. I felt I was being initiated into this place beyond space and time, beyond death, and that there could be no going back. I had a feeling of being stuck in a confusing puzzle, with a feeling of shame that I was lost, which only made me more confused and lost.

In moments of lucidity, I looked out and saw that we were gathered in what felt like an ancient circle, the circle that has always been, and that by our focused human ritual, we were assisting the process of creating the world. It was clear to me that indigenous people had participated in such ceremonies aware in a humble way of their role in cocreating life.

I was rolling on the floor, babbling. The group leader was asking me to move to another place where I could make noise and be less distracting to the others. The prospect of moving seemed inconceivable, since I was experiencing myself as something like a gaseous mass of foam, without form. With his reassurance that I could do it, I felt feet and legs take form as my attention was directed to them, and I could walk, with assistance. As I saw my body manifesting from thought, the notion that "thought directs energy" took on new meaning.

Away from the group, I lay down, went very deep, and became aware of being pure awareness or consciousness—except for one tiny area of holding. This was not "me," in the ordinary sense, feeling tension somewhere in "my" body or mind. This was just some identity aware of something "down there." As my awareness touched the tension, it released and I was flooded with an orgasmic sensation and a feeling of ecstatic oneness. As I returned to more self-identity, it occurred to me that it had lasted a very long time and I was amazed at how sustained and nonspasmodic it was. (I later realized that I had urinated, that I had released all tension in my bladder.)

I was in a very confused state again, moving my hands in front of me to the music and playing with being God or being related to by God, talking and singing aloud. I realized that I was crazy, and that this is what people are put into asylums for. I was experiencing true madness, yet I was comfortable with it. I realized that I was lying in a separate room from the group because of my madness, in the same way that people are placed in asylums so their madness won't bother other people. I felt a connection with inmates in psychiatric wards working through similar processes. I was conscious that I had an advantage, being in a supportive environment, and that I was in a process of working through my madness to true sanity.

I felt great compassion for my mad colleagues as I patiently danced through spiritual development. I was coming to terms with a paradox of being God and being related to by God at the same time. I also explored the nature of the guru and how people can relate to the guru as God at the center of the universe running the show. I played with asserting my godness against the guru's godness. I understood that those who have gone mad experiencing things along these lines have been doing humanity a service. I knew that I was moving through a stage, and that I would soon be able to relate my godness in more skillful ways than lying in a bed waving my hands in front of me, giggling and talking with myself. But I was content with my present condition.

I was dealing with infantile processes. I was learning, without concepts of what I am, that I was distinct from everything else, learning to express or assert my distinctness. I saw that my "orgasm" was very much the way a baby would just let that bit of tension go, to rest in the oneness.

A little later I realized that I was tired and that I was returning to time-space reality. My judgment mind started to question whether I had learned what I needed from the experience, but I also knew that it was time to assimilate, rest, and reconnect.

Five or six years later, I was actively working with people engaged in fostering dialogue between Jews and Arabs, working to bring an end to the Israeli occupation of Palestinian territories. This vision has given me insight and empathy for the pain and fear at the root of Israeli behavior. I understand the primacy of healing the heart for peace in the world.

During this session, which was in a group ritual setting outdoors in the mountains, I did a conscious journey to the world below ordinary reality. I became aware of the entanglements of many past relationships with roots like knots, tight and painful, but they were being disentangled and untied. A weary, frustrated feeling filled me and this healing work seemed endless. I felt heavy in my heart. I remembered that in previous journeys, my heart had been the doorway to greater vision and awareness, so I moved into it with my breath and awareness. I became aware of my father and his father and the cold armor that separates us, as men, from certain emotions, especially painful emotions. I could see the stiff, defensive heart posture that prevents me from having deeper relationships with women, and I felt this armor dissolving and releasing.

I decided to go to a deeper level to explore the lessons that underlay this experience. I immediately sensed my Jewish ancestors and became aware of the collective Jewish heart that connects to all individual Jews, including myself. I realized that part of my early disaffection with my family and the Jewish community was an aversion to the heart-pain of Jewish suffering. As a young person, I sensed that this unspoken pain was a cause of the separation of "my people" from "the other," the *goyim*. Since I rejected this separation, I also rejected the pain, but now I was able to feel the agony of centuries of persecution, alienation and isolation, of being the stranger in a strange land, and of the Holocaust.

For the first time, I understood, felt empathy for, and accepted this pain in my heart. Instead of being overwhelmed, I felt expansion, ease, and comfort in accepting my place in the scheme of things. In accepting my connection to my people, I was accepting myself as I am. I recognized that I chose to be born a Jew and that there was a karmic purpose to this choice. Without any clear instance of past life memory, I felt that my own heart-path was in tune with the group awakening now going on amongst the Jewish people. I felt a merging of my karma with my people's experience. I recognized that my work as a Jew was more than utilizing Hebrew ritual or prayer; it was to hold awareness of this connection and to open my heart as an act of planetary importance.

The lesson of acceptance of purpose and ancestry could not have been clearer and I knew I could avoid it only at my own peril. I asked my ancestors what I could bring forth from this experience and I was told, "Open your heart, open your heart, so that I and you and all our people and this planet may be healed."

Almost twenty years later, I am teaching workshops and leading groups with the theme of the compassionate warrior. The goal is to open to the deep sources of spiritual strength and compassion within and integrate this with engagement in social and political work in the world. As I began teaching these classes, I realized that I have been developing the skills and awareness I need to manifest my vision. I recognize that such inner work is vital to bringing justice and peace into the world. I feel deep gratitude for the mushrooms and their teachings. They have shown me ways to be present with strength and love in the face of great darkness and evil.

It Was the Divine Play of Hide and Seek

Jason Serle

Journeying with the mushroom in a focused, humble, sacred manner brought this man to a profound state of timeless emptiness, filled with knowledge. The sense of a separate self falls away and he feels ecstatically merged with others.

Although I had taken the sacred mushrooms on a couple of occasions previously, this was to be the first time that I approached them as a sacrament for the purpose of healing. I was dealing with a certain disease within myself that manifested as a subtle confusion as to who I really was and where I was going. This is no doubt the dilemma of mankind in general, but for each individual these fundamental questions find their own particular expression or focus. For me, the question that played a leading role in the play of my mind for some years was that of free will. Although I could conceive of many possible answers, I could settle on none. So it was with this question that I approached the sacred mushroom one night in May.

My partner was on holiday and I was at home alone. I had prepared the room with a simple altar of objects of personal significance and a comfortable mattress with plenty of pillows. It was about ten o'clock on a Sunday night, so everything was silent and the room was in pitch darkness. Having spent the day fasting in quiet contemplation and having bathed as an act of ritual purification, I ingested 5 grams of *Stropharia cubensis* in the silent darkness. After slowly chewing the mushrooms and sipping on freshly squeezed orange juice, I lay back to await the effects.

There was a slight nervous tension in my stomach and after what seemed to be only a short while, I began to feel the occasional shiver shoot up my spine. This sensation grew stronger and before long I felt and heard a high pitched hiss of white noise that seemed to be moving up and down the length of my body, turning my solid frame into a rarefied field of coherent electrical pulses. Several times I touched myself to confirm my existence. Even though I could clearly feel the boundary that was my skin, I knew that this feeling was merely the result of electrical transmissions being interpreted by my brain. This recognition dominated my sensations.

As my material self continued to break down, my body image shattered and its constituent parts were rearranged. My extremities had been removed and reattached to different parts of my torso. My head now issued from where my legs should have been, my legs from my shoulders and my arms from different places on my sides. For the duration of perhaps a minute, every time I moved a certain part of my body, I felt it moving in this strange new configuration. It was disturbing to feel so deformed, but I was fascinated by this unique perspective, which felt as real to me then as what I am feeling right now.

I was attempting to relax and surrender into the experience and was quite unaware of any disturbances in the visual field. When I shifted my attention into this area, I began to see faint geometric patterns but little more. By now I could feel surges of energy moving through me, increasing in intensity, and I felt a slight fear at being overwhelmed by the experience. The shivers continued and I experienced a restlessness that caused me to constantly change my position. I also found myself yawning with an unusual frequency.

Suddenly the two-dimensional blackness of the room opened out into an infinite three-dimensional void in which I was suspended, yet free to move in any direction I pleased. In the absence of anything to verify my motion and with nothing to measure the passage of time, I dwelt in a state of timelessness, an eternal realm that until then had been mere speculation.

It became clear that this great emptiness actually contained the sum total of all possible experiences. I began traveling into my past to relive events from my childhood as if they were actually and presently taking place, in the true fullness of the five senses. The mere thought of a person would bring me to them instantly. In a relatively short time, it seemed that I had visited anyone who had ever meant anything to me. It soon became clear that I could not only visit people I have known, but I could actually *become* them.

It became apparent that my own choice was falling away and there was a strong sensation of being *led* from scene to scene. The entity leading me seemed to know me better than I did myself, for as each experience unfolded I was amazed that it was exactly the experience that I wanted and needed. It was as if something were reading my thoughts even before they surfaced in my own conscious mind.

My awareness drifted from person to person, becoming them and living as them before morphing into somebody else. Family, friends, lovers, and acquaintances, I became all of them and I was astonished that the basic sensation of existence was identical for all. Thoughts changed, the mechanism of apperception and the paradigms from which things were beheld were surely different. These things are forever changing in all of us. Even so, there was no discernible distinction between being myself and being someone else.

There are two reasons for this that have since occurred to me. One is that my consciousness was one hundred percent identified with the person I had become, so there was nothing outside of that to make a comparison with. It was not that there was a "me" pretending to be "them," or a "me" plugged into the five senses of another. It was more like the "me" had *become* "them," therefore the "them" was now "me."

The second reason is that perhaps I had identified with the one Ground of Being, the great ocean of awareness that gives rise to the feeling of "I am" in all of us. It was this feeling, prior to all thought, that was identical in all those whom I became. At one point I became my mother giving birth to me, or perhaps it was me giving birth to my mother—I could not tell—but the experience was as real as any I have ever had: the contractions, the mixed feelings of pain and joy, and the relief at it all being over as I cradled the baby in my arms, holding its head to my swollen breast.

All traces of fear and anxiety had left me and in their place was an ecstatic feeling that grew in intensity. As it unfolded, I was being stripped of boundaries and liberated into an ever-widening awareness of the universe. The point that I had been, floating in an infinite void, expanded to include all things, all worlds, all planes, all levels, all beings, and all manifestations, all taking place inside of me. At one point I lifted my hands above my head and felt my body reaching from one side of the universe to the other, containing all things in between.

As these revelations continued, I realized that my question of free will had been answered: free will did exist, but there was only one. There was only One Will, which choreographed and directed all things, despite their apparent separation. Separate free will was a myth, for nothing existed separately from everything else. There was only one Super-Organism, whose body was the universe, and all manifestations were merely modifications of itself. It was the divine play of hide and seek, where mankind's own false notions of personal free will were no more than the cunning method of the One for hiding from itself so as to allow the seeking and the finding.

Hand in hand with this most liberating insight was the knowledge that everything is exactly as it should be. This was the natural consequence of recognizing a singular Will, for if there is only One, then there can be no Other to oppose it. Things are the way they are because that is the only possible way that they can be. There is nothing amiss and nothing out of place. Although each of us as individuals could find a hundred things that we would change if given the choice, this is only because we fail to see the bigger picture. A limited viewpoint sees imperfection due to its own limitations, and not for any other reason.

This experience with the sacred mushroom was of great significance to me. In all honesty, it has, more than any other event, changed my life for the better. The insights that I took away with me remain to this day. They have also deepened, as I have had the chance to observe their validity in my day-to-day life.

Shortly afterward, when my partner returned from her holiday, she undertook a similar rite, with much the same effect. Subsequently, we both attempted to repeat the experience and we each passed through ordeals that taught us an important lesson. Since we had no real reasons to journey, apart from the desire to again behold the beatific visions, after a brief glimpse we were cast out from paradise and left to dwell in a strange place that was neither here nor there. It was a dislocated reality that gave us the impression we lost our sanity. Much to our distress, we remained there until the effects of the mushroom had worn off.

Neither of us has taken the sacred mushroom since—not due to fear, but because we realize that the entheogens are Teachers who have no time for students who wish only to fool around at the back of the classroom. The Teachers are to be called upon only when there is a meaningful question to be asked and a sincere desire to know its answer. If that time comes, I will once again approach the Teacher in humility and surrender. If not, then perhaps I have already been taught everything that I need to know.

The Power of the Heart in the Face of Darkness

Mindfire

A bold Canadian woman poet of forty-nine years backpacks into the California wilderness to ingest a large quantity of mushrooms— and nothing happens. Twenty-four hours later she apparently encounters a frightening entity and finds a deep source of compassion.

What if the entheogens, our plant allies, all the visionary plants, offer us an opportunity to heal ourselves and elicit a healing and maintenance of balance in the planetary body and natural world itself? Beyond the phenomenology, which allows criteria-based thinking with regard to experience, lies a subtlety of immense power: the power of Love. Imagine Love as an idea, a heart consciousness, an ability to live in and of the heart, not ego-driven nor fear-based, in dynamic equilibrium with all that is: Love as a resonant frequency.

Some years back I backpacked into the Ventana Wilderness in California, the ancient land of the Esselen people. My intent was to journey with the sacred mushroom and to invoke the healing powers inherent in the fusion of interdimensional energies—with possibly far-reaching implications. After focusing my attention upon my intent, I ingested a large quantity of psilocybe mushrooms and relaxed into the unknown. Interestingly, there was no grossly perceptible change in my awareness. Just being in nature has a way of enveloping me in the unity of diversity, but I went to sleep that evening wondering at and accepting the apparent lack of connection this time around.

The next morning, and for the entirety of that day, I eliminated a lot of shit, to put it indelicately and literally. I was thoroughly cleansed, but I never entered into high strangeness until that evening, upon retiring to my tent. I was jolted twice by an enormous surge of energy that leapt from the ground through my base chakra, up my spine, and out through my crown. Not to be confused with a kundalini awakening, this energy was fierce in strength, yet ambiguous in intent. It was power uploaded from the Earth, awaiting translation through me.

As the eerie hooting of a horned owl announced his guardianship of the night, these powerful surges were followed by an enormous crashing through the woods and the heaving, rasping breath of an unknown beast. It was certainly not a cougar, bear, nor deer. All alone in the wilderness, my initial reaction was, to say the least, fear-based. I felt I was in imminent danger, yet it dawned upon me that this energy or entity might be a consequence of the previous day's ingestion of the mushrooms. I bucked up my courage and resolved to open to the essential nature of the encounter.

At the nearest point of rasping encroachment, I consciously shifted into heart-centeredness and "asked" for this entity to communicate its intent. At the moment of shifting to a trust of the heart, opening to Love and the relinquishment of fear, I no longer heard the rasping breath as a threat, but as the gasping of a wounded beast.

I felt an enormous wave of compassion suffuse my being and I reached out to the beast in acknowledgment and love. I asked, if I could be of assistance; what could I do to ease its pain? I projected unconditional love and acceptance. The rasping beast ceased its crashing and I heard it shuffle quietly away.

In the poignancy of this moment, I was exquisitely aware of the power of heart in the face of darkness. I was reminded of St. John of the Cross, who wrote:

> "My dove, turn back,
> For now the wounded stag
> Is climbing up the slope
> Freshened by the breeze of your flight."

I was painfully aware of the everyday world of our reckoning, where the so-called "beast" is clothed in the raiment of man; a world wherein it seems so difficult to soothe the wounded stag. We live in a world where dark powers of immense interdimensional energies pale in comparison to our inhumanity.

Within an hour of this encounter, lightning began to strike and a torrential downpour ensued, ending a four-year drought in the immediate region.

In the next morning's sun, I emerged from the womb of my tent to find hundreds of mushrooms of a variety I had never before encountered, arrayed in a Fibonacci-like spiral around me. Later, the young fellow who was to pack me out was not the one to arrive, but it was his grandfather, the eldest surviving of the Esselens.

Did I understand his look and nod as acknowledgment, perhaps even gratitude? Did it speak of all that had transpired? Could it be that the pain of its unacknowledged and unloved existence had trapped that wounded beast of indeterminate origin? Was it the source of drought in the region? By my act of acknowledgment and loving acceptance, did I free it, thereby freeing the blocked energies of the matrix?

Perhaps much of our journeying in our modern search for enlightenment is no more than narcissistic pursuit—and perhaps these allies have been working in tandem with our conscious, service-oriented, loving intent, to allow humankind to assist in the maintenance of a dynamic equilibrium, to heal ourselves, the Earth, and perhaps even other entities locked in frequencies of coengagement. This possibility takes tripping into a whole new dimension.

I consider it a privilege to partake of the mushroom sacrament and at the same time I am profoundly aware of the responsibility of doing so with great sanctity of intent. The warp and weave of the cloth of hope with which we may craft the fabric of a new heart conscious reality may truly be found in the symbiotic woven threads of hyphae and the awakened heart.

Encounter and Metamorphosis with the Sirenian

Leopold

A sixty-three-year-old professional finds himself shape-shifting and then confronting an ancient or futuristic sea-mammal deity.

I was comfortable in my own home with a gentle companion to watch over me. As the effects of the medicine commence, my hands and arms begin to feel shorter, stubbier, and clumsy. My hands appear to metamorphose into palmiped, elongated attachments, like a modified flipper. I feel a physical transformation is taking place in my body. I experience some trepidation as well curiosity as to what is going on. Certainly it is very odd, weird, and alien. I tell myself that it might be some sort of rebirth or perinatal experience, but that does not ring true at all. What is happening to me is a physical metamorphosis of an alien kind, with no connection to a birth memory.

Then I begin to sense/feel/see him in front of me and I realize I am in the presence of a very alien being. He has a broad, powerful human chest. I intuit that he has two hearts, rather than just one. The neck is very thick, short, and muscular. He has short, reddish-blonde hair, which I think may hide some horns, but I don't see them. He is obviously male. He is doing a peculiar deep and threatening breathing, which sounds like a cross between human lungs pulling in air and some sort of gill breathing. The rest of his body is not very clear, but it is vaguely the shape of a merman. His forehead is very broad and contains a third eye. I sense a great, mysterious intelligence in this alien being.

The eye scrutinizes me and holds me in thrall. He is slightly threatening and feels like a sea mammal, but not a regressive vision to an earlier stage of evolution. On the contrary, he seems to be from the future, or at least he seems more evolved than the human race. I fear being in the presence of something much more powerful and more evolved than I: a god?

The metamorphosis of my hands can be explained: I am becoming him. I am in the presence of a Sirenian and I am becoming one! I am he. The thought is both terrifying and exhilarating. The thought of a sea god, the image of Capricorn comes to mind, in all its power!

Gradually I surrender myself to the transformation, accept it, and wonder what it means, what the image is telling me. As I transform, he remains in front of me.

With time, as the experience subsides, I consider the Sirenian image as the physical manifestation of an archetype. For the first time in any of these experiences I not only see but am also transformed in the archetypal image. I am cautious about being possessed by an archetype, as there is danger in it, but no damage results from this experience, so I take it as empowering.

The net result is of wonder, amazement, and gratitude at the gift of understanding how incredibly complex and mysterious are the worlds we live in, inner and outer. The vision and my own metamorphosis were gifts of understanding the peculiar forces around us, and a way of becoming them and joining them. It was a feeling of at-oneness.

My experience stretched my imagination much beyond normal rational boundaries. I think of Einstein's remark that imagination is more important than knowledge. This experience certainly pushed my limits. There was very little of my normal persona when I was transformed. All ego constructs had collapsed, with all their attendant worries, anxieties, and small concerns. I was not just in the company of something much bigger than I; I was one of them. Overall, it was an exhilarating, empowering experience and my envelope is now larger than it was. An image has been indelibly imprinted on my memory, which I can access in the future when I need it.

My Role, However Humble, Was Necessary and Cosmically Inspired

Phil O. Cybe

A middle-aged teacher remembers to dance the eternal dance again and opens to the upsurge of radiant life energy.

I enjoy eating dried mushrooms like potato chips. I do. I just love their taste and crunchy texture, so I guess that makes me a fungophile. I am an experienced one at that, since I know that even a few of these mushroom chips can prove to be too much. Much depends upon dose, mind set, and the setting in which you've placed yourself. These chips have a kick that can send you spiraling out into the cosmos or, if your ego desperately insists on resisting and clinging to what it thinks is so, plummeting into the hell realms. Then again, these "little flowers," as they are sometimes called, can be gentle, playful, and instructive, true dear friends who can help you remember to dance "The Dance" with the eternal, luminous, wonder-filled Divine, from which everything is continuously arising and returning, expanding and contracting, like a heart beat.

So it was with some trepidation and much respect that I returned for another encounter with that which the Aztecs called *teonanácatl,* "divine flesh." I was in a traditional circle with a very experienced, masterful guide who maintained a sacred context, a kind of spirit canoe in which I and others could safely journey.

Soon after ingesting 3 grams of the little flowers, they came on like a raging, tumultuous river. The mushrooms were as I had remembered them: overwhelmingly powerful and relentless. In fear and trembling, I desperately tried to avert the rapid onslaught of brilliantly colored geometric imagery and the rapid-fire thoughts that accompanied them, but I could not do so. There was no escape; I was along for the ride. With the help of our guide's crystal clear, softly murmured instructions, I remembered to return to my heart center, relax, breathe deeply, and open to this upsurge of radiant life energy.

Over time, it softened and subsided. Acting as my own compassionate witness, I experienced that which I call "I" being dismantled, dismembered, and pursued by a hunt-and-seek power that was absolutely determined to leave no stone unturned. It would not take "no" for an answer. Letting the mushroom spirits do their thing was like having a really good body session with a very skillful body worker who intuitively pinpoints and unearths every deeply-held psychological and physical kink and knot, and undoes them in a way which is at times painful, exhilarating, and deeply healing.

At one point, the mushroom energy came on like a rolling California earthquake, leaving me involuntarily undulating on the floor. I was a Kundalini-inspired serpent. My movements uncovered, dislodged, and disclosed those places, within as well as without, to which I needed to pay attention. My relationship with my son came through very strongly. I could see with great clarity that he was indeed my son, and that he already knew it, through a process of nature-based self-initiation, a fact that I sometimes missed in my dealings with him.

I also saw that much depended on my upright behavior. I was a kind of linchpin, a hub upon which so much depended. I needed to heal. My role, however humble, was a necessary and cosmically-inspired one, called forth by the medicine way to uphold and defend. By personal example and practice I could be a standard-bearer of that which was required to restore a sense of connectedness to the luminous house within. This was also the case with other psychonauts who have been summoned to help heal that rupture into dualism which plagues and threatens us today.

With mushroom-inspired awareness I saw how to get in touch with effortless effort, by letting go and allowing things to unfold of their own accord, while observing and seeing into the deeper meaning. To do this, I needed to stay alert, to keep myself from being distracted and ensnared by worry, anger, resentment, and other samsaric states of mind. I realized that I needed to come from that heart-centered, balanced place within, that radiant source of sources from which everything is endlessly arising and returning.

The mushroom helped me see that to do that which I've been called upon to do, I need to enjoy myself and to drink regularly and deeply from the refreshing, bubbling wellspring within. A flattened, repressed life is too hard, too dry, too dispirited to live. Give me laughter and Zorba-like friends! I must say, "Yes!" to good wine, wonderful women, and dark chocolate. "Yes!" to Dionysus!

I have learned that the journey begins well before the medicine is ingested. I look for it in preactivations of to-be-examined issues and images. I notice it in brighter and resplendent dreams and in the extraordinary events that often precede a medicine session proper. This time, a day before the medicine circle gathering, Coyote trotted by within a few feet of my home, looking magnificent and regal. He looked at me, paused momentarily, winked, and then disappeared into the brush. The spirit of the Trickster is at work! It's tracking you, too, dear reader! Just say, "Yes!"

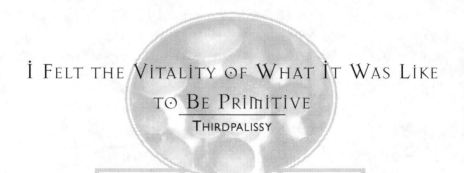

I Felt the Vitality of What It Was Like to Be Primitive

Thirdpalissy

A young man in his twenties takes mushrooms in a cow pasture in Southern Louisiana and has a vision of the Moon as the pregnant Cat Goddess Bastet; he was struck by parallels to the vision of Sekhmet, the Lion-Headed, reported in the book on Ayahuasca experiences.

I grew up in southern Louisiana, where from March to October cow pastures blossomed with psilocybe mushrooms after every rain, especially in the spring and fall. One day, about thirty years ago, Marc, my best friend, and his older brother, John, and I decided to try the Magic Mushroom. I had never done them before, though I had dropped acid a few times.

We went out to a known Psilocybe haunt and out of rotting cow manure picked a paper grocery bag full of them. On that occasion and all hunts afterward I noticed that I had to be somewhat detached. It was as if they presented themselves only if I were not too greedy to find them.

We took them back to John's house and cooked them down for 2 or 3 hours, boiling them in water, adding more water when needed. In the end we had a little less than a gallon of 'shroom juice. In those days we used to add grape Koolaid mix in with the juice to make it more palatable. We each drank a cup, settled back in our living room chairs, and listened to psychedelic rock music.

It's been a long time, so I cannot accurately describe coming-on, except to relate it as the sensual initial beginning of the psychedelic experience. Colors were brighter even though we were in a relatively dark room. The music enfolded us. John had one of those fake Persian rugs that were so popular at the time. As I succumbed to my own visions, creatures and what I can only describe as Terence McKenna's logos emerged three-dimensionally from the designs on the carpet.

I was transported to a time before we were top predator. I felt the vitality of what it was like to be "primitive." I was in a cave with the keen knowledge of hunter and knowing the dynamic threat of being prey.

At the first intermission, John pulled us together to talk a little about our experience. Then we drank another cup of the magic fluid and decided to go outside. We stood and talked in the driveway under a full Moon. I looked up and beheld a wonderful sight: the Moon, still the Moon, was also the pregnant belly of a bejeweled, cat-headed woman, staring and smiling back at me. She had many jeweled and pearl necklaces around her neck. I asked something to the effect of, "Wow, is anyone else seeing this?" Marc identified the exact same vision as I had but John could not see her, as hard as he looked. Marc and I jointly maintained the view of this seeming "goddess" for several minutes. She was not made of cloud but seemed solid and alive, smiling back at us. It seems as though she was showing us something in both of her hands but I cannot remember what it was.

Suddenly clouds obscured her vision and a wiggling, undulating "worm hole" made of cloud opened up between the Moon and ourselves. Marc and I both felt we were about to be sucked up by the Moon, so we increased our gravity (?!) to stay down, and eventually the sky returned to normal. I still wonder what would have happened if we hadn't grounded ourselves.

Her image is still in my mind. It was nearly ten years later when I came across an image of the Egyptian goddess known as Bastet, a statue of her with a couple of necklaces on. I was absolutely amazed. It was indeed the goddess that we had seen, though in our vision she had a couple of dozen necklaces.

My vision of Bastet certainly aligned her with the Moon. Though I have not found any scholarly research linking her with the lunar, still in all, it is very strange to consume magic mushrooms in Louisiana and see an Egyptian goddess.

Interestingly enough, Bastet is known as "the devouring lady." Gurdjieff believed that the Moon eats us when we die. But foremost she is protectress, especially of those who care for cats (neither Marc nor I had a cat at the time). Later she became the life-preserving goddess of joy and the protector of women. She took on an appearance of "cat as sex symbol." I would have to describe the vision I had of her as "sexy." On another note of interest, she defended her father Ra, the Sun, against his only real enemy, the serpent Apep.

I'm a fifty-year-old potter now living in North Carolina. I have a great interest in pottery from around the world and I love to visit museums and view their antique clay collections. One of my favorite museums is the Field Museum in Chicago. They possess a wonderful pre-Columbian pottery collection. Viewing the work of Mississippian clay from the state of Arkansas (where I was born and lived until I was twelve) I came across a bowl with a catlike head on one side and a snakelike tail on the other. Now, I cannot help but think of that bowl representing the Moon. If a twentieth century man in Louisiana can see an Egyptian goddess in the sky, I have no reason not to believe that pre-Columbian north Americans could. And those mushrooms were more than likely growing in the gulf south all the way into Arkansas then, as they do now.

I Saw My Entire Worldview and Value System Realign

David S.

A fifty-two-year-old writer and publisher endures intense physical suffering and then is able to open himself to and release negativity and find self-acceptance.

Every time I have a session with the mushrooms, I view it as a sacred ceremony, as a sacrament. I prepare by fasting and meditation. My sacred place is a rural home in a hilly, forested area in western Sonoma County, free of traffic and noise. There are fresh flowers set about, aromatic natural plant oils are being burned, and harmonious music is being played to create a retreat for deep inner work.

I always have a guide present to give me support, to redirect me if I wander or become anxious, to help me process if I become confused, and to provide an atmosphere of safety. The guide, usually silent, is also a witness to my healing and my life-changing insights.

The mushroom is a preferred friend because of its gentleness, its harmony with my natural surroundings, and because I believe it talks to me. My intention was to deal with my core negativity and harsh worldview, and to seek solutions to my dire economic predicament.

Initially I had a lot of physical discomfort and anxiety and I was glad there was music to draw off some of my confusion. I tried focused breathing, but I was losing the struggle as waves of generalized fear and hopelessness swept over me. At the same time, part of me knew that I would be well because I saw my guide quietly reading a book in the corner. Part of me also knew that this was the ego relinquishing control and sounding the psychic-physical alarms. Still, I was suffering.

A break came at about 70 minutes, when the vista outside started to pulsate and throw off beams of light and color and look more dimensional and radiant than usual. It was one of the most beautiful sights I had ever seen. I was elated and commented to my guide. She nodded appreciatively and encouraged me to hang in there. But nothing else happened. I was drawing a blank in a beautiful environment. I became more miserable as the anxiety and body aches came back. I started to despair and told my guide that nothing was happening, all I had was anxiety. It looked like this was going to be a rough one. She calmly reassured me and said, "David, open to yourself. Just open to yourself."

I determined to follow her advice. I told myself to open to myself and to turn into my anxiety. Almost immediately, powerful muscle spasms hit me in the back and neck. It was as if I had become spastic from repeated electric shocks. I felt I was trying to form a backwards circle. It seemed as though I was short-circuiting, and I flopped off the sofa and onto the floor in uncontrollable spasms.

A singularly powerful knowing swept over me and totally overwhelmed me, mentally and physically: that this world is a beneficent place and the source of all goodness. The power and simplicity of this realization astounded me. It was not part of my belief structure. Where had I been all these years? I had been in self-absorption. I saw my entire worldview and value system shift and realign. *The world is a beneficent place.* An immense relief came over me as I realized that I was free from the captivity of my previous worldview and attitudes. A new perception was manifesting, and it made sense. As waves of gratitude and awe washed over me, I went into more contortions and spinal muscle spasms.

Now came a knowing that things were going to be all right in my life. The term "all right" was the driver. Everything was *all right* in my life, starting now. At first I was shocked at the fact that I knew this on such a core level. It wasn't a case of believing it or hoping for it; it was simply *knowing* it. I was *experiencing* the knowledge and not merely thinking it. I tried to verbalize this, but I couldn't get the words out. I realized that I was having a world-life-view shift, and that I was blowing out a lifetime's worth of negative dross and sediment from my system.

My guide maintained her distance and silence as I flopped around on the rug like a huge fish out of water, attempting to talk with a thick tongue. What was happening to me physically didn't matter because I comprehended the significance. The negative karma of generations was being broken and removed. There was another way to see.

Powerful sobs wracked my body and there was a tremendous letting go of years of misery as next came the knowing that I was *all right* just the way I was. I was *all right*, period. Without qualification, rationalization, justification, negotiation, performance, or explanation. This was the simple truth. Throughout my life, on a deep level, I have always believed that there was something wrong with me. Now, for the fist time, I was simply *all right*. I experienced being *all right*. As the magnitude of this sank in, a great calmness came over me. On the outside I was a blubbering mess of tearful gratitude; on the inside I felt the purity of the truth. This made sense. This is the way it is. These knowings repeated themselves many times before the spasms subsided.

As the day slowly moved into dusk, I was filled with a deep gratitude for the wonderful gifts that I had received. Things were going to change. I didn't know how, but I knew that they would. Things had already changed: I was filled with grace.

I have left my previous occupation and begun writing and now I publish a quarterly newsletter. The difficulties of life are still here and my fears are often operative. What is different is that though things are somewhat the same, they look and feel different, feel positive. My negative self-talk is diminished. I have greater self-acceptance and am more at ease. I smile more. The world looks better. There is a calmness. I have a new reservoir of strength to draw from—I am more myself.

Pondering the Separation between What I Experience and What Actually Is

Mark Bryan

This twenty-five-year-old philosophy student laboriously enters a hell realm and then reaches a complex but functional understanding of God through the comparison between what is and what he experiences in mundane reality.

With some trepidation, on this early morning in my home I embarked upon my first solo, high dose mushroom trip, augmented by marijuana, and, at one point, smoked DMT.

I made mushroom tea by putting 5 grams of chopped mushrooms into a tea ball, then pouring separately three cups of boiling water over it. There was a flavored tea bag in the cup to mask the mushroom taste. I allowed about fifteen minutes for each steeping and after drinking cup number two, I knew that I had reached the limit of what I could handle. I decided to drink one more cup.

I recall sitting on my bed with my duvet covering my legs, witnessing its clumps and creases transform into a vast mountain range viewed from high above, as if I were flying over it. I experienced God and was very, very fearful, overwhelmed with pure suffering, pure shame, pure denial. It *hurt*, especially when I resisted the experience. I had a lot of difficulty giving myself up to what seemed to be the Christian God but, upon doing so, I came to the realization that *I am God*, and that I was simply viewing myself from the inside and the outside simultaneously.

As I flew across the duvet mountains, they changed from craggy peaks into barren hills, then to sand dunes, and finally into extremely arid land. I kept flying until I reached what seemed to be the Nile River in Egypt. There was desolation, azure sky, and sand for as far as I could see.

Due to a personal issue of the time, I began to feel guilt, which increased in intensity until I was also experiencing fear, remorse, and other such emotions in their purest forms. It was no longer just a feeling of being guilty *about* something; it was undifferentiated guilt with no object, no cause.

Next I became Christ descending into Hell. I experienced the sins of humankind and was punished for them all. Humankind *was me,* and equally I *was humankind.* This lasted for some time, with the struggle focused on the issue of my non-acceptance of the Christian God. The more I refused to yield to God, to recognize its presence and superiority, the greater my tortures. (Strictly speaking, "sin" is the choice of ignoring God in any action.) If God is immaterial then, when translated into a Buddhist context, the denial of God is the refusal to give up all of one's attachments to materiality—this is suffering, which is what I was experiencing as the disbelieving Christ.

Upon my eventual submission and full repentance I discovered that in actuality, because I *am* God (but have forgotten it), the whole experience was a trial to force me to give up my great attachment to a dogmatic belief that God was an impossibility. I was forced to sacrifice my understanding of reality. Relinquishing my day-to-day reality core led to my comprehending reality-as-it-is, not the mere experience of it.

I began pondering the separation between what I experience and what actually *is.* Thinking of *maya,* the veil of illusion, as a kind of television screen, my consciousness and thoughts became distinct from my body. For example, I could observe myself instructing my hand (located on a television screen) to move, without being *in* the action myself. (In day-to-day reality, I am *in* my actions, in that I am not *consciously deciding* to perform most of them.) On a pad of paper I wrote with some difficulty, "I am seeing my hand inside a TV—I am thinking and it is writing."

During the year prior to this particular mushroom experience, I had smoked DMT a number of times. Many of these trips included guiding presences that revealed information to me. I had been interpreting these presences as being external entities that were communicating with me, but during this mushroom trip I realized that the information was *not* external in origin, but was self-revealing. What in day-to-day reality I subjectively interpret as "I" already knew all of the information of which I was being made aware.

Time started running backwards. I had difficulty operating within such an unusual modality where I was perpetually forgetting (for it is rather difficult to remember what just un-happened). I was disoriented. Just as a child must learn how to operate in this physical reality, I had to learn how to function in a realm where time was running backwards. I could not remember with whom I had spent the previous evening, how long I had been high (an hour, a day, week, month, or year?), where I worked and even what that work was, whether my university professors existed. Had I ever learned anything? Did I know anything at all? Who was I? I? I? . . . ?

I saw many fleeting, fast-paced images, culminating in my shifting from the inside of my head into the head of an "insane" person locked up in a padded cell. Everything I had ever (thought I had) experienced (and also all future experiences, such as writing this in my room right now) was a fiction of a psychotic, deluded imagination running wild. For all I knew, this was the case, but I could not tell for sure right then, so I continued . . .

I decided to play with my strobe light. With the light flickering rapidly, the thought-words of my internal voice were flowing in sentences. With each flash of light, a frame was created wherein time ceased to flow. I was thus able to observe each thought, word, or concept individually and fully experience and explore it as a materially manifested object. I could climb over and around it, sensing the texture, shape, and form of the pieces of thought.

Overall, the experience was hard work, mentally and physically grueling. Much of the experience was extracted like the bitter liquid from an orange rind. This was most apparent during a period when I was squeezing complex original musical compositions from my head.

This was one of the most important breakthrough experiences of my life. Ever since I discovered that Santa and the Tooth Fairy were not "real," I had rejected the existence of God, reasoning that if my parents had lied about the first two metaphysical beings, why not the third? During my late teens, I became interested in Buddhism, which, of course, lacks a "god" altogether. I had never considered my adamant denial of God to be an attachment, until this trip. When I was forced to confront this, I learned to accept things that seem impossible or unreasonable, even to love that which I hated. This has benefited me in everyday life. With this trip, my understanding of Buddhism deepened and I have developed an abiding interest in messages presented by various other schools of thought.

I Remember What It Was Like before I Had This Face

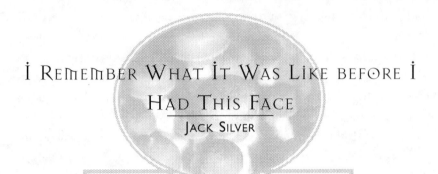

Jack Silver

This forty-four-year-old environmental activist and attorney is initiated
through a series of purifications and enters the place where energy and matter
meet.

Less than an hour after ingesting 2.5 grams of dried mushrooms, I am
in a state of total meltdown, consumed by the fire of purification. I am
frightened, but willing to face the fire. The "I" does not want to die or
give up control, so this purification has a deep type of pain that pene-
trates down to my being. Yet I know it is the resistance to the purification, not the purification itself, that is so painful.

I find myself in a room without dimensions, which makes no sense
unless you're there. It has dimensions, but they are made of energy fields,
so when I approach them, they shift and change. Here I meet my
teacher/guide.

He appears to me as an Indian. He says that I always screw up the
pronunciation of his name and then he laughs. He is kind but strict. His
people have a language that is absolutely precise, in which a word *is* its
total meaning. The evocation of the word evokes the reality. The language is one that I recognize: it is used to elicit and exchange
reality/experience, soul-matter.

We visit sacred places, temples, monuments, and places of sacrament where we do ceremonies of purification. This is where one pre-

pares to receive the sacrament of the soul. Every time I return to this place, I remember everything, even my teacher, although I still have not mastered his name.

I open myself up and asked to be purified, to be cleansed of all resistance. My teacher instructs me in the Ghost Dance. He simply says that when we are like this, we do the Ghost Dance. He instructs me to dance.

I ask, *Why do we dance?*

He says that he does not know why, we just do. I understand that he actually knows, but my question is inappropriate. I need only to dance and to be the dance.

I crawl through an igloo-shaped entrance about six feet wide and four feet high. Its floor is white fur. The ceiling is lined with dead rattlesnakes with their heads hanging down and their mouths open so that the fangs are prominent. If I rise up, I will certainly be pricked by their fangs.

My teacher muses, *Be careful to not touch the ceiling! Sometimes live rattlers come and crawl among the dead!* He laughs, but I think he is serious.

Next I enter my teacher's hut to participate in a shamanic journey. I lie down on blankets and furs. My teacher holds a prayer stick, a short staff about eighteen inches long, an instrument of transformation. The power end of the staff resembles the head of a raptor, but it is invisible. As my teacher moves the staff past me, I can see in complete detail the raptor head as energy is displaced around it. As the staff passes me, I am turned into a bird flying above a great valley. I remember not knowing where I am or what is happening, then realize I am the bird. I do not see as I normally do, but as the raptor sees color and shapes, with multidepth perception and heat as shape.

I hear my teacher's voice and I am back in the room. He says, *I have given you the gift of flight. You will always possess it.*

I experience the liberation of my spirit as a very young child, unfettered by matter, personality, or genetic legacy. It feels good and I do not want to go back to my life.

I am in a place of energy. All of reality is in this field of energy and I am consciousness in flux. I have been here before. This is the totality of my being. In this place I am reunited with Self. No time, no space, infinite in effect and reality. I enter a world not yet made. I am looking into the universe from the back, seeing where all the energy is coming from, in waves. I see where energy and matter meet, where form moves from potential into actuality. I am privy to all creation. All is energy, yet form emerges because form is a dimension, energy perceived as function.

Slowly I become aware of self again. I feel nausea and pain and disgust and recognize these as part of the creative force, unique qualities born of the experiential, to be realized fully. It is necessary to feel the nausea of nausea, the horror of horror, the disgust of disgust, all in their pure forms. Out of this same spirit come beauty, love, and compassion.

We are wired for the creative energies. They flow through our bodies and souls, into the world to bring forth never-before realities to delight and enrich all beings who share in the feast of life.

I see the universe as a fabric, with my self woven into its delicate and beautiful threads. As the fabric undulates, I experience the shifts and movements as part of a large current flowing. I understand I am being born into the fabric, forming a pattern in its weave, with its many threads all responding to the movement of the universe.

Like the knight in pursuit of the Grail, each of us who enters the forest through these doors of perception walks a path of our own choosing. We must pay attention, as we are opening up the gates of heaven and hell. We go where our attention is directed or distracted. The universe is infinitely diverse, with many dimensions and unimaginable complexity and beauty. As consciousness-possessing beings, we are able to transcend realities and travel through these dimensions. As we become transparent to transcendence, we travel the cosmic void. Drawn into its current, lost to self, washed up on the shores of an alternate reality, we are floating through the cosmic currents of creation.

This experience is one of many that have awakened my soul and allowed me access to an expanded realm of consciousness that I had not heretofore experienced. I feel I have reconnected with the worlds that interpenetrate this reality. I remember what it was like before I had this face.

We Are All Actors and Directors in a Giant Cosmic Drama

Mark A. Schroll, Ph.D.

A young man skeptically eats mushrooms at a wedding party and suddenly encounters a profound realization of the playful drama that is human life.

When I was in my twenties, I was invited to a friend's wedding reception to be held at a home in the country several miles from the city. My friend mentioned that some close friends were going to be taking sacred mushrooms and asked if I would be interested in joining them. My friend assured me the experience would be quite safe. I replied that I had never taken psychedelic mushrooms, but that the possibility had always intrigued me. I was especially curious about the claims that psychedelics could produce profound mystical experiences.

Each frozen mushroom cluster was approximately one ounce in weight. My friend recommended that I eat half of one, because of their potency. Picking one out, I bit into it. It tasted awful, almost like eating dirt. I chased it down with beer. In the hot July weather, the remaining mass of frozen mushroom began thawing in my hand. I thought to myself, "How potent can something like this be?" Fifteen to twenty minutes after eating the first half, I felt unchanged. Deciding that there was no harm in eating the other half, I chewed and swallowed it, too.

During the next hour I waited for something to happen. I was really beginning to doubt the literature concerning psychedelics and mystical experiences. I also began to scorn the critics, whose negative media campaigns frighten so many people about the dangers of psychedelics. This bitterness toward the government and the ignorance of the society I had been born into continued to swell within me as the time progressed. I was experiencing a slight increase in visual, auditory, and mental awareness, but nothing that seemed significantly beyond normal awareness.

Then, in the midst of all this doubting and critical reasoning, all at once a remarkable awareness came over me. Looking around the room at the party that was still going on, the understanding that we are all actors and directors in a giant cosmic drama became vividly real. The personality constructs and social games we create became unquestionably obvious. I felt I was able to see right into the very core of my own personality. This extended to an awareness of the personalities of everyone around me. I recognized that our social constructions of self are perceived as real because we grant each other permission to create these images and impressions. I became totally fascinated with the thought of the human ego's ability to assume any character it chooses to express. Indeed, we not only grant each other this permission, but daily we are completely taken into believing that the social roles we create are genuine and authentic.

Contemplating this thought, I began thinking about the shadow consequences of our ability to be both actor and director in this extraordinary drama. I contemplated advertising, which appeals to our shadow tendencies toward constant consumption by never allowing us satiation. Defining our self by the objects we own and the things we still must obtain keeps us in a constant state of deficiency motivation. We are always grasping for more objects to make us whole.

These thoughts were interrupted when I became aware that my ability to pay attention to conversations going on around me had been expanded. I began participating in three separate conversations, remembering each of the stories that I was hearing and participating in them like we usually do when participating in one conversation. This intensified my awareness that we are both actors and directors in this cosmic drama.

I was then compelled to begin shaking everyone's hand in the room, congratulating them for creating such a convincing dramatic illusion that it truly seemed real, saying to them, "Great acting, you are really seeming to be authentic in this creation of your self!" When I arrived at the last person in the room, the sun had set and the sky was filled with the stars of the new moon sky. I reached out to shake his hand and looked into his face with the night sky shining in behind him through a window. My awareness of figure and ground shifted, and his body seemed to merge with the wall behind him. I then found myself looking past him into the night sky, letting go of all the social constructions of self going on around me, melding with the star-filled universe. It is still one of my most profound transpersonal experiences.

Sometime later I roused from this vision and found myself outside the house. I had lost my glasses in the yard and people were looking for them with flashlights. Even though it was night, I could see each blade of grass with extreme clarity, like during the day. I found my glasses and picked them up. I wandered off from the crowd, crossed a road and a barbed wire fence, and found a soft place to lie down and sleep. The next day I awoke on a golf course putting green with a crowd of golfers staring down at me, wondering if I was okay. Initially I was quite startled, but I got up mumbling some nonsense and wandered back to my friend's home.

Over the past twenty-five years I have continued to reflect on the meaning of this experience. When I remember, my awareness of the world around me becomes expanded and my perception of the social constructions of self going on around me increases. Being human, I often forget to use this vision to guide my social interactions. In *The Book: On the Taboo Against Knowing Who You Really Are*, Alan Watts discusses life as a drama and relates it to the Hindu myth of the universe, *maya*. Reading it brought the awareness of my sacred mushroom experience rushing back into my conscious memory. Abraham Maslow's discussion of deficiency motivation and growth motivation gives me a vehicle of expression that helps keep my mushroom experience in my awareness. My interest in deepening the understanding of my mushroom experience and other transpersonal experiences has led to my continuing exploration of questions related to humanistic, transpersonal, and eco-psychology.

I am a forty-three-year-old male writer and teacher with a Ph.D. in philosophy of science. One of my life's guiding principles continues to be that the foundation of our discussion of transpersonal experience needs to be grounded in our direct experience of sacred plants. Indeed, cutting our selves off from this direct encounter with knowledge from the plant kingdom has contributed greatly to humankind's increasing alienation from Gaia consciousness.

THE LITTLE BEINGS TELL ME THAT
LAUGHING IS ALSO HOLY

KARIN RIESE

This forty-year-old physician and sex therapist, who lives in Germany, light-heartedly joins a mushroom circle ceremony at a transpersonal conference in the Canary Islands. She has a merry time with the mushroom creatures and experiences the exquisite vulnerability of the cosmic infant.

The guide opens the ritual by placing four candles in the four directions, representing the four elements. He follows by blowing a Tibetan conch horn, smudging with sage, and expressing gratitude to the spirits of the mushrooms for placing their powers at our disposal. All of this strikes me as a beautiful and important preparation. For the first time, I see the significance of a ritual like this, whereas before I had been rather skeptical toward rituals, especially in groups.

Some structural guidelines are given: everyone is to preserve the circle; one could dance, go outside, sing, speak, but must always return to the circle. Everyone in turn would hold the talking stick and say with what intentions they are undertaking this journey. For me, it is the first time with this kind of journey and I want to simply explore other worlds and share my experiences with the others. I have no anxiety because I feel trust in the group, the ritual, and in our guide's confidence.

About ten minutes later, the effects begin. I lie down and immediately totally new worlds open for me:

Geometric forms, triangles, jagged forms, lines, bands . . . all seemingly forms without life making a kind of interconnected web. But then, the joke is that these forms *are* alive, after all. Furthermore, they are curious about me, very interested in everything, and incredibly amused.

They separate themselves from the geometric web and are moving toward me. They all want to sit on my abdomen, but then I won't be able to breathe. Strangely, although they look very light, they are actually quite heavy. It's incredible how heavy they are. I chase them off my abdomen and lie on my side. Immediately I feel better. The little beings become irresistibly funny and even somewhat disrespectful, which I really like.

Then I suddenly see a Jeep in front of me. I say to the little beings, "Well, you've probably never seen something quite like this!" Immediately they all gather around and want to climb into the Jeep. In no time, the Jeep is filled with triangles, bands, and lines, till they are looking out the window and we all have to laugh. Really—they're laughing.

At this point I open my eyes and look at our circle. Everyone looks so peaceful, earnest, and holy. This sight makes me laugh some more. I'm practically rolling around with enjoyment, but at the same time I have a bit of a guilty conscience, since one isn't supposed to laugh in a holy situation. The little geometric beings are also laughing, and they tell me that laughing is also holy. So they give me a certain amount of cover. I proceed to crawl around in the circle—which is not really permitted—but my mood is merry and light-hearted; I find myself in front of one of the candles, having a conversation about the sense and nonsense of sitting in a circle. It is a quiet conversation; and at last the candle makes clear to me that the circle form is the right way to do it. I don't have a clue why, but it is the correct form. So then I go and lie down at my place.

Now I'm feeling like a newborn baby: very small and soft, with very thin skin, through which everything can pass without any possibility of defense or resistance. My whole body consists of perceptual awareness, a very clear perception, with a mixture of amazement and terror about everything that is going on around me.

I put my finger in my mouth and make myself into a round ball, so that my tummy is more protected; my back seems more stable. Someone in the circle clears his throat loudly. The sound is shocking: it goes like a knife throughout my whole body, and I'm unable to defend myself against it.

Then our guide arrives, crawling on hands and knees, snuffling around my head like a great warm mother mammal that protects me and soothes me. Immediately, I feel at peace again, and now also I'm curious. He crawls and snuffles around to everyone in the circle.

Now there are curved lines and sweeping shapes that coalesce into a great blue wave that contains many curved and sweeping lines and shapes, becoming larger and larger. Now this great wave arrives at where I am. I am dissolved into it—am both here and then not here. At first I find this quite acceptable. After a while, though, I begin to feel uneasy at the relentlessly soft and sweeping forms. I think that clear, linear forms also have their place. Just at this time, they could provide structure and holding. So I begin to draw straight lines in the air with my finger, and right angles on the floor with my foot. Already I feel better.

Now our guide is sitting in the circle and begins to chant an invocation of many names, rocking back and forth. I perceive him as an archetypal feminine being, yet in the body of a man. He calls each one of our names and the names of others who are not in the circle, but part of our community; we feel their presence as their names are called. Then he calls Odin and Freyja, Isis, Osiris . . . many gods and goddesses, and at the end, Odin and Freyja again.

Thus the journey comes to an end. There is a closing circle ritual, in which each one relates something significant from their experience. I am deeply touched by what each one speaks. The journey has been a great gift for me, from the "little princes." I thank them all.

And finally, we do the dance of the moccasins, based on the Native American proverb, "Don't judge another until you have walked for a day in his moccasins." Each one of us dances first in the place where we have been lying or sitting; then proceeds to the place of the one to the left and dances in their moccasins. And so I become in turn each one of these human beings, understanding a little better what they are. At the same time I see myself in the eyes of the others: alive, lively, sensual, and joyous, but also silly, exaggerated, ridiculous—as many shadings and varieties of me as there are humans who are dancing in my moccasins.

After this dance, the circle dissolves. We all disperse into the night.

Fifteen years later, upon reflecting on this and other experiences, I see that my encounters with the "little princes" initiated a new phase in my life and consciousness. They showed me worlds of unique and special beauty that I could never have imagined. This feature alone would have made these encounters worthwhile for me, but beyond that, I have been shown depths, treasures, and insights into my own existence. These function like time-released explosive charges, gradually transforming my attitudes, behavior, and feeling nature—in short, my entire worldview.

I have become more authentic, self-confident, less interested in mainstream conventions, less impressed by the material realm. I believe that without the painful insights into my own story and without the challenge of transforming these painful aspects into something new and better, the beautiful visions would not have been accessible to me. I find it good that it is so.

One thing I can say for certain is that my relationship to nature, and particularly to plants, has been drastically altered. Where before nature was basically alien and exterior to me, I now experience it as a living whole, of which I am a part. Plants are my relatives: I can meet them, communicate and learn from them. I have the most profound respect for their ancient and enduring wisdom.

Perhaps some people approach such journeys in consciousness with the expectation that they will become happier. I can't say whether I have become happier; that would be simplistic. My life has acquired greater intensity and authenticity: when I am happy, my happiness is greater than before; when I am unhappy, there are deeper dimensions to this state also. Because of this, I have had to learn how to bring more balance into my life, in order to be able to contain such intensities.

What I have learned from the plant and mushroom spirits, the visions they have given me, I count among the greatest gifts I have received in my life.

Mushroom Magic in the Lightning Field

Martin Goodman

A single mushroom takes this forty-two-year-old English writer on a little walk into a magical landscape where he finds his song and gives it to the mountain and the sky.

"*Quemado*. What does it mean in English?"

"Burnt!"

So we speed from the town of Burnt, turn onto a dirt road, and cruise through mile after mile of brown grassland. Gates are opened and closed and we surge through pools of mud, heading further into the hinterland. The first of the steel rods of the Lightning Field appears and beyond it, a wooden cabin.

The Chevrolet wheels around and pulls up at the front door. In fact, it is a good house: solid and commodious, my first log cabin. The tables, ceiling, walls, floor, chairs, everything in it is made of dark wood. No picture, no rug, no cushion, no cloth spoils the effect of wood on wood on wood.

Wooden rocking chairs on the back porch give views across the grassland to a ring of distant mountains. Between the log cabin and the mountains stretches the Lightning Field. The house is wood; the Lightning Field is steel. I see a poetic contrast of cabin, field, and mountains, wood, steel, and stone.

The Lightning Field is one of the world's largest art installations, placed here, in New Mexico, by the artist Walter de Maria in 1977. Four hundred lightning rods, shining steel poles that rise to a sharpened point, are set in a quadrant one mile by one kilometer. In all, forty-five rows of sixteen rods, each set so perfectly that if you face a line of rods just so, they all disappear behind the foremost rod's four-inch width. The same in the diagonal directions. Each rod is around twenty feet high, adjusted to the level of land into which it is set, so that the points form an exact plane on which an imaginary sheet of glass might rest in perfect balance. We tread through this forest of steel poles, feeling small and somewhat lost. The Lightning Field is on a scale beyond aesthetics, somehow.

We discover another element when we walk out into the lightning field: water skims the surface in patches, turning the earth to bog. We hunt for a missing element: fire. I see the first sign of it: a thin jag of lightning threads into the tip of a steel pole to my right.

It is the peak of New Mexico's lightning season. Some nights lightning blazes across the southern skyline. Sheets of it fill the night and contrast trees, mountains, and clouds in sharp silhouettes. Branches of it reach from high with multiple sizzling fingers that stab down across miles and miles of landscape.

I have learned something of the lore of lightning. Enormous winds swirl within thunderclouds to generate sparks of electricity. Bolts of up to a million volts shoot out at the speed of light, up to twenty-six of them at a time fusing into what we perceive as a single lightning flash.

I know to stay away from metal objects. I know that these giant lightning rods are anchored into the ground in deep stacks of cement, and know a lightning strike spreads high voltage through the ground. Lightning strikes at least a thousand people off the globe each year, plus those many beyond the reach of official records, innocents on some pampas, some tundra, some steppes or taiga or desert or grassland. Two thousand thunderstorms are sporting themselves around the planet at any given time. A small one contains ten times as much power as the atom bomb that flew from here, New Mexico, to destroy Hiroshima.

Thunder echoes inside a cloud beyond the range of mountains to the south. Dark clouds begin to pile up over to the west. The Lightning Field no longer seems a safe place to be.

We sit on rockers on the verandah of the cabin and wait for the show to commence. Thunderclouds gather over the mountains, but the sky above the plain remains fairly clear. Our anticipation dims a little.

I take out a small plastic package. Inside is a mushroom, given to me by a friend for my birthday. I have never "shroomed" before, taken the journey where magic mushrooms lead. The package contains one cap and one stem, the length of my little finger from knuckle to tip. It is dry, a fairly dark brown, and as I say a prayer and pop it in my mouth, I am surprised by its taste. I expect no taste at all, but here is the strong flavor of mushroom. It is pleasantly grounding and natural that a magic mushroom tastes like a mushroom. I chew, activate the strands with my saliva, and swallow. Psilocybin, the mushroom's hallucinogenic ingredient, is now in my system. I am on a chemical journey with no turning back. The dose is supposed to be a small one. Some lightness, some sense of opening should come.

The company of the others suddenly seems a little harsh. I wish to observe the mushroom's effects in solitude and go to my room. My bed, single and smart beneath a bright red blanket, is in an annex built to lean against the cabin's rear wall. I lie down and close my eyes.

The effects are physical at first. There is a click of release inside my ears. Heat gathers inside my jaw then turns to numbness. Then the visions begin.

The Lightning Field lies several walls away, on the far side of the cabin, but I see it clearly, eyes open or eyes closed. I tour the field from within and from a distance, turning to view the rods in different formations, from different angles. Lightning slips down from the sky with exquisite accuracy to pass in through the points of the giant steel needles. As I study the sight, I note how the rods absorb electricity from the sky, but they also spit it back. I watch twin forks of lightning shoot from steel tips to jag heavenward.

I watch the show for some time, absorbed in its wonder, before I suspect I am being ridiculous to have traveled all this way out into the wilderness, and content myself with a vision inside a closed room. The scene is so real I presume it is happening in the outer world also. I get up to join the others and share the experience.

One person is reading. Others are chatting. Another is staring out across the field. The mountains have captured the threat of the storms, so just the occasional bulk of white cloud drifts in the blue sky over our heads.

I decide to let the mushroom take me for a walk. It's a lesson I learned on ayahuasca, one I often ask my body to do on its own. I accept that there is a physical consciousness as well as a mental one, so I still my mind to let the physical have precedence for a while. I am hesitant at first, checking that my normal mode of decision-making is not completely over-ridden. I walk slowly. Perhaps fear is playing a part, for my body turns to the right, skirting the field entirely. Eventually I veer left and pass near a high steel rod to enter the lightning field, on a course toward its core.

This route is dry and the ground stays solid underfoot. Two slender mushrooms grow to my left, rooted in a cowpat, likely to be hallucino-genic. I bend over and touch them, wondering if this is the purpose of my walk, this opportunity to bend in reverence to the living form of the mushrooms that are active in my own chemistry. But my body urges me to rise and walk on.

I look some distance ahead of my feet as they set a regular rhythm and start to breathe in time with my steps. The breathing asks to be given voice. I try some sound, showing a song the way if it wants to fol-low, and soon the open-throated song of my body is loud all around me. My song, my walk, and my breathing all share one rhythm. The walk has arrived at its destination, for it is walking within itself. I look out to see what is attracting it.

A mountain, the most distinctively-shaped of the mountains that ring the area, rises in the west with a flat peak: Mount Allegre. I am pleased to be in the center of a march that is directed at a mountain, and my song sings louder. It started as open-mouthed calls, its notes swooping and plummeting, but my tongue is working now and form-ing words. I am singing in a language I almost recognize but don't understand this language of my body.

My song is so full it surprises me to hear another voice, a gentle command from within which says, *Stop!* Like taking the foot off the accelerator, the command sets itself against my momentum. My foot-steps slow. I pause and grow silent. I listen. I have been the center of my own attention, but it's clear to me that other forces are present. I won-der how they will show themselves.

Sing! my body tells me. *You are here. There is no need to march. But sing!*

My song resumes, sure of itself, with its lyrics in the language I don't know. I sing to the mountain, then raise my head and sing to the sky. My feet resume their march, treading on one spot in time with the song, as my hands rise from my sides. My fingers straighten and spread; my hands begin to shake and the fingers to shiver as they reach high to clouds lit white and rounded with shadow racing across the sky.

I am singing to the sky as my feet beat the rhythm of the song into the Earth. I know the song now. It has verses and a chorus and a shape. It has a beginning, passes through a middle, and in the natural way of things, it comes to an end. I stare into the sky, leave my hands to hold the moment of silence, then bring them back down to my sides. I am still following the promptings of my body, so I simply wait.

Look, my body says. *See what you can see!*

I look ahead, where Mount Allegre stands. I wait.

It comes in the air across to my right. The mental part of me notes disappointment in the plainness of the apparition, but I keep on watching. First one small violet-blue ball appears, the way I would imagine a molecule to be, then others follow to form a small ring. It revolves at an angle, then glides down and to the left, turning to present me with the full circle of rather than the sidelong oval.

It rests on the ground in front of my feet, still revolving, and as I watch, the circle expands. A broad avenue between the lightning rods opens between the mountain and me. The circle expands along it. It stretches to form an oval and twists to form a figure eight. Its violet-blue molecules are always spinning in a flow of energy, so that even as the circle twists and flattens along the ground, the tiny globes that form it still revolve around its perimeter.

Its pathway is complete. At one end of the pulsing, spiraling avenue is the mountain. At the other end is myself. This molecular stream is the energy that flows between us. There is nothing for me to do now but to stand and appreciate. I had thought, I had hoped, that my walk would lead me to the mountain. This stream of violet light is happening outside of my hopes. My walk has led me toward the mountain, but the mountain has also come to me.

As with the song, this encounter with the mountain has a beginning, middle, and a natural ending for me to play out. With the stream of violet light still winding between us, I acknowledge the mountain, thank it, and turn away. My body has declared it is time to walk back.

I had picked up a stone on the way out, a rough white one, and slipped it into my pocket. On my return I spot another stone, this one a blushing pink in the shape of an ear. I bend toward it and recognize it as a stone belonging to the journey. Laying the white one down, I take the ear stone in my hand and walk on.

The song returns. I drop the stone into my mouth and sing the song from beginning to end, for the ear stone to absorb.

My route home takes me through the Lightning Field, beyond the outer rods with the log cabin ahead of me. I pause and look to my right. A young rabbit stands at the edge of a patch of marshland, using its paws to wipe its face, bending its soft ears forward. A little further on I reach a broad stand of thistle, crowned with purple flowers. I kneel beside it for a moment, place my ear stone on the ground at the thistle's roots, and walk away.

I turn to Mount Allegre before entering the log cabin. The sun is dropping behind it, sheathing the sky in crimson.

At the time of this experience I was completing the manuscript of my book, *I Was Carlos Castaneda*. That book contains an account of an ayahuasca trip into the jungles of Peru in which the beneficial effects of hallucinogens were poisoned by the dark side of shamanism. The account given here marks my first return to psychedelics since that experience, and it was enormously cleansing. Mushrooms open me to the natural world in a very healing way and return me to a path of sacred mountains that is very real for me. I have revisited the mushroom once since then, a journey that surprisingly extended my experience with ayahuasca of personal transformation into the form of a jaguar (perhaps guided by the presence of a photo of a South American shaman dressed in jaguar skin that hung above the platform where I took the medicine). The effects of the mushroom help me seal a major experience of the past, whilst simultaneously giving me strength for further shifts that are to come.

I invite readers to visit my website, which is found at: www.MartinGoodman.com. There I would be glad to share experiences as the journey continues.

Martin Goodman is an English-born journalist and novelist, whose books include *I Was Carlos Castenada* (New York: Three Rivers Press, 2001), *In Search of the Divine* (San Francisco: HarperSanFrancisco, 1998), and *On Bended Knees* (London: Pan Macmillon, 1992).

BIOGRAPHICAL INFORMATION

Ralph Metzner, Ph.D., obtained a B.A. in philosophy and psychology at Oxford University and a Ph.D. in clinical psychology at Harvard University; he also held a postdoctoral fellowship in psychopharmacology at the Harvard Medical School. He worked with Timothy Leary and Richard Alpert on psychedelic research, edited the *Psychedelic Review,* coauthored *The Psychedelic Experience* (1964), and edited *The Ecstatic Adventure* (1968). He is also the author of *Maps of Consciousness* (1971), *Know Your Type* (1979), *The Well of Remembrance* (1994), *The Unfolding Self* (1998), and *Green Psychology* (1999). He has pursued research in altered states of consciousness and cross-cultural methods of consciousness expansion and published more than one hundred articles on consciousness, shamanism, alchemy, transformation, and mythology. He is a professor of psychology at the California Institute of Integral Studies in San Francisco and maintains a private practice of psychotherapy in the Bay Area. He is president and cofounder of the Green Earth Foundation, a nonprofit educational organization devoted to healing and harmonizing the human relationship with the Earth. He is also the editor of essays and experience accounts on ayahuasca, the Amazonian visionary vine. His book *Sacred Vine of Spirits: Ayahuasca* will be published by Inner Traditions in 2006. Dr. Metzner can be contacted via e-mail at: ralph@greenearthfound.org. His Web site address is: www.greenearthfound.org.

Diane Conn Darling is a freelance writer, editor, ritualist, and long-time psychonaut. She is the former editor of *Green Egg, The Green Man,* and *PanGaia* magazines and lives in Northern California. She can be reached via e-mail at: dcdarling@saber.net

Printed in the United States
By Bookmasters